As I pulled a blanket from the linen closet and headed for the stairs, Charlotte Topping, one of the night nurses, hollered, "Help! Code!" just as the Code Blue alarm began.

"Code!" I yelled as I flung the blanket on the desk and ran to grab the crash cart. The Code Blue procedure had not yet been covered in lecture or lab; I still had never seen CPR, and panic was twisting in my throat.

I was just steering the crash cart through the doorway when the head nurse got out of the elevator. "Stay at the station. Direct the Code team," she said.

In the background the operator's metallic voice called over the intercom, "Code Blue, Three North!... Code Blue, Three North!... Code Blue, Three North!"

CODE BLUE
A NURSE'S TRUE-LIFE STORY

BARBARA HUTTMANN, R.N.

BERKLEY BOOKS, NEW YORK

This Berkley book contains the complete
text of the original hardcover edition.

CODE BLUE

A Berkley Book / published by arrangement with
William Morrow and Company, Inc.

PRINTING HISTORY
William Morrow and Company edition published 1982
Berkley edition / February 1984
Second printing / May 1984

ISBN: 0-425-07579-6

A BERKLEY BOOK ® TM 757,375
Berkley Books are published by The Berkley Publishing Group,
200 Madison Avenue, New York, New York 10016.
The name "BERKLEY" and the stylized "B" with design
are trademarks belonging to Berkley Publishing Corporation.
PRINTED IN THE UNITED STATES OF AMERICA

TO LANI

Author's Note

In observance of the Florence Nightingale pledge, ". . . to hold in confidence all personal matters committed to my keeping, and all family affairs coming to my knowledge in the practice of my calling," characters and places have been disguised, and in some instances the experiences of other nurses have been used to illustrate my own.

Contents

Prologue

"I can top *that*," Faith said. "Have I told you the one about condom catheters?"

"Foley catheters? Same thing?" Charlie asked. Playing can-you-top-this was their favorite sport. Faith Mason was a head nurse at Oakmont, thirteen years at the bedside. Charlie Kelly was a student nurse, Vietnam War vet. According to both, they had "seen it all."

Around them, Lani and I felt like we had spent our lives in a tunnel. We just listened and laughed.

"Not a Foley," said Faith. "Both collect urine, but the condom cath is just what it sounds like—a condom with a tube in one end that drains to a collecting bag just like a Foley."

Charlie gave her a ho-hum look. "Must not've had 'em in 'Nam. We had sophisticated stuff." There were some few things in nursing Charlie didn't know yet, but he didn't like to admit that around us.

"So, Faith . . . lay it on us . . . thought you said you could top mine," he said.

She started giggling. "You're not gonna believe this. You guys think you do stupid things! When I was in school there was a ding-a-ling . . . Miss Perfect . . . goody-two-shoes. One day the teacher assigned her to a young guy in ICU. He had one of the condom caths, only she had never seen one. It was lying there on top of the sheets and she was too simple to guess that he had pulled it off for her benefit . . . he was always doing that . . . liked to embarrass the nurses."

The student wasn't too sure how to replace it, but it looked pretty straightforward. It simply went on as a glove goes on the hand—but rigid fingers are much easier than a flaccid penis.

She was having trouble. "How do other nurses do it?" she asked the patient.

"Simple . . . just follow my directions."

He told her to hang the bag on the bed rail, with the tubing connected, and to put the condom on the bed right next to his left thigh. "Got that?"

"Got it," she said, ever so grateful for his help.

"Okay. Now, clasp your right hand around the penis, at the base . . . not too tight. Just close your hand in a firm, gentle grip." He rested his shoulders back on the pillow and fixed his eyes on the ceiling. "Got that?"

"Got it!"

"Good. Now keep ahold and pull toward you . . . then back . . . then toward you. Perfect! That's just right."

"How long do I do this?" she asked.

"I'll tell you when to stop . . . speed it up a little . . . smooth and fast . . . perfect . . . I'll tell you when to stop."

"She was *so* naïve." Faith laughed. "Can you imagine anyone being that stupid?" When the nursing instructor happened into the ICU (intensive-care unit) while the staff stood at the desk mesmerized, watching what the student was doing, she thought they must all be watching some earth-shattering event on TV. "What's up?" she asked.

"That's what's up," said one of the nurses, pointing to the student still stroking away.

"Get her out of there," the instructor hissed, but no one moved a muscle. In less than a minute, the patient's penis was flaccid again and the student was in the same predicament as before—only worse!

"She got kicked out of the nursing program," Faith said. "Anyone that *naïve* doesn't belong in nursing."

Unfortunately, I could see how such things might happen—we had all done something almost as stupid. Like cooks who follow a recipe without thinking how each ingredient might alter the taste, we did most things by rote, just as we were instructed, confident that perfected technique spawned knowledge, rather than the other way around.

Perfected technique as a nurse was a goal that came late to me—the night Faith told her "penis" story, I was almost forty, and eight months away from achieving the goal. It was an October Monday, rainy, almost snowing. The four of us were sitting in the Albatross Pub behind the Oakmont County Hospital. You could tell how tough the day had been by how many doctors and nurses were in the pub. We played darts, told hospital tales and drank coffee—not a very lucrative business for the pub owner, but he made the best of it.

By the time I got home that night, it was nearly midnight. Dean and our three kids were asleep. In the quiet dark of the house, it was more difficult to keep ominous thoughts submerged. I would have liked to hurry back to the noisy pub.

It was a temptation to awaken Dean—for twenty years he had been working magic on my frantic feelings. But that night, I had frantics that he couldn't cure. Three days earlier, the doctor had told me I had cancer—two months to live.

My impending death was not the problem, actually—most condemned patients never hear the sentence when the doctor first says it. What had me frantic was the doctor's advice that I have surgery: "Tonight . . . this can't wait . . . you're a nurse. You know what we're dealing with here."

I told him I needed time to think, that I would call him Monday. Monday was almost gone. I could not bring myself to call, nor could I tell Dean what the doctor had said. Dean would have scolded, "If he says you need surgery, you need it!"

Could I say, "I can't . . . I'm too terrified . . . terrified patients are poor surgical risks . . . sometimes they die"? Hardly. He would not have believed that I was eight months away from being a registered nurse and still terrified of hospitals, doctors and anything to do with being a patient.

* * *

Hospital phobia was something our family acquired honestly, through seventeen hospitalizations that seemed fraught with horror tales. "It's fear of the unknown," I told Dean. It was something I desperately wanted to conquer. When I awakened during an operation (a peak on the terror scale), the doctor said it was because fear had made me resistant to anesthesia. When our daughter Laurie had a near-fatal hemorrhage following an operation, the doctor said, "Terrified patients are poor surgical risks."

The seventeenth hospitalization was our son, Alan's. He was fifteen then and a patient for the third time, which should have classified him as an old pro, but practice at being patients never helped any of us—chronic creeping terrors grew in proportion to the number of times we walked through the hospital doors. Dean and I sat beside Alan's bed watching the nurses come and go while Alan talked about the spaceships flying by his window. He was hallucinating, the foot of his casted leg was turning black, it was Thanksgiving Day, and the doctor was unavailable. At that moment, I decided to become a nurse so I would know how to get Alan out of such a situation if there was ever a next time.

At first, my decision was little more than a whim—an impulsive reaction to a bad situation. Six months later when Alan still had not recovered, I was casually saying to friends, "I'm going to be a nurse."

"A *nurse?*" they would say, looking incredulous. Dean was a corporate executive, climbing the ladder—corporate wives were thought to be too busy for careers. They also spent too much time moving in and out of houses. We had been transferred fourteen times by then.

When I was obviously serious about becoming a nurse, friends then would say, "Well, let me tell *you* . . ." If I thought I had cornered the market on hospital horror stories, I was wrong. Anyone who had ever been hospitalized had plenty to

14

say about doctors, nurses, hospitals and the whole concept of medical care. "It's fear," I told them. "Fear of the unknown." The more I thought about it, the more convinced I was that being a nurse offered the best solution. Once I found out what went on behind all those closed doors of the hospital, I could reassure other people with hospital phobia as well.

"Until I'm a nurse, no one in this family will ever be a patient again," I told Dean. "No more Huttmann hospital horror stories for us!" It was a vow that became an obsession, and those were words I would be forced to eat.

PART ONE

1 The Beginnings of a Nurse

"What do you think? Do I look like a nurse?" The uniform was blue and white pinstripes, with a white tucked bib. I thought it was smashing.

"Where's the hat?" Dean was amused, and slightly proud.

"Can't wear the cap on the street, can't chew gum, can't go braless, can't wear open-heeled shoes . . . sounds like the convent regulations!"

After a month on the Oakmont University campus learning the very basics of nursing, this was to be the first day at Oakmont County Hospital, the launching that felt like it should have a bottle of champagne cracked on it. My white pointy cap was in a small plastic hatbox I carried the way Mr. Phelps on *Mission Impossible* carries his briefcase with the secret tapes. Nurses stopped wearing caps about the time students started rioting on campuses. "Our brains aren't in our caps," they said, but mine was. With the cap on my head, I saw a cool, competent, compassionate nurse in the mirror. Without it, I was any old anybody.

At first, the cap's wide cuff was without stripes. At the end of the first year, it would have one. When we graduated, there would be two. It was a three-dollar symbol worth a million, at least to me.

The hospital was known as a "venerable institution," a huge complex of buildings where nurses and doctors were educated, famous scientists did their research, and the city's ill came to be cured. That morning, when I paused on the wide marble steps while I pinned on the cap, it struck me that I was about to be an insider in this building, which, in my mind, had taken on the characteristics of the White House. Walking into the Oval Office wouldn't have been any more thrilling.

Insidership sanctioned me to read all the charts, open any closed doors, talk to doctors and nurses whenever I liked, and come and go in spite of visitors' hours. Such freedom in a world previously shrouded in mystical rites and foreign lingo buckled my knees and fluttered my heart—I *loved* it.

The part I loved best—walking down the hall feeling as if I carried the keys to the kingdom—faded rapidly when I looked at the chart of my first patient, Herman Otis. He was a seventy-year-old with terminal cancer, beginning his fifth hospital day. On the first page of his chart there was a small square for writing in expected length of stay. Someone had written "five days."

If you really think doctors are gods, that they have special access to some vast ocean of mystery, and that they have the ability to predict everything, then you can understand how I, who believed all of the above, came to the conclusion my patient was going to die that day.

His disease was terminal, he was expected to stay for five days, this was the fifth day—this man was dying *today*. Maybe not this minute, maybe not until noon, but sometime today.

I found my instructor, Susan Erin, behind the nurses' station. Though she was a foot shorter and ten years younger than I, my feeling that she was the authoritarian parent was a safety shield she reinforced by her consistent ability to anticipate when I might be about to commit a blunder. Other students considered her the smartest of our six instructors. She was also the toughest, but underneath the tough there was gentle compassion with just the right touch of humor.

"Mr. Otis ... my patient in 311 ... he's dying today," I told her.

"Yes?"

"Well, I'm not sure what I'm supposed to do. Is there something special I do?"

"Look in the policy and procedure manual, under postmortem care. Do whatever it tells you." She hurried off to another ward.

Every hospital has volumes of manuals with instructions for any procedure, including cleaning dentures, but the nursing station was a bustle of nurses and doctors beginning a busy day—no one had time to tell me where to find the manuals.

"Hey, Huttmann, trade ya patients." Charlie Kelly was walking around the station looking as frustrated as I. Since the first day on campus, we had been drawn together by our distinctions—he was the only male in our class of eighty, I was the only "senior citizen," pushing forty fast.

"Why? What have you got?"

"I've got a woman and you've got a man."

"So? Mrs. Erin assigned them. Doesn't she know who's male and who's female?"

"She knows. C'mon, Huttmann, gimme a break . . . let's just trade patients."

"Mine's dying today. Still want to trade?"

"Whatever he's doing, I want a male patient."

"We can't trade, Charlie. Do what Erin says."

"Can you see me bathing a twenty-five-year-old blond knockout? Jeezuz, Huttmann! I can't do that." Charlie was twenty-five, unmarried, and also a knockout, in his own impish way. Usually he was unflappable.

"Kripes, Charlie, did you go into this program thinking only males get sick? Go ask Erin. If she says we can, I'll gladly trade." Later I understood how he felt—bathing males my own age still isn't all that easy.

When he couldn't find Mrs. Erin, there was nothing left but to get on with the day.

By the time I got to Mr. Otis's room, I had convinced myself he would not die that morning. He would wait until night, when he was asleep and his metabolism was slowest—at least that's what the textbooks suggested.

I picked up his breakfast tray from the cart in the hall and timidly opened his door. "Good morning, Mr. Otis."

Oh God, I thought, *how could this happen to me?* Sue Barton's patients never died. Twelve volumes about her nursing days never mentioned patients dying. I backed out of the doorway, pulled the door closed and leaned against the hall rail.

Lani Sward rushed by, carrying a breakfast tray. "Isn't this neat?" she whispered, smiling as if she were having the time of her life. Lani was blond, pretty, the perfect nurse of my mind—the Sweetheart of Sigma Chi kind who draws people to her without even trying. She and Charlie were the same age. If she hadn't been married to Lee, an accountant, Charlie would have been first in line.

"This is not neat," I muttered, after she was past.

Mrs. Erin came hurrying down the hall, clipboard clutched to her chest. "Huttmann, what are you doing? Are you sick?"

"Yes. Well, no ... no. I'm not doing anything, but I think I'm sick ... or I'm going to be sick."

"You look like a ghost. Did you eat breakfast this morning?"

"Yes. It's not that."

"Well, what is it," she hissed. She was so impatient. "Where's your patient? What's the problem?"

"The patient's in there ... in bed."

"And you're out here! Is there a reason you're just standing here and all the others are working?" She was getting angry, a bigger threat than a dead patient—almost.

"My patient is dead, Mrs. Erin ... and I really don't know what I'm doing here. I can't go in there ... I've never seen a dead person ... I really should go home ... this is not for me."

She heaved a frustrated sigh and led me to the nurses' lounge. "Look, patients die sometimes. It's part of nursing. Are you afraid of death?"

Such a thought had never crossed my mind. "Afraid? Maybe

22

I am." I chuckled nervously. "It's for damned sure I'm afraid to go back in that room!"

"How do you know he's dead?"

"I looked at him. He's dead."

"Did you take his blood pressure?"

"No." Good grief. How could I take his blood pressure when I couldn't even go near him?

"Did you take his pulse?"

"No."

"Could it be that your patient is sleeping?"

"No. I don't think so. He looked very dead."

"Did you call a Code?"

"Code?"

"Code Blue . . . did you let the operator know you need the resuscitation team, the Code team?"

"No."

"You came upon a dead patient and didn't call a Code?"

"His chart says he's going to die today. The doctor must know. Why would anyone wait for me to call a Code?"

She pursed her lips, rolled her eyes skyward and drew in air as if sucking tolerance through a very skinny straw. "Let's go have a look."

"At the patient?"

"Of course."

"I can't, Mrs. Erin. I'm really sorry . . . I just can't."

"Do you want to go home?" That was no sympathetic offer—it was a calculated threat that I was about to be dumped from the program. Spots in nursing programs weren't so easy to get—keeping them was almost as difficult. "What are his respirations?" She knew what my answer would be and was already opening his door when I caught up with her. While I lingered at a distance, she walked straight to his bedside, put her hand gently on his and called, "Mr. Otis. Good morning, Mr. Otis . . . time for breakfast."

He opened his eyes, blinked a few times, looked around.

"This a hospital?" His whisper was what you would expect from a frail little gentleman who looked like a Norman Rockwell painting.

"It is," she said. "Oakmont County Hospital. Mrs. Huttmann will take your temperature and feed you your breakfast now."

Mrs. Huttmann is going to anxiety-attack herself to death in the first semester, I thought. If I couldn't tell the difference between dead and sleeping patients, heaven only knew what terror I might come up against next.

Much later I learned that all hospitalizations have an expected length of stay for insurance purposes, based on national averages. For instance, the national average for a hernia repair is three days. Some insurance companies refuse to cover the bill for a longer stay unless the physician has requested an extension. I also learned that no one is really able to anticipate the hour of death—often no one can anticipate the day, week or month, for that matter.

Mr. Otis *did* have terminal cancer, but cancer is known to go into remission for months at a time, which is exactly what happened to him. In his prime he had been a successful stockbroker, widowed, with two sons. When the sons moved to Chicago, Mr. Otis decided to retire to the country. By the time we met him, he had just begun treatment for cancer. It was his first hospitalization—the beginning of worse times yet to come.

"C'mon now," Charlie said, when I told him about the incident with Mr. Otis. "Surely you thought about facing dead patients *before* you decided to go into nursing."

I hated to admit that I hadn't. Nor had I thought about delivering babies, watching operations, irrigating colostomies, giving blood transfusions, changing dressings on wounds, administering medications, cleaning up when patients vomit or are incontinent, giving enemas, prepping patients for surgery, starting intravenous feedings, scheduling diagnostic tests, X-rays and various treatments, testing stools for blood, making beds—the technical tasks of nursing.

"So what are you here for?" Charlie wanted to know.

It seemed too sentimental to tell him that I was going to be the compassionate nurse who dispensed comfort the way I wished it had been dispensed when I had been a patient. The particulars of "comfort" didn't matter—whatever it took, I intended to do it.

"Beats me," I told him. "One day I was a corporate wife, Girl Scout den mother, chief cook and bottle washer for a family who thinks we're the Brady Bunch. The next day nursing sounded more fun . . . so here I am."

When he pressed for a better answer, I told him about the time I awakened during surgery, and about similar incidents that had happened to Dean and our kids.

"So! It's *revenge*. Which anesthesiologist are you after?"

I laughed at the thought of revenge—me standing in the operating room with a scalpel at the anesthesiologist's throat. "I'm here to see what *really* happens . . . what's real and what were Fig Newtons of my imagination. Hospitals and doctors couldn't possibly be as terrifying as they've been in my mind all these years."

"We know why Charlie's here," Lani quipped. "Where else could he find a hunting ground of eighty girls, with no competition from other guys?"

"Knock it off, Blondie!" Charlie cuffed her playfully on the shoulder. "I only have eyes for you."

Charlie was there because he didn't like taking orders from RNs, or so he said. "They do the fun stuff and make the aides and orderlies do the scut work." As an orderly in the emergency room, Charlie was without the education or license to do many procedures, start IVs, give medications, or supervise the work of other nurses, but those were tasks he had been allowed to do in Vietnam.

Of the eighty students in our class, Lani and I were the only ones who had never worked in a hospital as an aide or LPN (licensed practical nurse) before beginning the RN program at Oakmont. For us it wasn't a question of whether RNs did "more fun stuff" than the others—we simply wanted to do what RNs do and know what they know.

For patients the various titles of nurses are sometimes confusing. Aides, orderlies, nursing assistants, attendants—all are titles for people who are not required to have some special education. They usually do the routine tasks that don't require knowledge about medicine. LPN is an East Coast title that is the same as LVN (licensed vocational nurse) on the West Coast—a nurse who has completed a year of community college education and works under the supervision of an RN.

Registered nurses (RNs) all take the same exams for licensure, but some are educated in universities, some in community colleges, and some in hospital-based programs that are not affiliated with educational institutions. The head nurses, supervisors, infection control nurses, and instructors at Oakmont all held master's degrees in nursing. The director of nurses, Rita Treece, held a doctorate. As in any other profession, the higher the education, the wider the scope of responsibility.

There were five hundred nurses on the staff at Oakmont but how many were working at one time depended on the shift, how sick the patients were, and which nurses were available. On the third floor where Charlie, Lani and I were assigned for the first semester (four months), there were forty-four beds and the same number of nurses.

Some of them liked students—others thought they were a pain in the neck, always asking questions and adding to the confusion. Even nurses who usually liked students weren't too crazy about Charlie being a nurse. "What's a nice guy like him . . . ?" In a female-dominated profession, he was definitely suspect.

"If you don't like taking orders, you ought to go to medical school," I told him. "Then you can *really* be the boss." He said being boss wasn't really what he was after. It was "the fun stuff" he wanted. "Making decisions, doing complex procedures, making a difference in what happens to the patient," he said.

From the beginning, Charlie was in trouble with doctors, probably because he had such a hard time staying off their toes. Some doctors didn't want suggestions from nurses. If Charlie said, "I think this patient would do better with less insulin," the physician might say, "Oh? When did you get your MD? What medical school are you from?" Female nurses sometimes got similar treatment, but not as often as Charlie.

About a hundred doctors had admission and operating privileges at Oakmont. As a group, they decided if or when another doctor could join the staff. For instance, the seven cardiologists decided to limit competition for patients by not allowing any more cardiologists on the staff. If an internist wanted a cardiologist to consult on one of his hospital patients, he was obligated to choose one of the seven already on the staff. It sounded like a business—limiting competition—which was one of the major surprises of being a nurse. I had never before thought of medical care as a business where no one makes money unless other people get sick.

Medical students who trained at Oakmont went on to be interns after they received their MD. After a year of internship, they became residents working under the supervision of staff physicians. The length of residency depended on the specialty. Peter Haynes was the surgical resident on the third floor when we were there, in his third year of a five-year program. He and Charlie had both been medical corpsmen in Vietnam, but Dr. Haynes was older, in his mid-thirties, and much taller. Wire-rimmed glasses and an expression of intense intellectual curiosity made him look scholarly, but a head of sandy-blond waves and curls gave him the little-boy look that kept him from seeming so serious.

The day we first met Dr. Peter Haynes was the same day I first heard a Code Blue called. In a sense it was something I had been waiting for during the three months we had been there, but it was also something I never wanted to happen. Charlie and I were sitting at the desk charting the progress notes on our patients, struggling with the medicalese that had no rhyme or reason—"void" is urinate, "stat" is immediately, "emesis" is vomit. We were arguing about the use of "ecchymosis" (bruise) when the panic in the operator's voice as it shrieked from the intercom right above my head stiffened the hairs on the back of my neck.

"Code Blue, Four North! ... Code Blue, Four North! ... Code Blue, Four North!" Within seconds, a flock of people—nurses, doctors, technicians—went running past us, headed for the stairs, their lab coats flapping about their bodies.

From where we were standing, the nurses' station in the center of the third floor, I could see down the four halls which radiated from the station like spokes from the hub of a wheel. Everyone in the halls stood still, poised mid-action, like a frozen frame in a movie. The only sound was the clomping of feet as the Code team raced up the stairs.

Months later, I understood the suspended animation—every nurse had a private file of patients in her mind that she scanned to see if the one in crisis was a patient who had affected her life.

In any hospital, Codes are the ultimate crisis. Some patient's breathing or heart has stopped and death is minutes away. The nurse who finds the patient in crisis dials the operator or pushes an emergency button at the bedside. While the operator announces the Code and summons the team from whatever they're doing, the nurse begins CPR (cardiopulmonary resuscitation).

Another nurse rushes the crash cart (a mini-operating room in a cabinet, with all the drugs, equipment and supplies for retrieving life) to the bedside. Any doctor who happens to be in the hospital rushes to the scene, which means there might be four or five doctors there within seconds. In addition, an appointed team of electrocardiogram and respiratory technicians, nurses and supervisors arrives within the first few minutes.

If the patient does not respond to CPR, several other procedures are attempted, including the most extreme one—opening the chest and massaging the heart by hand. Most patients who have been Coded are transferred to the ICU on the fourth floor when—and *if*—they have been stabilized.

For other patients in the hospital at the time of a Code, the situation is annoying. They have no idea they are waiting for a pain shot, or help to the bathroom, because their nurse is busy with a Code

Lani Sward came walking down the stairs that day, as we heard the last of the Code team reach the top. Her mental file had a patient who had been transferred to the ICU (intensive care unit) that morning. When the Code was announced, she was the first to shoot up the stairs. She walked back down with an all-in-a-day's-work manner that I envied—no matter what the crisis, Lani always looked calm and competent, even when she was a neophyte nurse.

"Who was it?" Charlie asked.

"False alarm," she whispered. "Boy, is Dr. Allen ticked!" The students in the class before ours had told us about David Allen, the chief surgeon, top on the doctor totem pole. "The astringent peacock," they called him. They also said he was a brilliant surgeon, and they didn't care about his gruff manner as long as he took such good care of patients.

"How could there be a false alarm?" I wanted to know. "Either a patient has a cardiac or respiratory arrest—it's a crisis or it isn't. What's a false alarm?"

"They had a new nurse in ICU," Lani said. "The panels behind the beds look like the dashboard of an airplane ... she pushed the Code button that connects to the operator's switchboard when she meant to turn on an examination light."

The Code team coming back down the stairs didn't look as amused as Charlie. "False alarms happen all the time." He laughed. "Sends a jolt of panic through the hospital ... that poor nurse must feel like a four-plus fool." Later I learned that "four-plus" is a term used to refer to extreme amounts. For instance, the sugar in a diabetic's urine could be reported as negative, one-plus, two-plus, etc. Four-plus is the most. The same scale is used to measure blood in stool. Four-plus means there is something drastically awry in the patient's body. Nurses use it in slang a lot: "Dr. Allen is four-plus nasty today—watch out!"

He was the last of the Code team to come downstairs, and yes, he was ticked. "Nurse! Call Dr. Haynes. Get me a sterile dressing kit. Which room is Newman's?" He was muttering about stupid nurses who couldn't read, why Code buttons weren't marked more clearly . . . The run up the flight of stairs, for a false alarm, would have been less provoking for a younger physician who wasn't carrying fifty-too-many-pounds on such short legs.

I looked around to see which nurse he wanted. Lani, Charlie and I were the only nurses at the station. At the same moment, Mrs. Erin, our instructor, rushed by. "You three . . . be on campus by three-thirty, in the lab . . . don't be late." She hurried down the stairs.

"I'll call for Dr. Haynes," Charlie said. "Get the kit, Lani. Allen's the honcho around here . . . get him whatever else he needs, Barb."

"It's three o'clock, Charlie. If we don't leave now, we'll be late." The one thing that angered Mrs. Erin most was tardiness.

Charlie shot me a gee-you're-a-dummy look. "Help Allen," he hissed.

Dr. Allen was flipping through the ward clerk's rack, looking for Newman's room number. "Where the hell is she?"

I scanned the diet list on the counter. "Judith Newman? That's the only Newman . . . room 317."

"Get a stump shrinker," he called to me as he was walking to her room.

I went to the utility room where Lani was searching the supply cart for a dressing kit. To find an unfamiliar item among the two hundred or more on the cart is some trick. "Have you seen a stump shrinker?"

"Never heard of it. Bigger than a bread box? Animal, vegetable or mineral?"

It could have been an instrument, a drug, an appliance, a bandage ... it might even have been a technician, for all we knew. At 3:00, shift-change time, there's never anyone around to answer questions.

We were still hunting when Peter Haynes arrived, bringing a stump shrinker with him. It was nothing more than a wide elastic band used to wrap the stump of an amputated limb. Wrapped properly, the stump shrinks and toughens so a prosthesis can be applied.

"Ever seen a stump?" Peter asked me. One of his best traits was the way he shared his fascination at the physiology of disease. New situations were a golly-gee marvel that awed him. "Imagine!" he'd say. "Can you believe the human body is so clever!"

I told him that I had never seen a stump. Though I was anxious to learn, my mind shrank from a few gruesome thoughts. An amputated limb was one of them.

"C'mon. You'll be surprised. Besides, we'll need some help."

I *was* surprised. It was like most other surgical incisions—neat, clean and very logical. The bone of the leg was removed, just above the knee. Then flaps of skin, one from the top and one from the back of the leg, were folded over the stump of bone and fastened with latex-covered staples. Though it sounds gross, there isn't much difference between the way poultry or roasts look that have been rolled or sewed and parts of the human body that have had surgery.

The only ghastly surgical incisions are the ones that become infected after surgery. When bacteria get in a wound and do their thing, the destruction of tissue, and the consequent odor and drainage, is almost unbelievable considering the microscopic size of the bacteria.

Sometimes people have limbs amputated because of an accident, but all the amputations we saw were results of gangrenous infection in diabetics. No matter how carefully diabetic patients watch their diet and exercise, circulation to their limbs can be impaired by the complex disease process. A slight infection that's hardly noticeable might become a gangrenous ulcer almost overnight. Unless the limb is amputated, the gangrene causes fatal infection throughout the body.

Judith Newman would have welcomed the fatal infection when we first met her. She was a small lady, almost eighty years old, with thick, snow-white hair and a pearly skin that looked more taut than that of most patients her age. An amputated leg would have been enough assault, but she was also blind and a survivor of a Nazi concentration camp where her two daughters and husband had been executed.

"I'm too old," she whimpered. "Please, just let me die."

If she was ever going to walk again, she had to toughen and strengthen the stump so she could wear an artificial leg.

"Push that stump, Judith." Dr. Allen held a pillow up against it so she would have a counterforce. The idea is the same as doing push-ups to strengthen muscles. "No, push, dammit . . . give it a hard shove!" Dr. Allen always talked to her as if she were deaf.

Dr. Haynes held Judith's hand, which angered Dr. Allen. "You have to be tough with cases like this, Peter," he said. "As of today, you're responsible for this case. I'd advise you to see that she walks." There was a threat in his voice that I didn't understand until later when Peter told me he was the resident under Dr. Allen. If he pleased Dr. Allen, he would be recommended for staff privileges when his residency was finished and he was ready to start his own practice.

Judith Newman had come to Oakmont County Hospital from Sunny Harbor, a nursing home where she had been living for ten years. Since World War II, when she emigrated to the United States, she had lived alone while running her own little millinery store in Oakmont. "When hats went out of style, I went out of style," she chuckled one day, but that was several weeks after we first met her. It wasn't too clear whether she went blind first or hats went out of style first, but damaged vision that resulted from uncontrolled diabetes had progressed to blindness, and she was no longer able to run the shop or live alone.

At Sunny Harbor she stubbed her toe on the doorjamb. By the time the toe was obviously infected, it was too late—there was no choice but to amputate above the knee.

Peter Haynes protested to Dr. Allen that he wasn't keen on ignoring Judith's right to refuse treatment, but Dr. Allen was adamant. "She was spry before she came in here a week ago ... a *good* doctor would see that she's spry when she leaves here. Get her walking, Peter!"

For a less conscientious doctor, Judith's refusal of treatment might not have presented such a problem, but Peter Haynes and our instructor, Susan Erin, had one thing in common— they considered the patient the boss. "The Patient's Bill of Rights ensures that there will be one boss only," Peter told us. "To treat when the patient says 'no' is to commit assault and battery. It's a moral and legal matter ... not just a whim."

A few weeks before we met Judith, Mrs. Erin lectured about the patient's rights on campus. "Too often we forget that the patient is a consumer of services we provide."

She had a clever way of putting things in simple terms. "What would you think if you took your car in for an oil change and the mechanic ended up doing a transmission overhaul?"

"I'd think I got a good deal for the price of an oil change." Charlie laughed.

Mrs. Erin ignored him and went on to explain that patients have the legal right to refuse meals, injections, diagnostic tests, X-rays, whatever. "Your job is to protect the patient's rights," she said. "You are the one who will be guilty of assault and battery if you give the patient treatment he or she is refusing."

She infused the lecture with dramatic words that ended up in my head as visions of policemen with clubs warding off assaultive doctors and nurses. Then the next day she assigned me to the burn center for a week and I got my first chance at practicing what she preached.

Everyone who entered the burn center on the sixth floor at Oakmont scrubbed and gowned in the anteroom before passing through the glass doors into the enormous room where the patients' beds lined the perimeter, all within view of each other. When I went in, a two-year-old in one corner was wailing pitifully for his mother through bandages that covered his entire body except for three holes for his eyes and mouth.

"He was in his crib . . . the whole house went up in flames," Marie Agostini told us. She was a feisty redhead with chiseled features, one of the six nurses (saints!) on duty that day. "The burns cover eighty percent of his body . . . it won't be long . . . there's no way he can survive."

The child's mother was in ICU, recovering from respiratory burns. "Scorched lungs," Marie said, "but she'll survive. She has minor burns on her hands too. The worst is yet to come, when she finds out little Sean won't make it."

It was a classic case of a smoldering cigarette on a couch—the result of an accident which would haunt them forever. The physical pain of burns is the most agony I have ever seen patients endure—the psychological pain must be even worse.

Of the six patients in the burn center, Sean was in the worst condition, but Bill Goldsmith ran a close second. He was a thirty-five-year-old policeman who sang with the Oakmont Opera Company. "He's iffy," Marie told me. "If he *does* get through this, his singing days are probably over." I wasn't crazy about being assigned to "iffy" patients, since I was still a neophyte, but she insisted I would do fine.

At a neighborhood luau where the host's yard was lit by Tiki torches, Bill had bumped one of the torches while running backward to catch a volleyball. Drenched in kerosene and ignited by the wick, he became an instant human torch with flames fanned by the autumn wind. Instinctively he rolled on the lawn to quench the fire, but his melting nylon clothes seared into his flesh and adhered as if they had been purposely glued to him.

Third-degree burns would have been relatively painless, since they would have gone deeper than his pain receptors, but Bill's burns were second-degree, and the slightest air current across his body caused excruciating pain. Thick, sandy-blond hair stood up from his head, as if he had been terribly startled. The ends were still frizzled from the flames. The rest of his body was swaddled in dressings spotted with huge dried splotches of his body fluids.

"A shot," he croaked, "please . . . I can't stand it . . . get me a shot!" While I hurried back to the anteroom for his shot, I wondered how on earth I would inject it through all the gauze.

"Can't have it," said Marie. "It's too early. Don't pay any attention . . . he'll keep after you, but you just have to ignore him."

"How can I ignore him? The guy's in pain!"

She was cool, aloof, efficient—the kind other nurses would say "really knows her stuff." ICU and emergency room nurses have that briskness in common with burn nurses.

"If he's always asking for a shot, he's not getting enough. Can I call the doctor and get the dose increased?"

She seemed impatient, as if I had invaded her territory. "Hey, the doctor knows what he's doing. Bill's got a long road to go. If he even survives, he'll be here months for skin grafting. He doesn't need to be a dope addict on top of it all."

"So cure him of the addiction when it's all over."

"The cure rate on dope addicts is two percent. Haven't you learned that yet? Just get those wraps off of him, cover him with a sterile sheet and wheel him down to the tub room. If he's late, you'll screw up their schedule down there."

I dreaded going back to him empty-handed. "It's too early, Bill. I can't give you anything for a while yet." "A while" was two hours, but I couldn't bear to tell him that. "I'm going to unwrap your dressings and take you down to the tubs . . . I'll be gentle, I promise."

"Don't touch me!" he snapped. "I'm not going to the tub room. No more for me . . . just bug off, all of you."

I was about to go ahead with unwrapping him anyway when I remembered Mrs. Erin's lecture—he had a legal right to refuse treatment. I had a legal obligation to protect that right. "You are the patient's advocate," Mrs. Erin had said.

"Bill, if you don't go to the tubs, your burns won't heal," I pleaded.

"They're *my* burns . . . leave 'em alone . . . no more for me!"

"Bill's refusing treatment," I told Marie. "Maybe if we give him some pain medication he'll let me unwrap him?"

She slammed the chart down on the counter in the anteroom and huffed over to his bed. "Listen, you . . . it's your choice . . . you can lie here and *rot* if you want. That's what'll happen to you . . . you'll *rot* . . . but it's your choice. We don't take you to the tubs because it makes *us* feel better!"

She seemed startled by her own outburst—in fact, the whole room, which had been a cacophony of moans and groans, became suddenly still except for little Sean whimpering for his mother.

"Bitch!" Bill spit. Then he muttered, "Go away . . . just let me die . . . get outta here."

Marie's shoulders sagged. She started to touch his bandages, then drew her hand back. "It's hell . . . I know." Her voice was kind and gentle, as if someone else were speaking. "I think I could stand anything but burns . . . it's really hell."

Then she perked up, as if putting on still another mask. "Oh, by the way, I forgot to tell you, Harriet called a while ago . . . said she'd be here to see you after you got back from the tubs. In a week or so, when you get those ugly bandages off your face, she can bring the kids to the anteroom so you can see them. Bet you really miss them."

Bill went to the tubs without comment, and was lifted by hydraulic hammock into a huge vat of warm water and chemicals that were meant to wash away the charred hunks of flesh so the skin underneath could heal. A nurse stood beside him in the water and scrubbed with a soft brush, in large swaths, as if mopping the deck of a ship. "We do this three times a week," she told me. Each stroke of her brush brought the contents of my stomach closer to my mouth as black particles floated to the top of the vat and left his entire body looking like a long tray of freshly ground raw meat.

The right side of his face was untouched by the fire—it was incredibly handsome, like the faces of men who pose for clothing store ads. Tears poured down that side while she scrubbed. The other side of his face was swollen and charred, as if the artist had gone mad after he finished painting the right side.

When he was wrapped up in a sterile sheet again, I wheeled him back to the burn center and the real agony began. With a wooden tongue depressor, I spread a white fluffy sulfa preparation over the oozing flesh while I planned a permanent escape. "That stuff burns, but it works wonders," Marie told me. "The pain is worth it."

Bill did his best to stifle screams, and I did my best to smooth it on quickly, without touching the tongue depressor to his body, but I knew I would never, *could* never, do it again. When he looked well frosted, like a giant sheet cake, I wrapped miles and miles of gauze around him and covered the whole with fishnet. The day after next, he would endure the same ordeal. And some weeks later, if he survived, the few unburned parts of his body would be skimmed for skin grafts, leaving the skimmed parts as miserably painful as the burns had been. That might take dozens of operations, and then there would be the painful physical therapy—loosening up joints, exercising muscles that had been unused for too long—all of it agonizing pain.

"How can you stand it?" I asked Marie. "All this crying, moaning, pleading, begging to die—how can you stand the torture they're all going through?"

She showed me a picture album kept at the desk, just for skeptics like me, with photos of an eight-year-old boy, from the first day, when he looked like a cinder that had sprouted blond hair, to the last day four years later when he looked like a human again—scarred but human. "It's a challenge," she said. "When you can accomplish things like this, you know that every day of pain, they're one step closer to looking human again. It's worth it!"

If there are special places in heaven, the burn center nurses will be there, but I will not be among them. Had Mrs. Erin looked for me the rest of the week I was supposed to be there, she would have found me on other sections of the sixth floor, making beds, emptying bedpans, whatever anyone needed—*anything* to escape the burn center.

Like Bill Goldsmith, Judith Newman had rejected treatment. "Just let me die," she insisted each time the nurses tried to get her to cooperate with them in exercising her stump. But then one day when I was with her for an entire shift, I realized she was often lost in the past. The phantom pain from a missing limb is said to be excruciating, but her physical pain was the barometer for her psychological pain which must have been even worse. The more the missing limb hurt, the more she thought she was still in the concentration camp thirty years earlier.

"The snow was so heavy at Bergen-Belsen," she murmured. "The girls were sentenced for smuggling . . . they will freeze to death, those girls without coats. Mala . . . my daughter. The SS man bound her hands behind her back . . ." In an emotionless stream of consciousness, she related the details of her daughter's execution as though such tragedies were a common consequence of life. More than a few nurses silently wept while listening to the monologues and bathing her.

"Most of the time she's out of it . . . still stuck in the concentration camps," I told Peter Haynes. "Do you really think she has the right to refuse treatment if she doesn't even know where she is?" She knew she was in a hospital, and she knew I was a nurse. For whatever reason, she trusted that I was not "the enemy," which was one reason I never told her my last name. Still she begged me to let her die.

"She has the right to refuse, unless we get two doctors to declare her incompetent," Dr. Haynes said. He clenched his teeth and wrinkled his brow. "God, this is sticky! If we don't work on that stump, she'll never walk. But I sure don't want to have it be a question of incompetence."

"What's the worst possible thing that could happen?" I asked.

Peter thought for a minute. "There's a lot of worsts. When her mind clears, she could sue us for letting her stump wither so she can't walk again. She could sue us for having her declared incompetent . . . see, if she had some relatives, the problem would be theirs . . . they would have to make the decision and get her declared incompetent."

"Dr. Allen made his decision . . . get her walking! What about that?"

Peter tried several times to reason with Judith in the rare moments when her mind seemed slightly unfogged, but in the end it would be a graver sin to let her stump wither than to treat her against her wishes or have her declared incompetent. "Let's wing it and hope for the best," he said, "see what we can do."

Keeping the stump from developing deformities, strengthening muscles, mobilizing joints, conditioning the stump and managing Judith's diabetes was a full-time job for an experienced nurse. For students, it was a three-nurse job that Lani,

Charlie and I rotated some days and worked on together other days. We put her limbs through range of motion three or four times a shift, pushed her stump against ever harder surfaces so the end would toughen, massaged the scar to keep the circulation going, turned her from side to side and then onto her stomach, lifted her to stand on the good leg, then lifted her back to bed—it seemed a backbreaking, thankless task at first, most of which caused her pain. The more pain, the more she muttered about the Holocaust.

"I thought I had seen it all in Vietnam," Charlie said one day, "but Judith's past definitely tops mine." He had been raised by a grandmother who had died while he was in Vietnam and, though he wasn't the type to display emotion, his tenderness toward Judith was like a grandson's toward a beloved grandmother. The affinity between them seemed always to have been.

We had worked with her almost three weeks and were nearing the end of our first semester of school when the fog in Judith's mind began to clear. Charlie was doing what he liked best—filling her blind eyes with color and action by describing what was happening outside her window.

"The one in the red sweater just clobbered the big bully with a snowball," Charlie said. "Whoops! She's running lickety-split."

Judith was chuckling as if she could see the scene herself. "Is she the short little girl with pigtails?"

Charlie was surprised that she remembered the description from several days earlier, and even more surprised when she said, "What a treat, listening to your movies every day . . . so kind you've been . . . what is your name?" From that day on, she could sense when he was in her room even before he spoke. "Mr. Kelly," she would say, never calling any male by his first name, "how dear of you to come."

Charlie related the story to us and Dr. Haynes in a very clinical voice—it was not his style to show his soft side—

". . . she's never out of it, never talks about concentration camps, definitely cooperating with treatment."

"Terrific! We're off and running . . . let's set a target." Maybe all doctors are as elated over a patient's progress, but Peter went around beaming like he had a brand-new son. "Do you think we can get her walking within a month?"

Charlie swept a dramatic bow. "Frederick Nightingale at your service, sir. These excellent student nurses will have your patient home for Christmas!"

"Speak for yourself," Lani quipped. "Barb and I haven't learned to work miracles yet."

"Blondie, you have no faith . . . we'll do it . . . Judith Newman will be home for Christmas."

For a while we were sailing on the euphoria of a competition between our skill and the calendar. Judith's spunk and determination made up for any lack of agility she might have had because of her age, and Lani and I played Jack LaLanne: "Up . . . up . . . get that leg up, Judith . . . hold it. Super! Let it down slowly . . . slowly . . . slowly . . . up again . . . perfect, ten times better than yesterday."

When her muscles were strong enough and she could pull herself up to a standing position on her one good leg, Dr. Haynes came in with the man from the company that had made her artificial leg. "Did you make it beautiful?" she quipped. "I always wanted beautiful legs." She was giddy while they were there, but after they left everything changed.

She slowly ran her hand up and down the cold plastic of the leg and wept without a sound. She talked about what a useless creature she was—blind, only one leg, not strong enough to get anywhere but from the bed to the chair and back again. "No good for anything."

Harsh reality always seems the most profound just before a giant leap to independence—it happens to stroke patients, surgery patients, anyone who has been severely ill and struggling through rehabilitation. Mrs. Erin taught us not to try and talk patients out of feeling crummy. "They've earned the right to indulge in self-pity," she said. "Judith has a greater right than any patient I've ever met."

Judith's spunk and enthusiasm were gone, which had drastic effects on her body. As she started to use her artificial leg, her blood sugar rose dramatically, she started feeling dizzy and nauseous, which made her balance poor, and she was convinced she never would get well again.

Charlie got frantic and made it his personal crusade to regulate her diabetes. He would inspect all her meal trays to make sure she ate the same number of calories every day. If the lab technician didn't get there to draw blood at the precise hour which would be best to give Dr. Haynes the data he required to calculate how much insulin she needed, Charlie would be on the phone bugging the lab.

"You're a pain in the neck, Charlie . . . there's more than one diabetic around here, you know." The lab tech acted angry, but most of the staff knew Judith and were touched by Charlie's devotion to her.

After a week of halfhearted attempts with her new leg, Judith snapped out of the slump as quickly as she had gone into it. "This is it, Barbara . . . today I'm walking out of this room!"

It took almost all morning to get her breakfast and bath finished, but she had everything planned—for the first time, she was the boss. "A catnap . . . that's all I need. At noon you and I are going for a stroll."

Of course, at noon every nurse on the third floor was standing at the nurses' station, watching her door as if Robert Redford might walk out any minute.

"Lani's on one side, Barbara's on the other, I'll take up the rear," Charlie told her. "Ready?"

"Ready," Judith said.

"Wait, hold it right there." Charlie went to the door and used his most dramatic voice to announce, "Ladies and gentlemen, distinguished nurses and doctors, we present to you Oakmont's outstanding patient of the year—Mrs. Judith Newman!"

He hurried back to Judith and whispered, "Okay now, this is it, straight ahead about ten steps and you'll be out the door."

"Let's split!" She mimicked Charlie's expression perfectly.

A heavier person would have had more difficulty than Judith, who weighed less than a hundred pounds, but still her steps were slow and frighteningly wobbly. Lani and I held her elbows while her new leg dragged more than it stepped, but she got to the door under her own steam and barely had one foot over the threshold when Dr. Haynes swooped her up in his arms with a yelp and buried his face in her shoulder. "For this I would walk every hour," she chirped.

It was a rare moment, when every nurse suddenly remembered why she wanted to be a nurse in the first place. Judith Newman would indeed be home for Christmas, with even a few extra days to spare.

2   A Few Surprises

"You can teach a monkey to nurse," Dr. Allen said to no one in particular. He was at the nurses' station, huffing around in his usual blustery way, his several chins tucked into his collarbone. Staff nurses who knew him ignored him or teased him into a better humor.

Student nurses often carried such statements into the classroom or the lab where we learned the intricacies of nursing. "Get a monkey in here to take my place," I told Charlie one day. "This is not for me!"

Susan Erin had lectured on the various syringes and needles, and the sites we should use for certain medications. Some drugs, like heparin (a blood thinner), go only in the abdomen, some in the leg, and a few in the arm. Because the buttocks are the largest muscles, most drugs should be injected there, for best absorption and the least pain for the patient.

Mrs. Erin passed around an orange and several syringes so we could get the feel of injecting. The trick was to hold the orange in one hand, plunge the needle in with the other and, with the same hand, withdraw the plunger of the syringe just a bit to see if the needle was in the vein. If we didn't hit a vein, we were to push on the plunger and inject the medication.

Part of my right thumb had been amputated in a freak childhood accident. For thirty years I had never noticed it—suddenly it was a handicap. My whole right hand seemed like half-thumbs, all quivering, when I sensed what Mrs. Erin was going to say next. "You can't do it to a patient until you've done it to a best friend."

No one had ever told me student nurses give each other shots, for heaven's sake. Charlie looked at me and snickered.

"It's nothing, Huttmann ... how come you look like you're about to spring for the door?"

"I *hate* shots ... always have!"

"Pretend you're throwing a dart, that's all. I did dozens, in 'Nam. I'm good at it ... I'll do it to you."

"Where?"

"Whatta ya mean, where?"

Oh my God, I thought. *Right here in this classroom, with all these fresh-faced, firm-skinned kids, this jelly-rolled old lady is going to have to bare her rear to the only male in the class.* "I've held the East Coast franchise on fear-of-shots for years, Charlie. I have to work up to this ... how about next week?" The syringe and needle suddenly looked like a bayonet.

"It doesn't hurt," he chided. "Charlie Kelly holds the world's record for swift, deft shots!"

"Who will volunteer for the demonstration?" Mrs. Erin asked. I scrunched my almost-six-feet down behind five-and-a-half-foot Lani who happened to be in the front row, directly in front of Mrs. Erin. I was thinking anyone would have to be crazy to volunteer. No one did.

Finally Mrs. Erin gave Lani a pleading look, and the class applauded as Lani hopped up on the hospital bed in the front of the room.

"Have the patient lying prone, toes pointed inward," Mrs. Erin instructed. "In that position the patient can't tense muscles that would impede absorption and cause pain." She pulled the waist of Lani's slacks down about two inches. "Never say, 'Drop your drawers,' to the patient. You only need a tiny space ... respect the patient's modesty."

I almost shouted, "Amen!" As a patient, one of my pet peeves had been the way nurses acted as if patients were not noticing when the sheet got whipped off and the gown pulled up. Some patients don't think about modesty, but for those who do, hospitalization is sometimes more than a little offensive.

Lani never winced or made a sound when Mrs. Erin injected

her, and I never made a sound when Charlie injected me—the pain of shots is mostly in the anticipation.

"Go ahead, Huttmann ... do it. I promise I won't whimper." Charlie made a frightened face and pouted his lips like a child. "Get it over with!" I suspect he's normal—also dislikes shots.

That night at dinner I told Dean and the kids about the shots. By then I was thinking it was amusing.

"How *could* you, Mom? How embarrassing!" Laurie was at that most-embarrassed age of sixteen.

"Bull!" Alan declared. "Next thing you'll be trying to tell us you have to take each other's tonsils out." He got up from the table and put his unfinished dinner on the counter. "Mom, why are you doing this? I can't think of one good reason why you should be a nurse!" Three traumatic hospitalizations had left him thinking that anyone who voluntarily walked into a hospital had to be stark raving mad. Sometimes I thought he was right.

Kim, our youngest, had a fascination with things medical that must have been genetically acquired. She was an aspiring physician—until that night. "That's it! Nope ... forget me being a doctor, Mom. If nurses have to give each other shots, imagine what doctors have to do to each other. Forget it."

"Who is this Charlie?" Dean wanted to know. The suspicion in his voice was vaguely painful—something that might pass if it were ignored.

At the end of the semester, two weeks before Christmas, Lani, Charlie and I were on our way to the campus for the last lab session. We had learned to take blood pressures, make a perfect bed, set up traction equipment, do bladder catheterizations (not on each other), draw blood, irrigate and dress wounds, gown and glove for the operating room, give perfect shots—the technical stuff of nursing—and I was naïve enough to think we had done it all.

"What's on the agenda today?" Lani asked.

"They saved the best for last," Charlie said. "I heard about this one from last year's class. The teachers want us to have the Christmas vacation to recuperate . . . we're going to learn how to give enemas!"

"You can't do it to a patient until you've done it to your best friend," Lani mimicked Mrs. Erin's singsongy voice.

"Enough," I said. "That's it! Charlie, give me your keys. I'm going back to the hospital. I'm nobody's best friend."

"Jeezuz, Huttmann. Who in this group is four-plus gullible, anyway? I don't know what's on the agenda, but it's for sure not going to be enemas."

It turned out to be N/G (nasogastric) tubes—better than enemas but not by much. Slightly smaller in diameter than a pencil, N/G tubes come in various lengths, depending on whether they are to go from the nose to the stomach, or from the nose to the small intestine. Their purpose is to empty or fill the stomach. For instance, the expression "pumping the stomach" refers to emptying the contents via an N/G tube attached to a suction apparatus. Often after gastric surgery, N/G tubes are used to keep the system free of normal secretions which would retard healing.

The tubes are also used to feed patients who, for various reasons, are unable to chew and swallow food. Since there is an opening at both ends, fluid can be injected by syringe or retrieved by suction. Once the tube is in place, it's irritating to the patient, but inserting it is the worst part.

"The trick is to get it past the gag reflex," said Mrs. Erin. "If you pass the gag reflex and the patient's still gasping for air, you've done it wrong . . . gone into the lungs instead of into the stomach."

"Let me do it to you first, Barb. I promise I won't make you gag." Charlie had never inserted one before—it was probably the *only* thing he hadn't done. "Hold still! I'll be really gentle." He dipped the end of the tube in lubricating jelly. "Okay, look, when I get it in your nose and down into your throat, swallow when I tell you. Pretend you're eating spaghetti . . . just gulp it down."

"You won't gag me? You won't get it in my lungs and choke me?"

"Knock it off and hold still, Huttmann!"

He started pushing the tube through one nostril, and it wouldn't budge. "Damn! You've got a deviated septum."

"What's that? I have an ordinary cold . . . my nose is sore."

"No, dummy, one side is clogged with cartilage . . . it's common. I'll go in the other side."

He tried again, and it burned like crazy. I pulled it out. "You're too rough, Charlie. I'll sneeze. Slow down." Finally he got the tube as far as the gag reflex, and I started retching. The entire class was a chorus of retching.

"Swallow! Swallow!" Charlie yelled. "It's spaghetti . . . gulp it down. Try, dammit!" Finally, after three tries, I swallowed it.

"Tape it to the bridge of the nose so the whole tube doesn't go down and get lost in the stomach." Mrs. Erin demonstrated with a fancy crisscross arrangement of tape.

Charlie was not good at crisscrossing. He taped my nostrils together and fastened the tape in a glob between my eyebrows. "A monkey could do a better job than that, on the first try," I told him.

"That's because a monkey wouldn't be in a hurry to get out of here for Christmas vacation."

The technical tasks of nursing are monkey-easy in terms of dexterity, after a bit of practice, but the skills RNs use the most have to do with making the right decisions at the right time. Often it's a matter of choosing the right words. What do you say when a patient asks, "Am I going to die?" What are the right words to coax someone like Bill Goldsmith into fighting for life?

In a sense, a student nurse is two people—the one she

thought she was and the one she *finds* she is. I thought it might bother me to empty bedpans, clean up feces or hold a basin while a patient vomits. There's a lot of what most people call "dirty work" in nursing, the kinds of things monkeys could do. But what was really exhausting me was what went on in my head. Why did I react so violently when I thought Mr. Otis was dead? How could I be a nurse if I was so afraid of looking at a dead person?

I thought it would be relatively easy to be objective about patients—treat people and send them home. Then along came patients like Judith Newman. We invested ourselves in her, became attached, worried about her twenty-four hours a day. When she hurt, we hurt. The worst was doing things to her that caused pain, like exercising her stump.

"If you become involved, you will be hurt," Mrs. Erin said. "The trick is to care what happens to the patient without getting too involved." That's easier in some nursing jobs than in others. Recovery room nurses rarely have a patient more than an hour or two, never see the family, often have no idea what will happen to the patient tomorrow or the next day. Still, it affects them when they get a patient who is going to wake up to disaster. Maybe a lady went to surgery to have a breast lump biopsied, and left the recovery room with both breasts missing and a terminal diagnosis. It's not a situation the nurse can whisk out of her mind very easily.

Does the patient have a husband? Little children who will be orphaned in a few months? A mother who has just that one daughter? Will there be someone there to hold her hand and comfort her when the doctor tells her she has only a few months left to live?

The doctor is with the patient maybe five minutes a day. That's not to say he has no emotional investment, but nurses have to know what to do after the doctor leaves, for the next twenty-four hours when the patient is suffering.

It's one thing for the doctor to say, "He can't have any more pain medication—he's getting enough," as with Bill Gold-smith. It's another thing to be the nurse, with the patient screaming for help all day.

Every patient has a different personality. Some react to fear by getting angry about little things like whether the toast on their tray is white or wheat. Others go into deep depression and won't cooperate with their care so they can get well.

Maybe they take out their anger on someone in the family, instead of the nurse. We saw that a lot. Terminal cancer patients might suddenly fly off the handle at an unsuspecting relative. The relative would stand in the hall in tears. Sometimes there would be screaming and swearing matches that ended in divorce before the week was out. Then the relatives were as much a concern to the nurse as the patient was. It's her job to try and help the family understand what's *really* happening, how condemned patients react to their situation. To help, you have to know how to interpret the needs of patients and families. Monkeys aren't so good at that.

As we got smarter, we were less offended by Dr. Allen's statements. Insulting nurses was his way of handling his own anger or frustration. One of the more mouthy nurses sometimes countered his remarks like the one about monkeys. When he asked for a cup of coffee, she would say, "Find a monkey. Only monkeys deliver coffee to doctors on this floor." Or he would tell her to give a patient enemas until the water was clear, and she would say, "That's dirty work. Find a monkey to do your dirty work." Usually he would smile, embarrassed, and call a truce. In every job, people have to learn how to handle coworkers, but it's probably much easier if you aren't trying to handle sick and dying patients, and their families, at the same time.

For student nurses I think the most exhausting part of nursing is worrying about whether or not they are doing it right—no matter what "it" is: Does the shot hurt the patient because it's being done wrong or because the patient's hypersensitive, or because the solution is so thick? Is Dr. Allen surly because his patient is dying or because I didn't give him the right lab results? Should I bathe the patient first or change the dressing first?

Worrying about the unknown is almost as tiring. In a Code will I do what has to be done fast enough? If a patient dies, is it going to haunt me forever? The most profound unknowns had to do with God. I envied patients who seemed to feel He was right there, watching over them, pulling the strings at the right times. Sometimes when report was given at the beginning of the day, there would be forty-four patients in such awful circumstances that I couldn't imagine how there could be a God. "Suffering breeds character," Dr. Allen once said, but I was not convinced. *Bill Goldsmith could care less about character,* I thought.

By the end of the first semester, four students had seen enough—enough disease and dying, enough studying half the night and racing from campus to lab to hospital all day, enough taking written examinations that always seemed vague, enough doing gruesome things to each other in the lab. When they left the program, it was another unknown—if they couldn't cope with what was going on, could I? It was something I worried about often.

Dean and the kids were beginning to worry too. "We don't care if you've been out playing around with Charlie and Lani all day," Alan said one day. "That's okay, Mom. Don't mind us . . . we'll just sit here and starve while you play." They were not complaining a lot, but my new world was definitely intruding on their Brady Bunch fantasy about the way life at home should be—had always been.

If I had loved nursing less and complained more, they might not have felt so abandoned, but despite the obnoxious parts of nursing school, I was having the time of my life. Patients came into the hospital acting just the way I had acted as a patient—terrified, childlike, totally out of control. Sometimes I could make them feel better, with just a few words and a touch of the hand. By combing a little old lady's hair and listening to her talk, I could get her calmed down. When I explained why and how certain tests would be done, some patients stopped trembling. When I did for patients what I wished had been done for me as a patient, it was like working magic—there is an incomparable sense of satisfaction when you can make a patient feel better.

"You could make your own family feel better if you stayed home," my mother said. "Mothers should be home with their children and husband." It was a guilt that had begun to gnaw at me.

3 This Was *Nursing*

Following Christmas we began the second semester of school. I felt like an old pro, in the sense that I knew I wouldn't faint dead away at the sight of blood or lose my stomach while emptying a bedpan. But I thought of what we had done in the first semester as a sort of dress rehearsal that would get us into the big leagues—the theater of blood and blades. Perhaps because most of my personal horror stories had had their beginnings in an operating room, I thought of hospitals in a very narrow way—you went in because you needed surgery and you came out when you had been *fixed.*

Some people came into the hospital with chronic diseases that surgery could not help, and they left the hospital without being fixed. Yet this seemed incidental to the business of hospitals. At cocktail parties people talked about "my operation" in the same tone of voice that actors and actresses use when speaking of "my opening night," but no one there ever talked about the time they spent in the hospital while suffering from pancreatitis. Surgery was glamorous, after all. Chronic illness was not.

Even the physician totem pole reinforced the glamour of surgery. The gastroenterologists, near the bottom of the pole, might have had more to do with relieving the pain and suffering of patients, but the surgeons were accorded far more deference and recognition. The surgeons even *looked* like the star performers. Most were dapper dressers with gregarious personalities, and, on the one occasion I happened into the doctors' lounge by mistake, the surgeons were the ones who were gathered around a table, engrossed in a game of poker.

Poker didn't fit my image of any physician, but I rationalized that the intensity of the operating room must be so fierce, Wednesday golf was not enough relief—the surgeons *needed* a game like poker. "Wednesday is golf, Thursday is gin and Friday is poker, unless business is good," Charlie said. At the time, I missed the sarcasm in his voice.

After surgery, patients talked about "my wonderful surgeon" and were anxious to display the "perfect incision" that was his handiwork, but hardly anyone ever talked about the internist who had pulled them through a near-fatal bout of pneumonia, which is only to say that I was not alone in feeling that the mystique of surgery and surgeons was the most seductive part of becoming a nurse. The operating room—the sanctum sanctorum—where I was sure all the answers to life's medical mysteries were stored, lured me like a golden finish line.

"Maybe I'll faint," I told Lani. "What if I pass out with the first slice of the scalpel?"

"You can't faint, Barb. You have to scoop me off the floor when *I* faint." There was a sturdy air of confidence about her even when she sounded scared.

We never heard of anyone we knew fainting in the operating room, but the myth circulated nonetheless. "If you start getting light-headed," Mrs. Erin lectured, "think first of the sterile field and fall away from it. The very worst thing you can do in an operating room is contaminate the patient's incision."

Nancy Wallace, the head nurse, was rushing past the double doors as Lani and I walked into the operating suite. "Students?" She didn't wait for our answer; the startled looks gave us away. "Pick some scrub clothes off the racks over there. Change in the locker room at the end of the west hall and meet me back here." Her rather abrupt efficiency was comforting—she would pilot this complex plane and we would be mere passengers. Nancy had been a student in our program five years earlier. Before she became an RN, she had been a scrub technician at the Mayo Clinic for several years. "Cool, sharp, tough," Mrs. Erin said. "She's the best!"

Peter Haynes came out of the doctors' dressing room as we passed by. "Lani ... Barbara!" He hugged us both and then started laughing. "You look like I felt the first day in OR [operating room] ... four-plus terrified!"

We talked briefly about Christmas vacation, which had been no vacation for him. He was on duty in the emergency room during the holidays, except for time out to take care of Judith Newman.

"Better change in a hurry," Peter said. "Report's in five minutes."

The scrub clothes were sweltering, wrinkled, blue-green twill uglies that were deceptively sexy if worn two sizes too small, which is how the other nurses were wearing them. When all the nurses were gathered for report before the day began, the room looked like it was the meeting place for contestants in a beauty pageant. Even with the scrub caps made out of windshield-wipe material, and the ugly floppy booties with electrical grounding tape straggling from their heels, the nurses looked like they had been chosen for their attractiveness.

The masks were more uglies made of the windshield-wipe material with four strings to tie over the caps, but they were the ultimate touch of seduction. The crew spoke with their eyes, the only part of their bodies not shrouded in scrub clothes—we didn't know then that the most significant messages exchanged in *every* area of the hospital were those in the language of the eyes. It was something we would have to learn without the help of our college teachers.

When we were all decked out and waiting for Nancy at the nurses' station, I looked at the huge blackboard above the desk and saw Mr. Otis's name among twenty others listed.

"That's the menu for the day," Nancy said. She was busy orchestrating the patients, staff and surgeons for all ten operating rooms, which were gearing up to begin action at 8:00. "Take your pick. What would you like to see?"

"I want to see all of them," I said, though many operations were listed in abbreviations, and I had no idea what they were. "On the other hand, I want to go home more than anything." Mostly I didn't want to faint and make a fool of myself.

Lani was worrying too. "Do the surgeons really throw instruments at nurses, Nancy?" That might be worse than fainting. It was the legacy of nursing school to hear horror stories of assaults on nurses.

"There's one tyrant, Dr. Allen, who loves to pick on students." We already knew about his temper flares.

"Herman Otis . . . is Dr. Allen doing his surgery?" I asked. "He was my patient a few weeks ago." Dr. Allen I wanted to avoid, but Mr. Otis might be awake and happy to see a familiar face.

"Dr. Stewart is doing Otis at ten. Look, you might as well get it over with. Start out with Dr. Allen and Dr. Haynes at eight. They're doing a cholecystectomy [gallbladder removal]," Nancy said. "Don't worry. I'll tell Dr. Allen you're new . . . to bug off. It's a good operation to see for your first one." She hurried off down the hall, calling, "Good luck!"

"We'll need more than luck," Lani exclaimed. "What if Dr. Allen asks about gallbladders? Do you know anything about gallbladders?"

"I don't know anything about anything . . . my brain's sitting on hold. If we just stand in a corner and keep quiet, maybe he won't notice us."

That was the last we spoke to each other the rest of the day. We were so awed we *couldn't* speak.

After ten minutes of scrubbing with stiff brushes and a thick amber antiseptic, we held our burning, dripping arms up, bent at the elbows like in the movies, and walked into the hospital's deepest inner sanctum, the operating room. Just walking in was a thrill. Too many times I had been wheeled in on a gurney, wishing I could see through the narcotized haze that made the room seem so ominous.

"Watch it! Don't touch anything," the scrub tech called, more out of habit than need. She helped us into sterile gowns and gloves, which was no small trick, since she was sterile herself and had to avoid touching us or our clothes. "Anything you touch below your waist is contaminated," she warned.

Lani and I carefully threaded our way between tables, Mayo stands, buckets on wheels and bulky equipment that looked like props for a science fiction movie. A slow tremble started with my hands and spread to pucker my knees. Panic? Or the freezing cold of the room?

"You! Students!" The anesthesiologist calling from his cockpit of machinery across the room gave me a quick intestinal collapse. "You can get a better view from over here once we get under way. There's a stool to stand on."

"Thank you," I called, grateful that he expected us to do something other than faint.

Everything seemed in suspended animation until Dr. Allen bustled into the room with Dr. Haynes behind him. Together they looked like Mutt and Jeff—Dr. Allen short, pudgy and abrupt, Dr. Haynes tall, slender and calm. While the scrub tech was helping Dr. Allen with gown and gloves, Dr. Haynes turned and smiled at Lani and me. So much for wishing we could be invisible.

As the patient was wheeled into the room, everything became a too-fast movie. The anesthesiologist hardly waited for the patient to be moved to the operating table before he slipped an IV (intravenous) needle into her arm. Two nurses appeared out of nowhere to scrub the patient's body, from neck to thighs, with the same thick antiseptic we had used.

The patient was a large lady in her mid-forties, apparently fast asleep before she was wheeled into the room. We hardly had a look at her face when a drape was suspended from high poles, blocking her head and the anesthesiologist from our view. In a sense, it seemed there was no person on the table—only a body.

Dr. Allen and Dr. Haynes stood on opposite sides of the operating table, arms folded above their waists, until all the drapes were in place. Without a word, the scrub tech pulled the instrument table over as she climbed a stool on Dr. Allen's left. The only sound in the room was the rhythmic bleep-bleep of the heart monitor buried somewhere in the anesthesiologist's machinery. She handed the cautery iron to Dr. Haynes and a scalpel to Dr. Allen.

Dr. Allen held the scalpel up like a baton—a thunderous roll of drums and a trumpet fanfare would have suited the moment perfectly. "Ready?" he asked.

He scanned the room and noticed Lani and me in the corner. *Oh God,* I thought, *here it comes!*

"Students?"

"Yes, Dr. Allen . . . their first day . . . first operation," Nancy said. She tried to introduce us but stumbled over our names. I opened my mouth to prompt her, but words were choked somewhere between my throat and my mouth.

"Can't see anything from over there," he growled. "If you want to learn anything, get over here!"

Lani and I moved like wobbly robots just a few steps closer to the table. Why didn't someone tell Dr. Allen new students faint . . . should stand near a wall . . . away from the sterile field? Dr. Haynes sprouted creases at the corners of his eyes, as though he knew what we were thinking.

Dr. Allen raised the scalpel again, then lowered it for the first incision on the side of the patient's upper abdomen. All the dramatic moments of my life were humbled by the long, swift slice of the blade. This was *nursing,* as the wedding ceremony was marriage—in the books, movies and TV dramas—I was totally unaware of the unbidden tears spotting the front of my scrub gown. Common old housewife Barbara was on the only side of the blade worth being on, about to have a peek into the medical wizards' own vast ocean of mystery—the human body.

The compulsion to see inside a human body washed over me like a wave from nowhere. There before me was the human anatomy in living color—the rectus sheath, greater and lesser omentum—down through the layers Dr. Allen cut, Dr. Haynes sponging and clamping as they went, like unwrapping a very common package.

The liver was peeking out from under the ribs; the gallbladder swelled from beneath the lower margin of the liver; all the parts were right where I had expected to see them. Still, it seemed miraculous, like the instant when a newborn baby arrives.

My stomach was folding back and forth over itself like cards in the hands of a magician. The odor of freshly cauterized flesh, the pulsating of exposed veins and arteries, the gurgling of blood as it was suctioned into waste jars—my body kept recoiling, as if all the instruments were assaulting me.

"It's okay to leave," Nancy whispered behind me. "Lots of students do, you know. Use the door near the scrub tubs." She pointed to the tearstains on my scrub gown.

"I'm fine," I whispered. How could I tell her the tears were more awed than sad? Or that it was an incredible high suddenly to feel that I was myself at last—Barbara the nurse—in a world where I knew I belonged. Me leave? Never!

"You!" Dr. Allen barked, looking straight at me. "From the top . . . the digestive system."

I pretended I was invisible.

Nancy leaned toward me and hissed, "Anatomy . . . mouth to rectum."

Before we ever applied to the nursing program we had to know that. It seemed an insult that he would ask anything so simple. "Mouth, esophagus, stomach, duodenum, jejunum, ileum, ascending colon, descending colon . . ."

"Wrong!" His eyes squinted at the corners as he looked at me.

"Ascending, *transverse,* descending, sigmoid colon, rectum, anal canal."

He was working with his hands inside the patient's abdomen and looking at Lani and me at the same time. It was nerve-racking, like being a passenger on a narrow, winding road while the driver points out the scenery beyond the edge of the cliff. We didn't know then he could have removed a gallbladder blindfolded, he had done so many over the years.

When the gallbladder was out, Nancy brought it in a stainless-steel basin so we could have a look before it was put in a container and sent to the pathology lab. "All tissue removed is sent to the lab for biopsy," she told us. "We're always looking for cancer, even if no one suspects it."

"Sew 'er up, Peter." Dr. Allen snapped off his gloves, tossed them in the trash bucket and left. The whole room seemed to sigh in relief as he walked out the door. Dr. Haynes went about suturing all the layers of the abdomen, then Nancy covered the wound with a dressing. Even before the drapes had been removed, the lady was coughing and sputtering, awakening from the anesthesia.

Within minutes, she was whisked to the recovery room, the soiled instruments and equipment were sent off to the sterilizing room, and a team of orderlies scrubbed the floor, table and counters for the next patient. It seemed too similar to what happens when one group of diners leaves the restaurant and the table is prepared for another group.

Lani and I were still rooted to the same spot when Nancy returned from taking the patient to the recovery room. "You look like you've just seen a ghost," she said, laughing. "That thoracotomy [chest surgery] . . . Mr. Otis? Dr. Stewart's going to do that in room eight, if you want to watch that next."

It seemed that watching one operation, our *first,* should have been enough for one day, even if it had only lasted an hour.

My body felt as though it had worked at shoveling coal for at least twelve hours straight.

Charlie caught up with us as Lani and I hurried to room 8. "Hey, you guys! You didn't pass out ... Nancy says you did great." He was assigned to the recovery room, next door to the operating room, and was hoping we would join him for coffee. "It's boring in recovery ... all the patients do is sleep!"

Just then I noticed Mr. Otis on a gurney across the hall. Most patients are out when they get to the OR, but he was sitting up almost straight, looking startled and curious. I clasped his hands in both of mine, then remembered I was all shrouded in the scrub clothes and mask—he wouldn't know who I was.

At first, he looked confused, then he smiled and patted one of my hands. "Hey, honey, I remember you. You held my hand that bad day ... I'd know your hands if I were blind." He reached up to pull me into a hug.

I almost asked, "What are *you* doing here?" but realized most patients think every nurse and doctor in the entire hospital should know what each patient is doing there. What I wondered was why a patient with bladder cancer was having chest surgery.

It had been four months since my first day in the hospital, when I mistook a sleeping Mr. Otis for dead. For that reason alone, he was at the top of my "most unforgettable character" list. The next time he was admitted to the hospital, about two weeks later, it was for his first surgery, and Lani and I were assigned to the twelve-bed hall where he became even more memorable.

He wandered from room to room, looking like a scruffy vagabond, in a three-sizes-too-big plaid bathrobe and a pair of crinkled leather slippers that flapped against his heels as he walked.

"Have bag, will travel," he laughed, carrying his catheter bag along like a briefcase. Actually he was a squeaky-clean, witty, wonderful little gentleman who was probably embarrassed at having to tote along a bag full of bloody urine for all the world to see. Joking about it seemed to shrink the significance.

Within twenty-four hours of a prostatectomy (removal of the prostate gland) which would have kept any other elderly gentleman in bed for several days, I found him rummaging around in the pantry near the nurses' station. "Listen, honey, where do you keep the tea bags these days? And how about a biscuit or two?"

When I explained that anesthesia makes the digestive system sleepy until a few days after surgery, and that food would not get where it was supposed to go, he gave me a quizzical look and said, "Listen, honey, if my stomach could talk, it would tell you it's tea and biscuits every day at four o'clock ... surgery or not ... for seventy-too-many years."

"Would you settle for tea, just until I can get ahold of Dr. Stewart and see what he says?"

"Sure, honey, if you can get him before my stomach notices."

It wasn't uncommon for doctors to forget to change diet orders so patients could begin to eat, and it wasn't uncommon for patients to do exactly what Mr. Otis did—ignore the orders and eat whatever he could find

"Listen, honey. I ate those old stale crackers in there," he whispered later. "This poor ole stomach just couldn't wait." It was too late to tell him Dr. Stewart had said he would have to wait, but if he had known how much Lani and I would worry about the consequences of the crackers, he wouldn't have enjoyed them at all.

When he was bored, which was almost always, he "helped" us by playing hall monitor, answering patients' lights and keeping track of which patient needed us next.

When he tired of that, he would walk in some patient's room and say, "Good morning there. Say, have you heard about the owl and the goat that had a hootenanny?" Some patients looked at him and said nothing, as if he were a crazy old crock who would go away if they didn't respond. "My brother said to me, 'Hermie, your hair's getting thin.' So who wants fat hair?" He just kept up the one-liners and finally got the patient laughing just because it was amusing to see how much Mr. Otis enjoyed his own jokes.

Sometimes I thought the hospital should hire a Mr. Otis for every hall, just to go around and cheer up patients who were frightened and lonely. He had a knack for picking out the ones who needed his humor most, and he was just as clever at knowing when it would help if he talked seriously and let them know he could still manage to make a bit of a carnival out of life even though he had a terminal diagnosis hanging over his head.

The day his humor went down the drain was the day the social worker, Cathy Ardmore, told him he would have to go to a nursing home at the end of the week. "Just for a while," she said. "Someone has to do your bladder irrigations and dress your surgery wound . . . just for a while." Cathy was tight-lipped and earnest, like a strict math teacher. Maybe she had a soft heart, but we saw her as a skinny, thirty-five-year-old jilted spinster.

"Talk to the boss," he said, "the tall one with the hat." To him, any nurses wearing hats were "the boss"—he didn't know only students wore caps in those days. "The boss will tell you I'm not going to any nursing home. I've been alone eighteen years . . . I'm *staying* alone!"

"His insurance runs out Thursday," Cathy told me. "We can't keep him after that."

"Give us a week," I argued. "Lani and I will teach him how to do his irrigations and dressings. How about sending a visiting nurse out to his place every day?"

"His insurance company won't authorize payment past Thursday. He has to go, that's all!" She seemed aloof and uncaring, but it was her job. If she didn't get patients out on time, her job would be given to someone else.

When I told him he would have to go to a nursing home, just for a while, he acted as if I had betrayed him. "But you're the boss . . . you tell that young girl I'm not going!"

The effects of fear, panic, hate, dread, rage and despair were known to Hippocrates two thousand years ago—they make a sick body sicker. There is hardly anything that can make someone like Mr. Otis sicker than telling him there is a nursing home in his future.

On Thursday I popped my head in his door just to see how he was before I got started with the day's work. His eyes were glazed and feverish. The water pitcher on his table had been knocked to the floor and he was plucking at the bedclothes like someone who is frantic for oxygen. It was a familiar scene—stroke patients look frantic and pluck at their clothing.

"Good morning, Mr. Otis." I hurried to take his blood pressure and feel his pulse to make sure he wasn't oxygen-starved.

"Did you have a bad night?" He turned his face to the wall and pulled the covers over his head. "C'mon . . . how about poking your head out here so I can take your temperature?" Had it been any other hour, I would have sat with him and tried to work things out as best I could, but it was shift change, and the phone at the nurses' station sounded as if it would ring off the hook. The night nurses were getting ready to leave, and I was the only day nurse there.

By the time I answered it, the voice on the other end sounded near hysteria. "Where are all the nurses up there, for God's sake?" I looked around and wondered the same thing myself. "There's a naked man, heading toward the turnpike, running down Central Avenue." I waited as if expecting the punchline to a joke.

"Are you there?"

"I'm here," I said. "What shall I do?"

"It's a patient. It's snowing, for heaven's sake . . . he'll freeze to death."

"Call security!" I shouted, trying to picture how I would tackle a naked man as he sprinted between the lanes of commuters on their way to work. "I'm on my way!" In the background I could hear the alarm on the fire door he must have used for escape.

As I pulled a blanket from the linen closet and headed for the stairs, Charlotte Topping, one of the night nurses, hollered, "Help! Code!" just as the Code Blue alarm at the station began its insistent "Bleep! Bleep! Bleep!" The elevator emptied out three nurses who were just coming on duty. God must have heard Charlotte's call for help.

"Code!" I yelled to them as I flung the blanket on the desk, placed the naked sprinter in the keeping of whatever Higher Power might be up there, and ran to grab the crash cart. It was stored in a seldom-used examining room that had a closet I wished would swallow me up. The Code Blue procedure had not yet been covered in lecture or lab, I still had never seen CPR, and panic was twisting in my throat.

I was just steering the crash cart through the doorway when Faith Mason, the head nurse, got out of the elevator. "Code!" I yelled. "Room 324 . . . I've never done one." She dropped her coat and purse where she was, grabbed the handle of the cart and went racing down the hall.

"Stay at the station. Direct the Code team," she called. "Watch the lights. Call Dr. Allen!"

The Code team arrived, huffing and puffing from running the two flights of stairs. "Room 324," I kept calling, while in the background the operator's metallic voice called over the intercom, "Code Blue, Three North! . . . Code Blue, Three North! . . . Code Blue, Three North!"

Lani and Charlie got out of the elevator just as I reached Dr. Allen's answering service. I pointed toward room 324, then noticed the patient callboard was buzzing away with about twelve lights flashing. "Wait!" I called to them. "There's no one to answer the lights. Help!"

"Dr. Allen's exchange . . . hold, please." The line clicked to the hold music that is supposed to be soothing but is infuriating when the call is urgent and the operator has no idea who is on the other end.

"It's a Code," I yelled into the receiver. "For heaven's sake, hurry up!" The lighthearted tune from *Fiddler on the Roof* seemed an incongruous insult, as did the operator's calm, cheery voice when finally she answered.

"Dr. Allen's exchange. Good morning . . . may I help you?"

"His patient has Coded . . . Oakmont Community Hospital . . . third floor."

"The patient's name, please."

"Room 324 . . . I don't know the name . . . just hurry, will you?"

"Hold, please."

"Couldn't you just tell him to get over here?" I said to the hold music.

Finally Dr. Allen came on the line. "Yes?"

"Your patient has Coded . . . room 324." I tried to sound calm and dignified, but missed by a mile.

"Patient's name?"

"I don't know . . . just a minute . . . I'll find out." There were forty-four patients on that floor, the ward clerk's desk was foreign territory to me—how would I find out?

"Never mind . . . it's probably Hank Cooper. Which doctor is running the Code?"

"I don't know. Just a minute . . . I'll find out."

"No, don't bother . . ."

"I saw several doctors going there, Dr. Allen."

"Be right over." The phone clicked dead. *No wonder doctors get frustrated,* I thought. When a Code is in progress, the ward clerk is away from the desk, and there is no one but a student at the phone, anyone who wants information is out of luck. It was at that moment that the ward clerk stepped out of the elevator, and I decided she was the most important person on any nursing unit.

"Code's going on in 324 . . . place is a zoo . . . Dr. Allen's on his way in . . . Lani and Charlie are answering lights . . . Mr. Otis is really sick, I'm going there."

"Gimme a break!" she laughed. "What did you do . . . come in early just to stir up trouble?"

"That's not all," I called to her, suddenly remembering the naked sprinter. Just then the security guard came out of the elevator with his arm around a frail, feeble, shivering Mr. Emory, who was also scheduled to go to a nursing home that day. He was naked indeed.

"Mr. Emory just wanted to go visit his daughter," said the security guard sympathetically. "Have you got a blanket for us?" He picked up the one I had intended to take out to the turnpike hours earlier (it only *seemed* like hours). To say that Mr. Emory looked cute might sound condescending, but there is no other way to describe how he stood there with his skinny knees knocking, his newborn-bird body quivering, and a surprised, inquisitive look on his face, topped off by a few stray white hairs sticking straight up on the top of his head. I hugged the blanket around him while I thought about what it must be like to be so desperate. Did the anticipation of going to a nursing home feel like abandonment, imprisonment, punishment—all of those plus more?

Charlie came along and was taking Mr. Emory down the hall for a warm bath and some breakfast just as the Code team came out of room 324, laughing and teasing each other while they pushed the patient's bed on their way to the ICU. They had successfully resuscitated the patient.

It was exactly 7:00 A.M., and the day had not officially begun. The narcotics would have to be counted, the diet lists checked for accuracy, the morning insulin injections administered, patients sent off to surgery; and the night shift nurses would need to report to the day nurses on what had been going on with each patient since 11:00 the night before. It felt like noon and the worst was yet to come.

When I finally coaxed Mr. Otis into talking, he told me, "Listen, honey, I'd rather be dead at home than alive in a nursing home. I'm an independent cuss ... that's all." He smiled weakly, almost apologizing for bucking the system, as if he had pulled some trick to give himself the 101-degree fever that would save him from being transferred to the nursing home.

"He's escaping into illness," remarked Cathy Ardmore. "His fever guarantees the insurance company will extend his stay, but he can't keep a fever forever."

It took a bit of manipulating, but his thermometer managed to register a fever until the next week when his surgical incision was all healed and he no longer needed the bladder irrigations. When he left, it was *not* to go to a nursing home—he was bound for his mobile home in the mountains.

Four months had passed between that day and this, when we found him sitting on the gurney in the operating room. "Are you still living alone?" I asked.

"Yep. That's the way it has to be."

He looked thinner, grayish and anything but well. Though his breathing was labored and shallow, he acted as if he had simply come there to check things out and have a look around the operating room.

I told him that Lani and I were going to watch his surgery, and then felt guilty that the thought was such comfort to him. Little did he know we were not the experienced nurses of his fantasy. "Thank you. Thank you," he kept saying as if he had just been rendered safe.

Dr. Haynes came along and told us he would be assisting Dr. Stewart with the surgery. "I see you've picked the best nurses," he told Mr. Otis. "Did your sons get here yet?"

Mr. Otis looked sheepish. "Haven't told them yet ... no

sense makin' a fuss." Lani and I stood on either side of the operating table, holding Mr. Otis's hands while the anesthesiologist started the IV, and Dr. Haynes talked about what would happen after surgery. "You'll be in ICU," he said, "and I'll be right there beside you when you wake up ... don't worry, we'll be watching you every minute."

"Count backwards from ten," the anesthesiologist instructed.

I gave Mr. Otis's hand a quick squeeze and sent him a huge love-courage message with my eyes. "Sweet dreams!"

The drugs injected through the IV line worked almost instantly. Mr. Otis's hand grew limp in mine as he counted backwards, and he was out before he got to six. There was a momentary flash of panic in my chest as I remembered how it felt to be going under the last time I had surgery. That sudden, involuntary surrender of control leaves one incredibly overwhelmed. "He's so vulnerable now," I said quietly, almost to myself.

"Poor risk," Dr. Haynes commented. "C'mon. Let's go scrub before Dr. Stewart gets in here." While we were at the scrub tubs, I asked what he meant by "poor risk."

"On a risk scale of one to ten, he's about eleven. It's bad enough that he's seventy years old ... he's a cancer patient, in remission now but immunosuppressed from radiation and chemotherapy. There's not a lot going for him, and he won't even tell his sons he's sick, let alone that he's in deep trouble now."

"Peter, you're keeping Dr. Stewart waiting. We're ready to start," Terri Greer called over the intercom. Terri was the circulating nurse for room 8. Pert and young, she was the bold, cheerful type who couldn't be bothered with obsolete decorum—like addressing Peter formally as Dr. Haynes over the intercom. I was an "old lady" in a profession of mostly young nurses, wed to the tradition of indicating respect for doctors by using last names.

"Let's go," Peter said, and we walked into the operating

room together, dripping puddles of scrub water behind us. The scrub tech handed us sterile towels, and we joined Terri and the rest of the staff for the operation.

When I saw Conrad Stewart, I realized no nurse—not even Terri—would call *him* by his first name. Though he couldn't be considered intimidating, there was an air of majesty about him. Perhaps it was his height, well over six feet, or the soft, intimate tone of his voice that invited one to listen more closely. His blue eyes were provocative in a way that was compelling but disarming. When he looked directly into your eyes, it was as if there was a shared secret . . . except that only he knew what it was.

"Ah, students," he said. We must have worn neon signs over our heads which made it obvious we were new. "Step right up here." Dr. Haynes introduced us to him and then indicated that Lani was to stand on the stool across from Dr. Stewart. I hesitated, thinking surely someone in that room would jump to our defense and tell Dr. Stewart we should stand away from the sterile field, preferably against a wall, but no one made a move. Dr. Stewart beckoned me over to the stool beside him. As I stepped up, I smiled and looked deeply into his eyes, hoping he could read the whistling-in-the-dark message.

"This is our first day in the operating room," I said in my most pleading voice. Any clairvoyant would have known I was saying, "This is too close to the action . . . I've never seen inside a chest before . . . Mr. Otis is a real, live human being . . . my first patient . . . very special . . . I'm not sure I can keep my head on straight while you cut him . . . oh help!" Dr. Stewart was not clairvoyant, but he was friendly and gentle, which was almost as good.

As he cut through each layer, he explained the instruments and what he was doing, why he had to crack the ribs to get to the lung, and which arteries and veins he would need to sever. I kept my eyes glued to the incision, pretending that it wasn't really Mr. Otis with his head just inches above where Dr. Stewart was working.

By the time the chest was open and the cracking of the ribs had stopped ringing in my ears, the lung, moving up and down in rhythmical breathing, seemed to pump a fog around me in a smothering swirl. It was one thing to watch from the foot of the operating table, and quite another to be right there trying to answer Dr. Stewart's requests to hold a retractor, move the sponge, release the clamps. He and Dr. Haynes worked quickly, and kept two scrub techs, as well as Lani and me, in constant motion.

The fog came and went in waves that finally subsided just as the line on the heart-monitor screen went flat.

Technically it was a Code Blue, the panic call in every hospital. Had the Code taken place anywhere but the operating room, an army of people with life-saving equipment would have dashed from all directions to organize the Code team. As it was, everything for retrieving life was right there. Dr. Stewart pushed the lung to the side and began massaging the heart instantly. There was a straight line for several seconds, followed by an erratic flutter, then several intermittent beats.

The bleeping of the monitor was an annoyance, like a car that acts as if it's going to start and then doesn't. Again there was nothing. Straight line ... more erratic flutters, several intermittent beats, and finally the restored normal rhythm. The tension in the room was almost tangible as the crew kept their eyes glued to the monitor until the normal rhythm had gone on for at least two minutes.

No one had spoken a word. Finally Dr. Stewart stood back from the table and twisted his shoulders around as if unwinding sprung muscles. "Okay, people, just keep calm ... we're doing fine here ... no need for panic." It was the only time his voice was gruff, as if chiding naughty children.

A few minutes later, Dr. Stewart muttered, "There it is ... just as I thought ... look at that!" He was holding Mr. Otis's right lung in his hand. The cancer that had begun in his bladder had metastasized to his lung.

Amid the noise of machinery and talking in the operating

room, the heart-monitor sound is subtle, like the ticking of a clock, and the rare variations in rhythm were something I felt before I consciously heard them. There was a hesitation, then a late beat, another hesitation, a faint little "bleep." Dr. Stewart began massaging the heart again. Only the startled eyes of the crew, all looking up at the monitor, gave away the fact that Mr. Otis was having a second cardiac arrest.

"Peter, did he ever get his sons out here?"

"I tried, Dr. Stewart. He wouldn't do it . . . said it would be making a mountain out of a molehill."

"Some molehill," Dr. Stewart muttered. "Maybe we should have called them anyway."

"Pressure's dropping," the anesthesiologist called.

"Terri, get us some more blood . . . how many have we got left?"

"Four."

"Push 'em all. Call up to the lab and see if we can get more."

"Do you want a pacemaker, Dr. Stewart?" Dr. Haynes spoke calmly, but his face was dripping with perspiration.

"Yeah . . . we're losing ground, Peter. Terri, get us a heart surgeon stat . . . see if they've got a pacer we can use in room ten."

The anesthesiologist sucked a huge gasp of air through his teeth as blood spurted up like a geyser and sprayed across the front of my gown. Both doctors had their hands in the chest, with an assortment of instruments flying in and out.

"Get it! Where is it?" Dr. Stewart yelled as they searched for the vessel that had burst. It didn't seem that anyone, even a healthy patient, could survive the loss of all the blood that was pooling in a throbbing, bubbling mass and overflowing onto the drapes surrounding the chest.

In the background I heard the hospital intercom. "Any cardiologist, to the operating room stat! . . . Any cardiologist, to the operating room stat! . . . Any cardiologist, to the operating room stat!"

Dr. Haynes would pluck a blood vessel from the pool of blood and examine it for a perforation while Dr. Stewart searched around for another—it seemed a hopeless task, like feeling for minnows in a muddy ocean. Nurses in scrub clothes appeared in answer to Terri's phone calls, which had coordinated an entire team without anyone saying a word. The respiratory therapist was there to draw blood gases, technicians from the heart team came to assist with the implanting of a heart pacer, fresh trays of instruments were brought from central service, huge lamps and microscopes were rolled in by orderlies, and the blood bank delivered a tray heaped with units of blood.

"Cancel the surgery to follow," Terri told the supervisor. "Put Dr. Stewart's other surgeries on hold. We'll see how this turns out . . . could take a while." Her voice was clipped but calm. In fact, the apparent calm of everyone as they moved quickly to assemble everything and everybody who might be needed to avert catastrophe was stunning.

"Got it!" The anesthesiologist's whispered exclamation signaled Dr. Haynes's success at finding the bleeder. The pulsating pool of blood was still.

"How's the pressure?" Dr. Stewart asked the anesthesiologist.

"Same . . . we're into this four hours now." Later I learned that the risks of deep anesthesia compound with time. It wasn't that anyone could have altered the progress of the operation— the anesthesiologist was keeping score, in a sense.

Two cardiologists were putting on scrub gowns at the door. "What's up?"

Dr. Stewart was tying a tiny knot, which would hold the culprit vessel. Without looking up, he said, "Bert . . . thanks for coming. We've got part of a lung out . . . heart's acting up . . think we ought to put in a pacer." He turned and nodded toward the scrub tech. She wiped the perspiration from his brow with a sterile towel. "Thank you," he murmured.

Perhaps because I knew I would have to be so adept one day, the nurses' ability to anticipate exactly what should be done next, even in such uncommon situations, without any verbal directions, both awed and frightened me. With all that was happening in that room, how did the scrub tech know to wipe the surgeon's brow at that precise moment? Terri had been injecting solutions in IV lines, gathering supplies and equipment as the operation progressed, summoning people from whatever tasks they might have been involved in, emptying various collection vessels as they became full, keeping the front desk informed on the progress—how did she know what to do when, in a situation that changed from moment to moment?

It seemed a waste that I was there, in the front lines, inadequate to perform. I offered my spot to the cardiologist, Dr. Lundford, just as Lani was offering hers to the other cardiologist. "No, no," said Dr. Stewart. "Students only learn by watching. Ever seen a pacer implantation?"

"No."

Susan Erin, our instructor, was standing in a corner. The expression on her face, as I was about to step down from the stool, kept me rooted at Dr. Stewart's side. She hadn't been there when the operation began, but I had no idea how long she had been watching. If I did what I thought she expected, I would continue to stand there, back ramrod straight, and watch like an intent scholar.

If I did what I wanted to do, I would crumble into a heap in some little closet that no one ever used. My body ached from the effort of disassociating what was happening above the drapes from the vulnerable human being I knew beneath the drapes. Even if he could survive the two cardiac arrests, the loss of massive quantities of blood, the partial removal of one lung, the implantation of a pacemaker, the row of cracked ribs, and the damages of such long anesthetizing, what would be the point? What was ahead of him could hardly be termed life.

Such thoughts made my hands tremble. I clasped them together tightly and continued to look like the intent scholar while I pondered the decision—to step down from the stool would be to leave nursing forever. To stay would be to separate intellect from emotion.

A pacemaker is an electronic device, about the size of the smallest transistor radio, which controls the heart rate by providing repetitive electrical stimuli when the natural rate regulators of the heart are unable to do so themselves. Some pacemakers are temporary, to control heart rate during surgery. The permanent ones are of varying design and usage, according to the type and severity of the condition they are intended to treat.

The one being implanted was a demand pacer, which would emit stimuli only when Mr. Otis's heart failed. Dr. Bert Lundford, the cardiologist, explained that the pacer would improve the blood flow to major organs (heart, kidneys and brain) and prevent a third cardiac arrest.

It seemed a simple procedure of implanting the electrode system on the outside of the left ventricle of the heart, and placing the generator in a skin "pocket" just above the waist. Perhaps in the hands of a less skilled surgeon it would not have seemed so simple, but Dr. Lundford worked quickly, in staccato movements that mimicked his appearance and personality—crisp, short, precise.

The other cardiologist, Dr. Banterman, never spoke. No one even acknowledged that he was there. Later Dr. Haynes told me that Dr. Banterman was the resident under Dr. Lundford. "Residents are thought to be invisible," Peter said bitterly. "Dr. Banterman is a better cardiologist than Dr. Lundford could ever hope to be, but while he's in residency, his role is to act invisible."

Whatever the relationship, the two cardiologists worked in perfect concert, as if implanting a pacer was something they had done together hundreds of times. Occasionally Dr. Stewart made an approving comment. He was standing with Dr. Haynes, among the anesthesiologist's machinery at the head of the operating table. When the implantation was complete, the job of putting Mr. Otis back together again was turned over to them.

Dr. Banterman and Dr. Lundford snapped off their gloves as they stepped down from the stools. "I've got a bypass about to begin in room ten," Dr. Lundford said. "Catch me there if this thing acts up." Whether it was because Mr. Otis was finally safe from another cardiac arrest, or because Dr. Lundford's brisk manner was a bit unnerving, most of the tension seemed to leave the room as the cardiologists strode down the hall.

Dr. Haynes and Dr. Stewart began the slow, tedious job of closing the long incision, layer by layer, which started in the center of Mr. Otis's back and followed the line of the rib cage up to the center of his chest. "Your mom must've been real proud of your embroidery," quipped the anesthesiologist. "You guys do good work." The remark seemed sacrilegious, like popping bubble gum in church, but my built-in hostility toward anesthesiologists made me very shortsighted at the time. Later I would come to appreciate any touch of humor that would lighten the burden of such intense situations.

In what seemed to me the final, brutal, assaultive gesture, Dr. Stewart thrust a stiff latex tube through the skin into Mr. Otis's chest with a plop that could be heard across the room. My inner gasp came out of my mouth before I could stop it. Too soon, emotion reconnected with my intellect, and again it was a human body lying there—Herman Otis, wanting tea and biscuits at 4:00. "Plop"—another tube, a couple of inches below the first, was thrust into the chest wall. Both came together to one latex tube connected to a gallon-size glass jar. The tubes would remove air and fluid from the cavity so Mr. Otis's lung could expand.

Finally an enormous dressing was packed around the whole, leaving the chest tubes sticking out, and the doctors began removing the drapes. Terri leaned over a bucket to lift blood-soaked sponges, shake them out full length and then drape them over the side. The scrub tech swished soiled instruments around in basins of water—the business-as-usual way the crew went about their work was one of the most stunning features of the day.

When all the drapes, sponges, instruments and equipment were removed, Mr. Otis looked like a lost soul in a maze of tubes, one from his mouth to the respirator that would keep him breathing; the catheter from his bladder so the function of his kidneys could be continually assessed; the chest tubes to the jug on the floor; and an IV in each arm to keep the fluids and blood running in to replace what he had lost. He was a pathetic sight if ever there was one.

Together we lifted him onto a gurney and, with Dr. Stewart following close behind, wheeled him to the recovery room where Charlie was waiting, not too patiently, for some action. It was the kind of case that suited Charlie—complex, challenging and fraught with the threat of impending death.

Almost before we had the gurney pulled into the spot that had been cleared for it, Charlie was attaching the monitor wires from Mr. Otis's chest to the overhead monitor. He pulled out his stethoscope, carefully arranged all the tubes and IVs, took Mr. Otis's blood pressure—all before we had time to step away from the gurney. Lani and I were probably the only ones who knew he was still one of "us," students who still had more than a year to go.

I wanted to stay and hover with Dr. Haynes and Dr. Stewart until there was some sign of life from Mr. Otis, but Nancy Wallace called over the intercom that Lani and I were to report to room 10 immediately. "Wait," Terri told us. "Let me get Dr. Stewart to sign the sponge count. I'll show you where room ten is." That's when I learned that a sponge is simply a gauze pad. Every sponge used during an operation is counted before and after, just to be sure none are left in the patient's wound.

"When there's a spurting bleeder like we had with Mr. Otis, it's easy to lose a sponge in all that blood," Terri explained. "Saving his life is more important than keeping track of sponges . . . but try and tell that to a jury when the sponge shows up on an X-ray two months after the surgery!"

For some reason it seemed presumptuous to ask the doctors if Mr. Otis would live, yet it was a burning question. "Will he live?" Lani whispered to Terri. She beckoned toward the door and we went out in the hall before she replied. "Nancy refused to assist with that surgery. She's betting he won't make it."

"How could she decide that *before* the surgery?" Lani asked.

"Surgery might give him time . . . that's all . . . just time," Terri said. "Personally, I'd *want* time. Nancy says if she can't have life with quality, she doesn't want the quantity."

It was a decision I would have to make for myself, sooner than I ever would have suspected, but at the time I thought of it as a fascinating moral issue that was something to be pondered, perhaps in terms of Bill Goldsmith or Herman Otis.

4   Too Much

The first day in surgery was too much—too much blood, too much life-hanging-by-a-thread, too much cutting, clipping and slicing, too much defrocking of the medical mystique all in one day. I was a different person when I arrived at the hospital that morning than I was when I left the operating room almost twelve hours later.

The wife Dean took to a corporate banquet that night was not someone he recognized either. He was the speaker. No one could ever call one of his speeches a "sleeper"—dramatic, witty, profound speeches were his forte. But I slept.

"You're too much . . . really too much," he said. "Have you ever heard of a speaker's own *wife* falling asleep, for Pete's sake?"

It was the beginning of a chasm that I was too myopic to correlate with the fact that several nurses in our class were in the midst of dissolving marriages. *What's Dean doing dragging me to these banquets?* I wondered. *Can't he see I don't belong there anymore?*

"Don't tell us all that yucky stuff," the kids would say. "Hold the gore!"

Friends and neighbors certainly weren't any more interested in my new world than Dean and the kids, which seemed an astounding revelation. Wasn't *everybody* eager to hear about wondrous scientific advances in organ transplants, breast reconstruction, surgery with laser beams . . . exciting stuff?

"No one will listen," I complained to Charlie one day. "All these traumatic, awful things happen every day and we can't even tell anyone. It's like nurses are on another planet where shocking events are a private movie in a foreign language that no one else can understand."

"What's so traumatic? I'll listen . . . what happened?"

It was the last day of our operating room rotation, and really no more traumatic than any other, but the urge to babble was always greatest when personal values were becoming confused with moral and ethical dilemmas. "That case we did this morning . . . Frank Bandini?"

"Oh yeah . . . the twenty-seven-year-old." Charlie rolled his eyes skyward and twitched his body as if trying to escape from the confines of a prickly blanket. I remembered the look of horror on Charlie's face when we pulled Frank's gurney up to the slot Charlie had cleared for him in the recovery room.

There is no law that says a young life has greater value than a life of one who has been around several decades, but except for orthopedic cases, it was rare to have a young patient in surgery. To have one so close to Charlie's own age was bringing tragedy too close to home.

Frank's official diagnosis, before surgery, had been "abdominal pain of unknown etiology." The pain wasn't new, but it had recently intensified and become something he couldn't ignore when frequent vomiting kept him from going to work. The surgery that morning, an exploratory laparotomy, was an incision that extended from his breastbone down the middle of his abdomen in order to expose an area large enough that the surgeon could explore all his organs for the cause of pain.

As the circulating nurse that day, I had to make sure he was the right patient, prepared for the right surgery, with the right chart forms and consents all completed before the operation began. Once surgery was in progress, I kept a chart of everything that happened, who did what, what medications were given, and how the patient tolerated the operation.

In addition, I counted the sponges, summoned other departments if they were needed, and kept the operating crew supplied with anything they might need from the storeroom. All the things that had been done by Terri Greer during Mr. Otis's operation—all the things I had been so sure *I* could never do adequately—were things I was doing during Frank Bandini's operation.

The circulating nurse often goes in and out of the room to gather equipment and supplies, which is why she is not scrubbed (sterile) and must stay as far as possible from the sterile field. This is why I didn't actually see Frank's exploratory laparotomy—something I would regret a few months later when the same surgery would be performed on me.

"As soon as they brought Frank into the operating room, Nancy Wallace flipped," I told Charlie. "She grabbed the chart from the orderly and started growling about the whole thing being an abomination. Then she wouldn't let them transfer Frank to the table, and she said she was going to talk to Dr. Allen. She never came back!"

There had been arguing in the hall, with Dr. Haynes taking Nancy's side, and a sudden hush when Dr. Allen appeared on the scene. Eventually Terri Greer came in to take Nancy's place, and Frank was scrubbed and draped without comment, as though there had been no disagreement.

"Nancy refused to assist . . . said it was unnecessary surgery," I told Charlie.

"That's how much *she* knows," Charlie huffed. "What proof has she got?" She and Dr. Haynes both believed that surgery releases cancer cells to travel throughout the body and hasten the terminal process.

"So, does surgery make it worse or doesn't it?" I wanted to know. Months later, when my own life was at stake, the question was even *more* urgent, but the answer was the same as Charlie gave that day: "Who knows?"

"Would you refuse to assist with surgery?" I asked him. "How could a nurse like Nancy presume to judge any surgery unnecessary? It's not her place to decide that."

"It's not only her place—it's her obligation!" Charlie said. "A lot of the nurses who work in this OR chose this hospital because they don't do abortions here. Nurses refuse to assist at surgery that's against their principles. Nancy believed Frank's surgery was too big a risk ... it was against her principles."

When I asked Peter Haynes what he thought about Frank's surgery, he hedged. "It's getting too much to think about. We spend half our time fighting over whether we're going to operate—whether the patient deserves quality or time. Anyway, Frank's terminal. There's no way to change that ... what's done is done."

Peter had objected to Mr. Otis's surgery, but as a resident he was in the same position as student nurses—you assist where you are told to assist. Unfortunately, Peter ended up being in the unenviable position of confronting Mr. Otis's sons with the news that his condition was grave. The most unfortunate part of the whole incident didn't surface until months later when Richard Otis, the older son and an attorney, turned guilt into grudge.

Dr. Stewart had telephoned Richard shortly after the surgery to tell him that his father was seriously ill. No, he wasn't in immediate danger, yes, his heart was causing problems, and yes, he and his brother should come immediately.

"You don't tell a son that his father has terminal cancer over the phone," Dr. Stewart said.

By the time Richard got to the hospital, it was almost midnight and Dr. Stewart had long since gone home. At the information desk outside the ICU, Richard demanded that Dr. Stewart be summoned. The clerk dutifully paged the nursing supervisor. The twenty minutes it took her to finish admitting a patient from the emergency room and then investigate the situation with Mr. Otis was about the same length of time it took Richard to decide Oakmont was a hospital where everyone moved too slowly to handle any crisis, let alone the crisis of his father.

Peter Haynes was the resident on duty that night, beginning his fourth stint of operating all day and being on-call all night. "It was a full moon," Peter told me later, which explained the fact that there had been no opportunity for more than an hour or two of uninterrupted sleep during those four nights—the emergency room in every hospital is at its busiest on nights when there is a full moon. Peter had crumbled into bed exhausted about a half hour before the supervisor called to tell him Mr. Otis's son was waiting to talk to Dr. Stewart.

In his rumpled scrub suit, looking almost as groggy as he felt, Peter arrived in the ICU waiting room to find Richard Otis pacing from the door to the other side of the room. By the time Peter had finished telling him that his father had bladder cancer, that two heart attacks during chest surgery had severely compromised his chances of survival, and that a portion of one lung had been removed, Richard wanted to talk to a *doctor,* someone who *really* knew what was going on, and he wanted to see his father *immediately!*

Though Peter Haynes and Mr. Otis's son were about the same age, in their mid-thirties, Peter had a sandy-haired boyish look about him that was compounded by the scrub suit. His lanky frame suggested he hadn't quite yet aged enough to put meat on his bones. By contrast, Richard was the three-piece impeccable-charcoal-gray-suit executive type with a thick neck and fullback shoulders. He looked competent and successful. Peter looked like a subject from an experiment measuring the duration of survival after thirty whacks with Lizzie Borden's hatchet.

When Peter told Richard Otis that he had been the assisting surgeon on his father's operation that morning, they were on their way into the ICU where the unequaled sensory assaults dwarfed any concerns Richard might have had about Peter's competence. He did what all other relatives do who enter the ICU for the first time—sucked a huge gasp of air in through his teeth, straightened his back and puffed out his chest, focused his eyes straight ahead in an unseeing gaze, and painted an expression of mastery on his face.

There is no way to prepare a relative of an ICU patient for the clanging, beeping, knocking, moaning, whistling sounds and sights of the ICU. Even more futile is any attempt to prepare the relative for how ravaged the patient will look, especially if, like Mr. Otis, he is attached to a respirator. Peter explained all the tubes and machinery that were supporting life, but two or three minutes after he arrived, Richard had seen enough and heard more than enough. He launched into a loud, abusive attack on Peter that was interrupted, just briefly, by the arrival of his brother, Jeff.

Jeff was younger by a few years, dressed more casually and taught German in high school. Richard's tirade embarrassed Jeff before he had a chance to notice that it was his father in the bed behind him, and he followed Dr. Haynes out of the ICU as if he had forgotten why he had come in the first place.

"How dare you!" shouted Richard. "Have you ever heard of informed consent? Did my father have *any* idea what the consequences of surgery would be? Why didn't you call me?"

"Rich . . . calm down." Jeff looked around nervously. "It's the middle of the night."

If Richard noticed that Jeff was even there, he ignored him. "This is a perfect case for the courts. Herman Otis is no fool . . . he would not have consented to a surgery like this!"

Later Peter Haynes told me there was no way to calm Richard. "He couldn't hear me. How can you hear anyone when you're over your ears in guilt?"

Richard's parting sentence that night, delivered with narrow eyes and in the thick, dry tongue that accompanies terror, was, "For your sake, and for the sake of this hospital, you'd better start thinking up some tricks that will save that man!"

It was through Jeff that Peter eventually learned that a squabble between Mr. Otis and Richard some years earlier had led to an estrangement that was "stupid . . . like two little kids

84

in a sandbox." The urgency to repair the breach was suddenly overwhelming when Richard realized his father might die before he ever had a chance to talk to him again.

During the week that Mr. Otis's life hung by a cobweb strand, Dr. Stewart and Peter were able to get through to Richard in bits and pieces, but it was difficult to explain to him that doctors cannot violate a patient's wishes. Mr. Otis did not want his sons told that he had cancer, or that he was having surgery, and the doctors would have been remiss had they done anything about it.

"How do you explain denial to someone who's never been through it?" Peter said. "By not telling his sons, Mr. Otis was essentially denying that he had cancer . . . he played ostrich!" Denial was a syndrome that I would have, within the same year, and Peter was right—until you go through it, it's nothing more than a textbook theory that has no emotion attached. Richard was not about to release the doctors from the responsibility of "withholding information."

Another thing Richard couldn't understand was why they had operated on Mr. Otis's chest when the cancer was in the bladder—something I had wondered about the day of the operation, and something Nancy Wallace and Peter Haynes disagreed with.

"Like almost everyone," Peter explained, "Jeff and Richard thought of cancer as something that eats away at the body, in a sort of organized clump which spreads like melting butter. When the puddle gets too big, the patient dies." I had heard patients say, "They got it all!" meaning surgery had managed to snatch the cube before it began to "melt," and thought, "Phew! What a relief."

No one is sure how cancer moves from one part of the body to the other, but it is not unusual for the spread (metastasis) to be predictable. For cancer that originates in the bladder, the lungs could be the next likely site. Why not the brain or the bowel first, no one knows. When Mr. Otis began having chest colds and infections, then found it difficult to breathe, Dr. Stewart was almost certain that cancer had gone to the lungs. Surgery was the final proof.

Chemotherapy and radiation sometimes slow the metastasis of cancer. In fact, I have heard of cancer patients who went through the treatments and never had a sign of cancer again for as long as twenty-three years after the original was discovered, but Mr. Otis wasn't so lucky. From the beginning he was considered terminal, based on the type of cell and the severity of the disease when he first went to Dr. Stewart, which was the crux of the issue between Dr. Stewart and Dr. Haynes and Nancy.

"Why operate when there's no hope anyway?" said Dr. Haynes.

"We can give him some time . . . and easier breathing . . . if we get that lung out," said Dr. Stewart.

Nancy's position was that chest surgery is a dreadful assault to the body, and that the cracked ribs and huge incision would make Mr. Otis so miserable during recovery, he would rather not have the extra time. "Any surgery depletes the body's natural defenses," she said. "I wouldn't have it! What's an extra week or two if you're too sick to enjoy it?"

Of course, hindsight is twenty-twenty, and I doubt Dr. Stewart would have operated if he could have anticipated the two cardiac arrests during the operation, but as Peter said, "What's done is done."

"Your father knew the risks," Dr. Stewart told Richard. "We would not have operated without his consent."

The issues involved in Mr. Otis's case were ones all the nurses and doctors discussed, especially when a lawyer-relative was pacing the hall outside the ICU almost around the clock, but it's very easy to be objective when the dying patient is not a relative or yourself. "Who ever *really* knows what choices we'll make until the time comes," Lani said. "Maybe Mr. Otis wasn't denying at all . . . maybe he thought he was saving his sons from trauma by not telling them."

She and I thought about talking to Richard. When we went to visit Mr. Otis at the end of each day, we would see Richard in the waiting room as we passed by. Every day he looked more haggard and less like a snappy attorney. Jeff might sit there reading a magazine, and sometimes we would see him in the cafeteria, but Richard was too distraught to read or eat.

"We could tell him about how Mr. Otis used to 'help' us," I suggested to Lani. "Remember his one-liners? It's pitiful to see a son so angry."

Richard had gone from anger with the doctors to anger at his father. From his perspective, Herman Otis had used the ultimate trump card in their squabble—he would die before giving Richard a chance to make a final statement.

"He thinks of Dad's death as a weapon, an 'I'll show *you*' trick," Jeff told Dr. Haynes.

Anger at the person who is dying is normal, a predictable response of relatives. They are being abandoned emotionally, and it's hard to intellectualize that as something tolerable. The doctors and nurses were trying to help Richard work through the anger, but sometimes there is nothing to do but wait until it passes.

There wasn't much we could do for Mr. Otis, either. He was in the netherworld of his coma, but still we talked to him each day as if he could hear. Lani and I usually went to visit in the ICU, around 3:30, when our work in the operating room was finished.

"It's almost four o'clock, Mr. Otis. We've brought your tea and biscuits."

There wasn't one day that I didn't pause, expecting him to open his eyes and say, "Listen, honey, that's all I've been waiting for!"

What bothered me the most, what *still* bothers me, was the slight hint that he heard and knew what was going on. I would smooth the monk's-fringe of white hair behind his ears, adjust all the tubes so he looked comfortable, and patter a little about what was going on in the world. Then I would put my hand in his and tell him to squeeze it if he could hear me. "Let me know if you're listening," I would say. Almost always his hand moved around mine.

"Can he really hear or is it involuntary response?" I asked Charlie.

"What difference does it make?"

"It's bugging me. If he hears, there's hope. If he doesn't, it's cruel to keep him breathing." Mostly I worried that he was in pain, from the infections and abrasions of all the tubes, and couldn't tell us.

"Why worry about things you can't help?" Charlie wanted to know, but I had come to the conclusion, watching Mr. Otis lie there helpless amid all the clang and clamor of the ICU, that there could be nothing worse than not being able to communicate. "Supposing his nose itches and he can't scratch it?" That would be the least of his problems, but it was something familiar to Charlie. Once when he was scrubbed for surgery, and unable to touch anything without contaminating his hands, the scrub tech had squirted a glob of K-Y jelly on his nose—just enough to dribble down in a stream that drove him crazy throughout the surgery. It was a retaliatory prank for one of Charlie's.

"Ask a neuro doc," Charlie suggested. "Ask Peter Haynes . . . they'll probably tell you what Mrs. Erin told me. Patients in a coma hear, at least a little bit. Beyond that, who knows? For God's sake, if you think his nose itches, scratch it!"

Sometimes Mr. Otis would stir a bit or grunt slightly. My hopes would soar. If only he would wake up long enough for Richard to talk to him for a few minutes and long enough for us to hear how we could make him more comfortable.

Sometimes at night I would dream that he awakened. "Maybe it's premonition," I told Dean. The next morning I would stop to see him before I went to the operating room, just to see if a miracle really had happened.

The third time was about six weeks after his operation. I

walked into the ICU and found a young blond girl in the bed where he had been. I hurried out to the waiting room. His sons were gone. Then I went to the information desk and scanned the census list. "Mr. Otis . . . Herman Otis . . . he's on the census list but he's not in bed six."

The clerk looked over the list.

"Otis," she said. "The one with the lawyer son?"

"Yes."

"Expired last night, after they printed the census. Yeah, he's the one. The mortuary came about an hour ago."

"His sons . . . were they here?"

"They were with him . . . Dr. Haynes was here . . . the chaplain was here. He went sour on the evening shift. They knew he was going."

The nurses would say, "It was a blessing." It didn't feel that way to me.

"What a way to find out," I told Dean that night. It seemed such an indignity to be shocked by finding a young girl in his bed.

"You're losing perspective," Dean said. "You're not his wife . . . his mother. Why should someone have called you?"

"I had a vested interest. He was my first patient. Lani and I kept him from going to a nursing home . . . we cheated the system for him . . . we were the last ones to talk to him just before they put him out in the OR." I still thought of death as a villain—something that should never happen, especially to someone so special to me.

During the six weeks we were in the operating room, Mr. Otis was the only patient familiar to us. The others came and went, always in a narcotized haze, which made our work seem almost like a mechanical kind of nursing. The patients who came for cataract surgery always had local anesthesia, so they were awake during surgery, but usually they were too drugged to talk.

It seemed ironic to me that most patients thought of an operation as the most monumental event in their lives, yet in the operating room, it was easy to think of them as another object on the assembly line. Some days we did nine hernia repairs. Other days we had six or seven open-heart operations. From start to finish, there was very little difference between one operation and the next, except when there was a case like Mr. Otis's, when everything happened at once. Maybe for full-time operating room nurses, that happens frequently. Otherwise, days seemed routine.

We watched more appendectomies, hysterectomies and cholecystectomies than I ever want to see again. Most operations were common. Then one day we had a kidney transplant. A forty-two-year-old lady was donating one of her kidneys to her brother who had been suffering from failure of both kidneys for several months. They were put in adjoining rooms, which had a passage between them so the crew could go from one room to the other without contaminating their sterile scrub clothes.

Since Oakmont only did two or three transplants a year, both rooms were crowded with medical students, residents and staff physicians who had never seen the operation before. The surgeon himself had only done one transplant before. Later, when it was over and both patients had a good prognosis, Peter Haynes talked about how risky it was for patients to have such traumatic surgery done in a hospital where the crew wasn't very familiar with the technique. It was something I had never thought about before.

"The actors are always better when the show is in its second week," he said. "Opening night is when they're working out the flaws in the play. For kidney transplants, it's always opening night in this hospital."

It wasn't as if kidney transplants were done every day in any hospital, but if I were having one, I would want to find the hospital where they are done the most often, by the surgeon with the most experience.

Open-heart surgery was the specialty at Oakmont County Hospital. Patients who came for that operation were in good hands. There has to be a first for everything—I guess the first few open-heart operations were plenty risky. While we were there, they were all-in-a-day's-work—it was the fad surgery of the year. Anyone who had a cardiac stress test that wasn't near perfect ended up having coronary artery bypass surgery. Since then, people have become more discriminating about whether or not they want to have an operation that might not change life for the better.

"No one knows what causes the arteries to get clogged in the first place," Peter Haynes explained. "It isn't like the surgery cures the problem . . . the arteries will eventually clog again." It seemed to me that an operation costing around $25,000 should offer cure.

"We're doing too much of it," Peter said. "Some patients don't need it."

I was more than happy to bury his opinions on useless surgery in the basement of my mind when we ended that rotation.

5 Beyond the Call of Duty

In the three months following our operating room rotation, Lani, Charlie and I rotated through the maternity and psychiatric wards, neither of which we really enjoyed. Maternity was a disaster for Charlie—the new mothers could cope with a male doctor, but male nurses were quite another matter. "Get him *out* of here," they would say. By the time we got to the psychiatric ward, he was not liking nursing very much.

The psychiatric instructor (not Mrs. Erin) was so busy shrinking our minds, we learned very little about how to take care of patients. When we were finished with that rotation, there wasn't a student in the class who was liking nursing very much.

By the time we got to Sunny Harbor Nursing Home for our gerontology rotation, we needed Judith Newman more than she needed us. She was doing fine on her new artificial leg, getting around with the help of a walker, and Charlie found himself in competition with the light of her life, Mr. Casper. Every night, Jules Casper played gin with Judith and let her win. He said it was the Braille cards that made him lose, but he was the adoring kind who loved watching Judith get all excited about winning every night, as though it were the first time.

He was a very "proper" gentleman, always in a white shirt and conservative tie. "You saved her life," he told us. "Thank you . . . she means so much to me . . . thank you very much." Whether it was deserved or not, we accepted his admiration, especially on days when nursing seemed to offer few rewards.

Throughout the two years of nursing school, Judith and Mr. Casper were talismans for us, prodding us along when we would rather have opted out. "Whoever rescues a single life, it is as if he had rescued the whole world," Judith would say as Charlie began to falter. "You have *so* much to give the world, Mr. Kelly." Charlie was definitely opting out, but Lani and I were too busy to notice what Judith had sensed all along.

It was while we were at Sunny Harbor that *I* first began to falter. Judith's roommate, Violet Fraser, was recovering from a broken hip. "Get her up," Mrs. Erin said. "She'll get pneumonia unless you can get her moving."

Elderly patients are more at risk from fluid in their lungs after anesthesia than they are from the condition for which they had surgery. The repaired hip was no problem, but Violet was reluctant to move. She was also still in a haze from the anesthesia—not too sure what was going on but very pleasant.

Mrs. Erin stood behind the wheelchair, ready to pull Violet in from behind while I swiveled her in from the front. I sat her up, her short legs dangling over the side of the bed.

I put my arms under hers and pulled her toward me. "Put your good leg down, Violet." Her grin was vacant. "Good leg, Violet . . . put it down!" Still nothing. "Good leg on the floor, quick!" My mind envisioned her hip shattering into tiny fragments if I dropped her or plopped her back on the bed.

"Put her back!" Mrs. Erin suddenly came alive. "You'll drop her. Put her back." Just then another student came to ask for Mrs. Erin's help. "Look, I have to go," she said. "Just put her back and let the staff nurses do it."

It was too late to tell Mrs. Erin that my back felt as if it had split into two jagged pieces. By the time I got bent over to put Violet back in bed, jolts of electrifying pain were shooting down my legs.

"Have you ever had a back problem?" That was the first, middle and last most important question for nurses. Bad backs were taboo!

"I've probably wrecked that lady's hip," I cried, when I went to the orthopedist that afternoon, "and now I'll get kicked out of nursing because of my back."

"You made a stupid choice," Dr. Dan Anderson said (no sympathy here), "wreck her hip or wreck your back. It wouldn't have hurt her hip if you had just dropped her back on the bed." I learned more about fractured hips and diseases of the spine just from the incident that day than I would ever learn about them in class.

I left his office in a back brace that strangled me from ribs to thighs and burst the blood vessels in my abdomen—but I could walk without pain if I was careful not to move a muscle in my back. Steel rods up the back, and plastic bones up the front, with miles of laces and elastic holding the two together, I was wrapped in a medieval torture corset.

It was a slushy spring, with pockets of ice-crusted snow in shady corners, piled against curbs, at the base of steps, wherever I had never bothered to notice before. I walked in the picky steps of the elderly, with all the muscles of my body focused on staying upright.

The doctor's parking area was shared with the lot of Oakmont Hospital. I had parked in the employees' section and was almost to my car when I heard a door bang and a man yelling. "You bitch you . . . you fuckin' bitch . . . how dare you treat Jesus Christ like this!" Chelsee Jones, one of our students and a part-time LPN at Oakmont, was struggling to get the man through the back door of the emergency room to the outside where another man sat in a wheelchair.

Chelsee's patient was in a restraining jacket, which mummified his arms against his body, and his legs and chest were strapped in the wheelchair. Still he writhed and tossed like a tiny boat on lashing waves. "Don't put your hands on the Lord God," he screamed as Chelsee reached down to adjust his jacket. "Keep your hands off, you fuckin' bitch." He hawked up a great glob from his throat and spit in Chelsee's long blond hair.

She wheeled him down the ramp where the other man sat slouched in the wheelchair looking as if he had slept in the gutters of skid row and hadn't changed his clothes for a year. The slouched one lazily turned his head up to Chelsee's patient and drawled, "Hey man . . . you ain't Jeezuz Christ . . . you're just a goddam crazy. I thought I was crazy . . . seeing you, I know what crazy *is* . . . I ain't crazy . . . you shut your filthy mouth . . . that's a *nurse* you're yelling at, you goddam crazy!"

The little man in the straitjacket gave a giant heave with his body and toppled the wheelchair over the ledge of the ramp, throwing himself in a heap beneath it.

I started to run to help Chelsee, slipped on a strip of ice I hadn't noticed, and was down on the ground without her even knowing I was in the parking lot. No one saw me, thank heavens, I would not have wanted *anyone* to see me wallowing in such a landscape of self-pity and pain.

Later Chelsee told me the emergency room had been jam-packed with patients when the slouched man was brought in by paddy wagon, out like a light from cheap wine. Before he could be taken to the alcoholic unit of the hospital, a physician would have to evaluate his physical condition, but there were lives to save before taking time for that. The drunk became belligerent while waiting and had been put outside to sober up without disturbing the other patients.

Meanwhile the man in the straitjacket was waiting for transfer to the psychiatric ward, and Chelsee put him outside too, because his spitting and screaming were even more disturbing than the belligerent drunk. Having crashed himself and the wheelchair to the ground, he had more problems than craziness. "Talk about a zoo!"—Chelsee's understatement.

That weekend, cinched into my medieval corset, I felt like a defeated warrior. Since I was forced to sit or lie still, the ravages of mother-abandoned housework, child rearing and wifery were far too obvious. Dust bunnies lined the edges of the staircase; the oven had an inch of burned tuna-casserole spillovers on the bottom; unwashed, ironed or mended clothes spilled from baskets stacked here and there; and several dozen minor tasks that had been pushed aside for over a year loomed like icons to the disaster I, the zealot nurse, had brought upon the once-peaceful household.

At dinner that night I said, "Uncle! I give up, you guys. I'm dropping out of nursing school." Pride prevented me from telling the truth—their mother would be booted out of school for having a decrepit back.

The kids were elated, thinking I had finally come to my senses, but Dean reserved comment. It was not his style to count birds until he had them in hand.

Though I really didn't believe in horoscopes or the like, and I wasn't sure whether or not there was a God, it seemed to me my back problem was just one more in a whole string of messages from Somewhere—nursing was for the young and strong, unmarried, childless woman with no other responsibilities. To be available for all shifts, day and night, weekends and holidays, with no possibility of planning life more than a week ahead—who could do it?

In other careers, women leave work a half hour early to rush a child to the orthodontist, or take an extra fifteen minutes on their lunch hour to dash to the bank. But nurses leave at least six patients every time they leave the floor. Sometimes that isn't a disaster for a half-hour lunch break *if* the day has gone smoothly. More often than not, the day has been a series of interruptions, mishaps and emergencies.

When a patient Codes or dies, the doctor and the supervisor arrive, do what they can, then leave. The chaos that is left—a family in emotional crisis, the ravaged crash cart, pages and pages of documentation about the incident—the myriad tasks belong to the nurse. The spent emotion also belongs to the nurse. For the nurse who has invested herself in a patient, it is not easy to pick up the pieces of a busy day and just keep on working after the patient has died. There is no time for the normal human emotion of grief.

In some hospitals, nurses rotate shifts, from days to evenings to nights and back to days, every two weeks. In *all* hospitals, new nurses work Christmas and Easter. New nurses always begin on the night shift. If shifts are permanent, the new nurses work nights until there is an opening on another shift. Sometimes it takes years to get a spot on the day shift.

While I was lying in bed in my torture corset, the day after lifting Violet, I had such thoughts for the first time: Whatever made me think I wanted to be a nurse? How on God's earth would I function if I worked on the night shift? Could Dean and the kids really tolerate my being gone on Christmas and Easter? What if every patient was as important to me as Mr. Otis or Judith Newman? How often could I tolerate the death of people who seemed almost as important to me as my own family?

"This decrepit back is an omen," I told Dean. "It's just not in the cards for me to be a nurse." In fact, it seemed a relief that I had an excuse to quit without being labeled a quitter.

The next evening, Alan came limping into my bedroom. His knees needed more surgery. The thought whisked the old hospital phobia into my mind. Memories of his last hospital stay were still all too fresh. My vow, that no one in our family would ever again be a patient until I was a nurse, was haunting me. Could I really quit now, when I had just a bit more than a year to get to the finish line?

More than the others, Alan resented that I was not doing what other mothers did—cooking, sewing, cleaning. Perhaps it was just that he was more vocal. He was also the happiest that I had declared surrender the night before. I must confess to manipulation.

"Well, Alan, your knee hurts because you need more surgery," I told him. "You'll have that limp until the next operation."

"Forget it . . . never again!" Hospital phobia flashed across his face.

"If I became a nurse, you wouldn't have to be scared. I would be right there the whole time . . . nothing bad would happen." Bribe—barter—negotiate. My voice sounded like a mother offering her kid a candy bar if he would only eat spinach.

"That's okay. I don't mind the limp. I can stand the pain."

"For the rest of your life? You want to be peg-leg forever? Never run? Never ski? Never play tennis?"

He limped to his room without answering. His knee problem seemed an omen too—an endorsement for the zealot nurse. I would *not* quit.

The next day, when I returned to school, I pretended a stiff back was my normal posture. Mrs. Erin's eyes grew four sizes when she saw me sitting in a chair, looking as if I had just been severely startled.

"You have a *back* injury?" She infused the question with all the suspicion of an investigator uncovering an extortion plot. "Nothing is more important to a nurse than her back."

There was a two-week bout of weeping and wailing, exams by the campus physician, X-rays, statements from my orthopedist, and a signing of several releases which would free the school and anyone connected with it from liability for past, present or future back problems. By that time, I would have signed anything to escape dismissal from the program—adversity fueled the zealot.

"Phew! That was close!" I told Lani. "Next time I act as if I want to drop out, remind me of today, will you?"

There were times when Lani wanted to drop out. She was working full-time at the phone company besides going to school and running a household. Like Dean, her husband, Lee, held the traditional view of how things should be—husbands work and bring home the bacon, wives do everything else. Lani didn't have kids yet, but the phone company job was as time-consuming.

Dean and the kids never commented on the fact that I had not dropped out of school as I had said I would, but sometimes silence is louder than comments. Though I would much prefer a loud tirade and a dramatic flurry of cards being laid on the table, things weren't going that way.

The night before an exam, when I had too few hours left to learn everything there was to know about certain body systems, a minor crisis invariably hit—Kim had an asthma attack, Alan's knee went out of joint, Laurie's dog disappeared, or my mother had a sudden need. Sometimes it was an impromptu corporate dinner with Dean's most important client. Cars broke down, clothes disappeared, an obscene-caller began harassing us, a sliding glass door shattered in the midst of a snowstorm, the plumbing backed up into the showers, jacket zippers broke, buttons magically fell off everything. You name it, it happened.

Then one evening about a month after the incident with my back, I was on duty at Oakmont County Hospital, wheeling a patient to the X-ray department. Mrs. Erin came hurrying down the hall with a frantic look on her face. "The emergency room is looking for you . . . it's urgent. I'll take your patient . . . cover for you the rest of the day."

The tone of her voice made my skin prickle. "Use the phone in the lobby," she said.

On my way to the phone, I remembered that Dean had left that morning on one of his frequent business trips, by airplane. It was the night before midterm exams. Disasters and midterm exams always coincided.

"This is Barbara Huttmann . . . is someone there looking for me?" The receiver was about to bruise my ear, it was shaking so hard.

"Barbara, listen . . . don't panic, everything's okay." Whenever anyone says, "Don't panic," my throat tends to twist into tiny knots. "Your daughter's on her way to St. Joseph's Hospital . . . the paramedics are on the radio. They want a consent to treat."

"Treat what? Oh my God, what's happened? Is she conscious? Can't they bring her here?"

"They're closer to St. Joseph's . . . calm down . . . she's okay."

"Okay" is relative, at least in medical parlance. I had seen some okay patients in the emergency room who never lived to tell how "okay" they might have been.

St. Joseph's was the closest hospital to our house. Knowing that there might be times when Dean would be away on business and I would be en route from hospital to campus, I had filed a consent form to treat our kids in St. Joseph's emergency room.

"That's the height of pessimism," Dean had said, but I thought of it as an insurance policy. No one would be wasting time looking for us while a child's life was hanging by a thread.

"They *have* a consent on file," I shouted into the phone. "Tell them to go ahead . . . it'll take me twenty minutes to get there." With my heart doing crazy flip-flops, I drove the twenty miles to St. Joseph's at top speed.

No one needed to tell me where to find Kim—her hysteria could be heard for blocks. There isn't anything quite as wonderful as the healthy, lusty, piercing, howling, raging scream of a child who, minutes earlier, you had thought might be dead. For a minute or so, I was too busy being relieved to be embarrassed that she was carrying on as though she had been dipped in lye and was being burned at the stake.

Kim was thirteen going on twenty at the time, except when she was frightened—then she was five going on four. We called her "Sarah Heartburn" when we teased her, only because there had been several incidents like the one at hand. She had a tendency to crush toes on the edges of doors, catch fingers in automatic car windows that were whizzing closed, and break bones in accidents which seemed the most unlikely that could be imagined.

The decibel strength of her hysteria had nothing to do with the extent of her injuries, and *everything* to do with a characteristic she might have inherited from her mother: an unparalleled fear of nurses, doctors, hospitals and the slightest hint that she might be at their mercy.

"Oh Mom!" she sobbed in deep dramatic tones. "Oh Mom, I was so worried they wouldn't be able to find you." Her dripping sobs ground to a halt, and then she smiled. "I think I was scared." She looked at her body as if checking to make sure it was all there. "I passed out . . . I got so scared I passed out."

"Kim, what happened? Where are you hurt?" Nothing was bleeding, no bones were protruding from odd places. "What are you doing here anyway?"

The smile faded, and she went into a fresh round of tears. "I can't believe I got so scared I passed out . . . Mom, how could I do such a thing?"

"Scared of what? What's going on? Why the paramedics? Are you hurt?"

"That's what's so stupid." She began chuckling. "I'm not hurt!"

"Dammit, Kim, don't tell me that. Don't tell me the paramedics brought you in here Code Three and you're not hurt. Do you know what Code Three is? Do you realize all the sirens blare and the driver of the ambulance jeopardizes every car on the road while he careers through the streets to get to a hospital in less than three minutes. Don't tell me you aren't hurt!"

"Don't be so mad, Mom."

"You have three seconds to tell me what the hell is going on. If you *don't* hurt, you're *gonna* hurt!"

She had been in a gym class at school when she felt one of her kneecaps slip off as she tumbled to the ground. The excruciating pain so frightened her that she passed out. By the time she awakened, the kneecap was back in place, and the fire department truck and the paramedic van had their sirens screaming as they pulled up to the door of the gym. When she looked up at the startled group of teachers and students gathered around her, she passed out again.

"They kept talking about shock," she said. "What's shock?"

I didn't tell her that the shock at hand was that her mother suspected what her father already knew—nursing was disrupting our family. When it takes a paramedic scene and an emergency room to get some attention from a mother . . . mea culpa, mea culpa, mea culpa! When Dean got home, he was not surprised.

Kneecaps slipping out of place were an inherited orthopedic problem that managed to cross generations in our family. It bypassed some offspring, but when it showed up, the first time was usually in the teen years. It was simply that the tendon which holds the kneecap originated from the wrong place. Once the tendon was surgically moved, the only reminder was a four- or five-inch scar on the knee.

Kim's surgery, about a month later, took place during my emergency room rotation, when Lani and I were seeing so many broken bones and injuries from snowmobiles, skis and auto accidents, Kim's plight seemed relatively minor. Both her legs were to be casted, from ankles to thighs, which is minor until one tries to go from a standing to a lying or a sitting position. Using the bathroom is a major problem, the *only* one I anticipated.

The night before surgery, Dean said, "You see, these kids are a full-time job. She'll be coming out of surgery about ten in the morning. You have an exam, I have a staff meeting. Would you like to awaken from surgery without a mother or father there?"

"You can't miss one staff meeting?"

"Not this one."

"But the kids need you when they're in the hospital . . . I'm too big a worrywart. You laugh and tell jokes, tease them into forgetting the pain . . . she really needs you."

"You're the nurse!"

It was something I easily forgot, unless I was dressed in my uniform, which wasn't something I could explain to Miss Jabonski, the nursing instructor who confronted me late in the afternoon on the day of Kim's surgery.

"What are you doing? Student uniforms are to be worn in the hospital where you do your rotations . . . you do not rotate here." She was from the same nursing school and instructed a group of my classmates at St. Joseph's Hospital, but I was never one of her students.

"My daughter just had surgery," I explained weakly. "I'm staying through the night. This way I won't have to change clothes before I go to Oakmont County Hospital in the morning." Her disapproval was silent . . . but clear.

That night as the group of nurses were making rounds to begin the eleven o'clock shift, a very large, gray-haired one who reminded me of an army general interrupted the report at Kim's bedside. "You'll have to leave," she said. "Visiting hours were over three hours ago. Don't worry, we can take care of her."

She whispered politely, so as not to waken Kim, and smiled at me before she hurried from the room with the rest of the group. Dean had warned me that I would not be welcome. "No, no," I had said. "That was in the olden days. Nowadays nurses encourage the family to stay . . . patients recover faster when loving relatives are around to assure them everything's okay."

When the gray-haired nurse came back an hour later, I was slipping a bedpan underneath Kim, which was no easy project, considering the heavy casts. With the flip of one switch she turned the room into a stadium of spotlights. "You can't do that . . . what are you doing? I'm sorry, but we don't allow anyone but nurses to touch the patient."

"I'm halfway there . . . a student nurse at Oakmont," I said, as if she couldn't recognize my uniform! I smiled at her politely. "I know how understaffed you are on nights . . . perhaps I could help by taking care of Kim? We've had our orthopedic training . . . I know about casts."

"Well, that's kind of you . . . I know you just want to help, but you know the rules. Parents are not allowed to stay all night with our patients." She was really *very* polite. "I'll call the security guard so he can unlock the front door for you to leave."

She bustled out, looking very efficient. I wondered what would happen if she told the instructor from our school. A student in bad graces could wind up with grades that were incompatible with staying in the program.

Still groggy from the anesthesia, Kim muttered, "Mom . . . please don't go . . . are you going?"

"You'll be fine, honey. These are good nurses . . . I can tell . . . you'll be just fine."

"Remember what happened to Alan, Mom . . . please don't go." Three years earlier, the same surgery had been done on Alan's leg. It was a six-month saga of pain, infection and agony that needn't have happened.

"I'm not going . . . you sleep, honey. I'll be right here next time you open your eyes."

The gray-haired nurse returned in less than an hour. "I'm sorry. I can't leave," I told her. "We've a long history of hospital horror stories in our family, you know, a bit more terrified and intimidated than most. It's not that you aren't *wonderful* nurses. We're just hyper people . . . I must stay through the night." It felt much like telling God I was going to walk on His gold streets with my muddy shoes whether He liked it or not!

"I see," she said slowly, narrowing her eyes. "Well, it's against the rules."

"I know that. It's something I must do . . . I won't touch her . . . I'll simply sit here. Please, pretend that I'm not here. I promise not to get in your way."

I sat in a chair in the corner through the night, in the dark, wide-awake, while a great patch of righteous indignation, fertilized by unutterable fatigue, grew inside me and blossomed into fierce determination. *When I am the nurse,* I thought, *mothers will get pillows and blankets, a cup of coffee, conversation—there won't be any mothers sitting at bedsides feeling like spoiled, belligerent brats who are damned if they do and damned if they don't!*

When the 7:00 A.M. group of nurses made rounds, they stood by Kim's bed while the team leader read from Kim's Kardex. "Hauser procedure ... Dr. Anderson's patient ... one-day post-op."

"What's a Hauser?" one of the nurses whispered.

The team leader gave her a withering glance. "Ankles ... he fixed her ankles ... congenital defect." She lifted the blankets at the foot of the bed to display the casts, verifying her guess that Kim had indeed had ankle surgery.

When they left the room, Kim said, "Ankles? What did he do to my ankles?"

"Nothing, Kim. It's your knees, same operation as Alan's." I had planned to go to school that day, thinking the first night after surgery was the risky part. If anything happened (too-tight cast, hemorrhage, adverse anesthesia effects, drug reaction), the indicators were usually obvious the first night. What could happen if the nurses were treating the patient for the wrong operation? I was afraid to leave for school.

In Kim's case it would not be a big disaster, but the incident confirmed what I already suspected—great dangers lurked among the menacing shadows of hospitals. "When I finish school, there won't be any menacing shadows," I told Dean. "If you and the kids can just hang on ... just one more year ..." The incident caused a break in our polite hostility. "We need a nurse," I pleaded. He smiled and hugged me. "We do, huh?"

Much later I learned that "Hauser procedure" is an obscure term that *no* nurse, and few doctors, would know. It isn't even in the dictionaries commonly used in the medical professions. Considering the number of people who work with each patient in a day (fifty-eight is average), gaps in communication are bound to occur, sometimes because of obscure terms, sometimes because of ignorance, and sometimes because nurses and doctors are human.

After Kim's second day of hospitalization, she seemed magically cured of hospital phobia. Part of it had to do with the fun of all her school chums coming to visit her, and I needed to believe that part of it had to do with my mom-nurse role. It must be tremendously comforting to have someone at the bedside who can separate fantasy and reality in a hospital.

"No, that's not a patient screaming, Kim. That's the wind howling through the crack in the window. No, you're not bleeding to death. When you stand, the blood in your veins rushes from your upper body to your toes . . . it only *feels* as if the incision on your knee has broken open . . . there's at least three layers of stitches holding that incision together."

Her recovery was so fast, and so perfect, despite the pain and hassles that naturally go with orthopedic surgery and having both legs casted, that I was more committed to nursing than ever. Neglecting Brady Bunch life seemed very nearly acceptable.

6 To Code or Not to Code

Just before Kim's operation, when Lani and I had begun our rotation in the Oakmont County Hospital emergency room, we had the advantage of being in Charlie's home territory. "This is the Oakmont Knife and Gun Club, m' ladies," he said, "where minor squabbles are settled swiftly." According to Charlie, the patient population of Oakmont couldn't be bothered with the usual verbal tomahawks for arbitrating disputes. "It's silver bullets and blades ... this is no place for weak-stomached nurses." He implied we wouldn't see anything but mayhem.

"Last night we had a patient who looked like one of those straw-filled targets at the rifle range, he was so full of bullets." Charlie thrived on the thrills of walking a tightwire—the more bizarre the incident, the greater the thrill—which was very comforting for neophytes like Lani and me. "The guy fed his neighbor's dog Drano, so the next time the neighbor saw him, he peppered him with bullets—twenty-seven of them!"

All twenty-seven bullets had managed to miss vital organs, surgery was successful, and the man was expected to recover as fast as someone who had twenty-seven superficial cuts from pruning rosebushes. "Of course, without the superior care of the Oakmont ER staff, he'd be a goner," Charlie said, with the pride and loyalty of one who truly loves his job.

"You take care of the knife and gun wounds," Lani said. "Barb and I will handle the colds and flu!"

On a typical day, all the examining rooms were full. A crowd in the waiting room grew restless, thinking they might never get treated. In fact, it wasn't unusual for a patient with a broken leg to sit five or six hours waiting while other patients were treated as soon as they arrived. "It's a matter of priorities," Charlie said. "The patient in the greatest danger gets treated first."

One night the paramedics brought in a wrestler type, a huge man in his late twenties, lying face down in a pool of blood. Besides a skull fracture, he had lacerations from one end of his body to the other. "Chain-saw attack," the police said. "Last time it was a knife stab. The time before that, someone shot off his kneecaps. Think you can patch him again?" It would take a whole night of surgery.

At the same time, an ambulance brought in Thomas Benjamin Edison, Esquire, and "Don't forget the Esquire, ma'am, if you please." Those were the only words he spoke other than a constant loud "Fuck you! Fuck you! Fuck you!" in a strict cadence that felt like dripping water in a bathroom with twelve-foot-high ceilings. He had jumped off the overpass of the turnpike. "He's soused," said the ambulance driver. "Booze probably saved his life."

Within minutes, we got a radio call from the paramedics. They were on their way in, sirens blaring, with the mayor. He had been speaking at a banquet when he began having pain he thought was gas. By the time he finished his speech, he felt like a two-ton tractor was crossing his chest. He said nothing, then slumped on the table. When the paramedics got there, a doctor from the audience was doing CPR. "Massive coronary [heart attack]," the doctor said. The most dangerous period following a heart attack, in terms of risk of recurrence, is the first two hours.

Who can decide priorities with three cases like those? The first two might have lost their lives from internal bleeding we could not see. The last was in impending crisis for two hours. Any of the three might have slipped away within minutes of their arrival. (All survived.)

Setting priorities was an even greater problem one night when the three of us first had our emotional involvement challenged. Judith Newman arrived Code Three, which means the same on the streets as a Code Blue does in the hospital. Over the radio the paramedics told us they were bringing in an amputee in respiratory failure.

Lani was in the tub room with a little girl who was suspected of having meningitis. If the child's temperature did not get lowered soon, she might have convulsions and permanent, maybe fatal, brain damage. I was in the next room, doing ice-water stomach rinsings for a middle-aged lady who was in danger of hemorrhaging to death from a perforated ulcer.

Peter Haynes and Loren Mulwards, the two physicians on duty, were doing everything they could to save an eighteen-month-old with severe croup.

Charlie and the only RN on duty, Penny Hammond, were at the desk coordinating the X-ray, lab and operating room staff that would be needed for all the patients. Charlie ran out the door to help the paramedics when they arrived. The first we knew about it was when we heard the rumbling of the gurney heading toward the trauma room (a mini-operating room) and Charlie's shout for Dr. Haynes, "Stat, Peter. It's Judith Newman, respiratory arrest . . . Peter . . . Code Three . . . Dr. Mulwards . . . anybody . . . stat!" Charlie was . . . *usually* unflappable. His panic, Judith in arrest—if ever I had wanted to leave a patient, it was the lady in that room with me. Her perforated ulcer suddenly seemed a terrible inconvenience. The ice-water rinses were still coming back red into the suction bottle. Not deep red—the bleeding was slowing—but red enough that she was still in danger.

In the hour between when I first knew Judith was there and I was free to go to her, I realized what Mrs. Erin meant when she said we should "care" about patients without getting "emotionally involved." Lani felt the same way. She had stayed with the child in the tub, of course, knowing that Judith was there. Any one of the cases that night could have used the entire staff. To have too many patients in crisis at once was not something our staffing patterns anticipated.

By the time we saw Judith, she was on a respirator, ashen, comatose—as close to death as anyone could be. "She'll make it," Charlie said. It sounded more like a command than a statement. He told us she was gasping for air, coughing, sputtering when she arrived.

"We did rotating tourniquets, two IVs, oxygen . . . she kept getting bluer and bluer. Finally we put a tube in her lungs, the whole bit . . . still we couldn't get her breathing on her own," Peter Haynes told us. "Her blood gases are looking better . . . she'll come around." The respirator would breathe for her until she could do it on her own. "Congestive heart failure," Dr. Haynes said. "What can you do with a brittle diabetic? Just fight what comes along."

"Brittle" diabetics get in trouble no matter how carefully their insulin, diet and exercise are controlled, but Charlie was not looking at it that way. An unofficial keeper of Judith's health, he expected miracles—her sickness was a personal defeat for which he felt responsible.

Judith's new problem, congestive heart failure, commonly strikes the elderly who have impaired heart function. It causes excessive fluid in the lungs, among other things, and produces the ominous death rattle in the late stages. Fortunately, the folks at Sunny Harbor had called the paramedics in time to avert disaster.

After a week in the ICU, Judith's mind cleared, and she was transferred to the general nursing floor where we visited her frequently. When she went back to Sunny Harbor, two weeks later, she was better but never the same again.

Judith was only one of many Code Threes—a lucky one. During our three-week rotation, there were more than I could count. More often than not, the patients were accident victims—auto, motorcycle, swimming pool—who were clearly beyond rescue, but it seemed the ER crew never made any distinction between cases that needed hasty, aggressive treatment and cases in which aggression was contraindicated.

"They save *everyone,*" I complained to Lani, "or at least they *try* to save everyone." The crew worked as hard to save an accident victim who had long since stopped breathing when he was brought in as they did to save the one who at least had a chance at survival. Often the one who wasn't breathing couldn't be resuscitated no matter how hard they tried, but there were cases they did manage to revive. One was two-year-old Jenny Tucker, who had slipped from her trike into the family swimming pool. By the time the mother retrieved Jenny from the pool, called the paramedics, and began resuscitation, brain damage was in progress. And by the time the ambulance delivered her to our emergency room, there were no signs of life.

"Breathe, dammit!" Charlie commanded as he did the chest compressions during the Code. He was infusing the child with every ounce of energy he had . . . the whole crew moved with awesome speed and skill. Once in a while they would see a bit of a heart flutter on the EKG (electrocardiogram) machine, which gave them renewed fervor to continue the effort.

In the meantime, the mother stood sobbing in my arms. "Breathe, Jenny . . . Oh God! . . . please make her breathe," she pleaded. "Breathe, Jenny!"

Eventually Jenny's heart began beating for prolonged periods, she would breathe spontaneously, and then suddenly she would stop again. After almost two hours, she was attached to a respirator that would breathe for her. "She's alive," Dr. Haynes said hesitantly, almost as if he were asking rather than telling. The crew watched the EKG scribble out a normal heart rhythm on the paper strip for several minutes before they looked up at each other and beamed. "We've done it!" sighed Charlie. "We brought her back."

As the mother's frame went limp in my arms, I felt the same crunching in my back that had put me in a brace when the lady at Sunny Harbor went limp in my arms. I slid her to the floor as best I could, while Lani ran to get an ammonia capsule to crush under her nose so she would take some deep breaths and revive. She awakened as if from a deep sleep, looked around with a puzzled expression, then suddenly remembered what had happened and began sobbing, "My baby . . . my baby . . . my baby!"

"She's alive," Lani told her as she gently smoothed the hair back from her forehead. "Your baby's alive . . . she's on a respirator and we're taking her to the intensive-care unit."

"She's alive? She's really alive?" She looked around at the faces of the crew and knew Jenny was indeed alive.

"She's in critical condition," Dr. Haynes said solemnly, "but you can be sure we'll do everything we can for her . . . everything." Only the staff knew what "critical" really meant—that Jenny would undoubtedly face devastating infection within a matter of hours from the pool water in her lungs. He could not bring himself to tell her Jenny's chances were slim.

"How much brain damage do you think there is?" I asked Charlie later, when Jenny and her mother had been transferred to the ICU.

"Brain damage?"

"Mrs. Erin said the patient who stops breathing for four minutes begins to suffer irreversible damage—brain cells do not regenerate."

"Who's to say she was without oxygen four minutes?"

"Think about it," I said. "By the time the mother realized the child was in the pool, kicked off her shoes, jumped in, untangled Jenny from the trike, pulled her onto the deck, and called the paramedics, don't you think at least four minutes had passed?"

"Huttmann, you're trying to uptight me! Mrs. Erin said the cells in the brain *begin* to die . . . but the brain has millions of cells. We don't even use all we have. So Jenny will have a few less . . . big deal!"

"How many less is a big deal? If it took five more minutes

for the paramedics to get there, and another five at the least to get her in the van and bring her to us, that's fourteen minutes, and that's assuming the mother was there within seconds of Jenny's fall, that they only live five minutes away from the ambulance garage, and that the CPR was done with skill. How many brain cells have to go before the child ends up in a vegetative state for the rest of her life?"

Such a question had plagued me from the beginning of the semester when I heard about a hospital across town where the ICU had seven cases, all very similar to Jenny's, in perpetual coma, for periods as long as three years. There was no hope of reviving the children from the comatose state, but their young hearts could be sustained by drugs and respirators almost indefinitely.

"She'll do fine," Charlie prophesied. "You'll see. We'll follow this case just to prove how pessimistic you are."

"Everyone deserves a chance," Lani said, but it seemed to me that the kind of chance we gave some patients was a moral offense. A typical example was a case similar to Jenny's. A very large lady, Maggie Hart, in her mid-sixties, was brought in looking doughy on every part of her body that wasn't blue. Even I, who had seen very little of death, recognized the signs of one who has long since stopped breathing.

"She's from the Catskill Home," puffed the ambulance driver, struggling to get the stretcher through the door. "Choked on a piece of bacon at breakfast . . . gone when we got there."

The Catskill Home where Maggie had lived was a place for those who had suffered brain damage that rendered them incapable of existing among others. They could function, move about, but they usually had to be told what to do and when to do it all day long. Most of them had violent mood swings that sometimes made them dangerous to those around them, and there were also those who never had any kind of swing and just moved about like zombies. Maggie Hart had lived there all of her adult life. "She could be a holy terror sometimes," Penny

Hammond told us later. The Oakmont County emergency room had many times repaired the results of the violence that sometimes got out of hand at the Catskill Home.

I stood in the corner and watched—for a student it's acceptable to do that . . . it's *preferred* unless the student is exceptionally skilled and helpful, which Lani was—my armor all hinged together and in place. Anger twisted in my throat while I watched the crew go about resuscitation as if their own lives depended on it.

"Why would you work so hard on someone so obviously dead?" I asked Penny later, stifling the urge to yell in outrage. "Doesn't anyone ever take into account how long it's already been since the patient stopped breathing?"

She gave me a stunned look, as if the question came from a green-horned monster. "Whatever comes through those doors gets Coded," she snapped. "It's that simple. Until the doctor tells us to stop, we give it all we've got. Have you stocked the cupboards in the clean utility room yet today?"

Like a reprimanded child, I stocked the cupboards and learned which questions not to ask aloud. It seemed rather heretical or sacrilegious to even *think* of not Coding a patient who was obviously gone, and I felt somehow perverted for continuing to harbor doubts. Had I been Jenny's mother, perhaps I might have felt differently—perhaps I might have implored the crew to reverse a decision that had been made by some Higher Power.

"We're tampering with God's work," I told Lani that afternoon. We had stopped by the ICU to see how Jenny was doing. As predicted, she had a respiratory infection that required potent antibiotics. She also had chest tubes draining her lungs, an IV in each tiny hand, a bladder catheter that ran to a collection bag hanging on the side of the bed, and an array of electrodes running from her body to the monitor overhead. In addition, the respirator equipment attached to her neck had a huge accordion-like tube which ended at a machine that was almost as big as her crib. Her eyelids were taped shut to prevent damage of the cornea since she was unable to blink, which seemed to me the ultimate assault.

"How will you know if she awakens?" I asked Ann Pruett, the head nurse of ICU. "The respirator keeps her from talking and the tape keeps her from opening her eyes . . . how would you know she's awake?"

"We'll see it on the heart monitor. Her heart will speed up and she'll begin to get restless." At first, her tone was that of a teacher. Then she said, almost under her breath, "But it's not going to happen . . . she may still be here like this months from now." She hurried off to another patient's side, which was just as well—I might have been compelled to ask how it felt to nurse a child who was never expected to open her eyes or utter a word.

"We probably don't understand the situation," Lani suggested, "but it sure seems to me it's morally wrong to Code everyone."

Charlie argued the question with us. "First of all, who says there's a God? And if there is a God, then it must have been His will that we should discover the techniques to resuscitate people . . . and when we've discovered the techniques, why not use them." There was no question in his voice.

A few days later, Lani and I were sitting in the cafeteria with three of the paramedics. At one time, they had all been nurses in the intensive-care unit or the emergency room. When the city decided to train nurses to replace firemen as paramedics, many nurses applied for spots in the pilot program, which was to be tested for a year. Six nurses were chosen from a large pool of applicants. The program had been in effect just a few months when we met them.

They told us the training involved physical feats such as scaling walls, running long distances and driving obstacle courses. The written tests were arduous. In fact, none of them passed the test the first time around, but eventually they were all licensed and began living in the hospital when they were on duty. In uniforms that resembled those of firemen, they carried walkie-talkies and roamed the halls of the hospital waiting for the next call.

"We're in the van most of the time," Janet Jenkins told us, "going to or from a crisis. Our response time is great—three minutes and twenty-eight seconds—much faster than the response time of the firemen." It was her contention that nurses were the best paramedics. "We've got at least two years of medical training more than anyone else who's a paramedic . . . why shouldn't we be the best? At the crisis site, we can do everything instantly. Other paramedics have to wait for radio instructions on what to do, or they have to bring the patient into the hospital before treatment can get started." I was awed by her stories of careering through the streets of the city, sirens blaring, to save a life, but something was nagging at me.

"If your response time is three minutes and twenty-eight seconds, then I guess the patient's survival depends a lot on how fast the person who placed the call to you moved?"

She missed the point, but then I wasn't being too clear. "There's no ambulance crew that arrives faster than we do . . . our patients survive!"

"Do you Code all of them?"

"Of course . . . unless they have vital signs and have been revived before we get there."

"What if the patient lives out in the sticks and it takes ten minutes to get there? Do you Code that patient too?"

"Of course! Our survival rate is terrific. Nurses are the next best thing to carrying doctors on the van . . . and if I were the patient, I'd prefer nurses. Nurses are the best at starting IVs."

"If the patient has not breathed for ten minutes, and you revive him, won't he have brain damage?"

Suddenly it was as if she saw me for the first time. She narrowed her eyes, looked contemplative and then shrugged her shoulders. "I guess I'm missing what you're asking. What's your point, Barbara?"

"Mrs. Erin told us you must revive a patient within four minutes to avoid brain damage. If your response time is almost that, and you add the time it takes for someone to place the call to you, every patient you revive is destined to be brain damaged. Don't you have some criteria by which you judge whether or not to revive a patient?"

"I never thought about it . . . we Code them all . . . it's our job."

"You never worry about condemning some patient to a permanent coma by Coding him?"

There was a look of distasteful mistrust on her face as she looked up at the clock. "Wow! It's really getting late . . . let me know if you want to ride the van with us someday. It's really a blast! I've gotta run."

By that time, everyone else had left the table, including Lani. I sat there thinking something was missing—there must be another ingredient. Janet Jenkins was a highly skilled nurse, according to anyone who ever mentioned her. I respected her more than any staff nurse I knew, yet she never thought about *not* Coding a patient. It seemed incredible that anyone could be a nurse for nine years and never think about that.

I had discussed such thoughts with Judith one afternoon at Sunny Harbor, without telling her about Jenny or any of the gory details. "Every new answer raises a new question," she said. "It's easy to poke a fire with someone else's hand." She seldom solved my problems, but I seldom brought her the solvable ones!

The problem was temporarily placed in the back of my mind, in a small steel vault marked "Do Not Open Ever!" but it would resurface each time I went to see Jenny. Several months later, it would become more important to me than any other topic I had ever pondered, which is how it is with the major moral and ethical dilemmas—they demand resolution when they have become personal.

Not all cases in the ER were Codes or terrible tragedies, but unless they were some kind of crisis, they probably didn't belong there. "There's good crisis, and then there's bad crisis,"

Charlie told us. The unexpected delivery of a baby, which we never saw, was what he considered a "good crisis." A heavily bleeding wound in the beginning stages was a "good crisis."

"If we see the patient before their condition is grave, it's a 'good crisis,' " Charlie explained. It was the last day of the semester, when we were sitting in the ER lounge with the staff in the first quiet moment we had had since we began our rotation. An ambulance driver wandered in and caught us by surprise.

"Too bad I can't be a nurse and sit around drinking coffee all day," he quipped. "Anybody want some business?"

"Good crisis or bad?" Charlie asked, knowing it had to be benign or it wouldn't have been treated so casually.

"Good. Well, it's good, but it's bad. We're transferring a twenty-seven-year-old cancer patient from his home. They haven't got a bed for him on the floor yet. Admitting says you guys can watch him until they have an empty bed."

The crew went immediately to attend to the patient, who it turned out was Frank Bandini. In the two months since we had watched his operation he had lost so much weight that we would not have recognized him except for the fact that young patients with his diagnosis are rare and particularly poignant. He had an intense impact on Lani and Charlie, being the same age, and the rest of the crew seemed to be trying to distance themselves from him.

Mrs. Erin appeared out of nowhere, as she always seemed to do when there was something she wanted us to see. "This patient is going to have a scan in about an hour." She looked at her clipboard to confirm his appointment. "The three of you should go with him . . . observe. You can tell the group at conference all about scans.

"Are you all right?" she asked Charlie. She always had a sixth sense and could tell when a student was battling emotion, but she never referred directly to what was going on. "Are you all right?" meant "I know this is difficult for you," which seemed sufficient compassion.

Charlie pretended he didn't hear Mrs. Erin's compassion and went off to find the resource book that would tell us everything we needed to know about scans. At the time, the diagnostic machinery was so new and expensive, only very large successful hospitals like Oakmont County owned one.

"Kripes . . . this is like being in a James Bond movie," Lani whispered as we wheeled Frank's gurney into the scanning room. There was something science fiction-like about the huge gleaming machinery in the center of the room, surrounded by cameras, TV screens and a computer. The spotlights recessed in the ceiling increased the feeling of a movie set, as did the partitions and glass behind which the crew worked.

"Maybe I ought to reconsider," said Frank, beginning to shiver. "That monster machine looks like it could swallow up an army without anyone noticing!"

"You won't feel a thing," Charlie told him, with the confidence of one who has been through the scanning himself. Only Lani and I knew Charlie had never even *seen* the machinery before, let alone felt it.

I held Frank's hand and smiled while we waited for the technician to transfer him from the gurney to the table that moved through the scanner. "I would be apprehensive too," I offered. "It's the size of the machinery . . . makes you feel like an insect, doesn't it?"

He became "our patient" while we stood there doing what we could to infuse him with courage we had a scant supply of ourselves. Down the road, Frank would tell us how grateful he had been to have us at his side that day. "The terrified leading the terrified . . . little did he know," remarked Lani. It was that ability to comfort patients as though we were the world's leading authorities on whatever was happening to them that seemed one of the greatest satisfactions of being a nurse.

Eventually the technician explained the procedure to Frank before doing anything, which was the education Mrs. Erin wanted us to have. "You won't feel a thing," the technician began. Charlie nodded his head proudly, as if to say, *See, I told you so!*

In simplest terms, the narrow X-ray beam makes a 180-degree scan of the body, one degree at a time, as the table on which the patient lies moves slowly through the scanner. In electronic computer language, X-ray photon absorption data are displayed as a digital printout on a TV screen. Photographs are taken of the screen image and stored on magnetic discs. Air appears black, bone is white, and soft tissue has various shades of gray, depending on density. A change in normal density indicates trouble, which in Frank's case suggested areas of the body to which cancer had spread (metastasized).

"We call it a CAT," she explained, "for computerized axial tomography ... a CAT scan. All we want of you is absolute immobility. Do you think you can lie absolutely still?"

"Like in a grave," he said, with a touch of bitterness.

"The clicking's the worst," he told us later. "With every click [and there were hundreds], I expected to feel a jab of radiation electrifying my body."

We were wheeling him back to the emergency room when his wife caught up to us in the hall. "Hey ... wait up! Who's the good-looking redhead on that gurney?"

"My wife ... Bonnie," he said to us. She was younger than he, probably about twenty, and had thick blond hair that hung almost to her waist. He grasped her hand, and she walked the rest of the way beside the gurney.

"How was it?" she asked.

"Not bad ... how long do you think we have to wait to hear the results?"

"Who waits?" she said. "God doesn't zap good guys like you. I already know the results are great ... you'll be back in the towers before Christmas!"

In the operating room we had heard his case was terminal—there wasn't anything that could save him. Yet Bonnie expected him to be back at his job as an air controller by

Christmas? Either she had never been told he was dying, she refused to believe it, or someone had been leading her to believe there might be a cure.

By the time we got Frank back to the emergency room, a room had been readied for him on the oncology unit. "What for? Wait ... aren't you going home in an ambulance ... today?" Bonnie asked.

"We have to wait for the results," Frank said. "Besides, you could use a break. Let's let the nurses do the work for a day or two."

She was pregnant and had been taking care of him by herself, but at the time that didn't strike us as odd. What *did* was that they both seemed to be going somewhere on different tracks while thinking they were going to the same destination.

Later Charlie remarked, "He knows he's dying, but he's not sure she knows, and if she doesn't know, he doesn't *want* her to know."

"Do you think she knows?" I asked.

"She's playing ostrich. Wouldn't you play ostrich if you were that young, that pregnant, and that close to losing your husband?"

"How close?"

"When he had surgery, they only gave him a few weeks ... it's been at least a couple of months."

When I thought about Frank after that day, it was the kind of thinking that creeps up on one in the dark hours of the night, when ostriches take their head out of the sand and look at reality. What would it be like to be on the brink of dying and becoming a father both at the same time? Did he lie awake at night, wondering if he would ever see his first child?

"Do you ever think about what it would be like to be dying?" I whispered to Dean.

"Aren't you asleep yet?"

"There's this boy ... only twenty-seven ... he's dying."

There was a long silence, a thousand miles wide, and then the slow, easy breathing of sleep.

7 Divine Destiny

It was almost July when we finished the emergency room rotation and took the final first-year exams. Seventeen students had opted out of the program. Two more failed the exams and disappeared. For those of us remaining, it was the halfway point of no return. "Leave now or forever hold your peace," Mrs. Erin said. For all of us, it was a temptation.

After final exams, each of us had an evaluation conference with Mrs. Erin. She probably had no idea that what she said might be the deciding factor. "You must deal with your fears," she told me, as if they were tangible objects one had to pluck from the skin like a tick. She never said, "You are going to be a *great* nurse," or even a good one. "Perhaps you should work as an aide during summer break . . . see what it's like to have six or eight patients on a shift . . . get desensitized to your fears."

That night, when I told Dean about the evaluation, I said, "Mrs. Erin isn't sure I'm going to be a good nurse. Maybe I'm not the type."

"Of *course* you're going to be a great nurse. What does she know?" It was like him to champion me before I started nursing school, but things had changed. He wasn't crazy about any kind of change. Now here he was again, back to supporting the zealot. Some days he said, "Corporate wives should not work!" Today it was okay.

"It's the halfway point. If I'm going to drop out, I have to do it now."

"That's crazy . . . drop out?"

When I told him I was afraid—of death, cancer, massive wounds, patients who had needs and diseases that seemed obscure, little children dying, doctors, and a series of unknowns that seemed to expand with knowledge, he agreed with Mrs. Erin. I should spend summer break working full-time at the hospital—see if it was possible to get desensitized to fear.

"At the end of the six weeks," he said, "decide if it's really what you want to do." It seemed absurd that I was so unsure after all it had taken to get that far.

The temptation to work at Oakmont County Hospital, just so I could keep tabs on Jenny's progress (or lack of it) and call on Peter Haynes and Charlie if I got into trouble, was not as great as the need to work close to home. St. Joseph's was just a few blocks away—close enough to meet the kids for lunch and give them a feeling I wasn't as "gone" as during the school year.

St. Joseph's was a Catholic hospital, much smaller than Oakmont, with a brand-new oncology (cancer) unit that boasted the latest in family-centered care. One room was furnished like a living room, with elegant furniture, phones, a refreshment center and a small alcove that looked similar to a shrine. If one could ignore the box of Kleenex on every flat surface, it might have seemed a very pleasant place. At least the intention was good—cancer patients and families could visit and forget for a few minutes that it was a hospital.

Lani was working at the same hospital, on the orthopedic unit, and liked it so much she had left her job at the phone company. "No turning back for me," she said—at least one of us was sure about the future.

Though I chose to work on the oncology ward because my deepest fears had to do with cancer and death, I came to think of the entire experience as Divine Destiny.

The nurse I worked with most was Lynne O'Malley, a Julie Andrews look-alike who was engaged to Dr. Loren Mulwards, the physician in charge of the emergency room at Oakmont. He was slightly taller than Lynne, always tan from skiing or swimming. Their wedding was to be at Christmas. If it wasn't the Cinderella social event of the year, it wouldn't be for lack of talk about it. They seemed the ideal couple.

I liked Lynne from the beginning, but I liked her even more the day she said, "Oh, I'm so glad you're here today—it's just you and me. I would *never* be able to handle this many patients with any other nurse." Such approval was just what I needed. Much later I learned that it was rank insanity for two nurses to handle twenty patients, but at the time I thought it was just par for the course.

Perhaps all oncology units are like St. Joseph's, with nurses, doctors, patients and families acting like one enormous family. A cancer remission for one patient was a triumph for the whole family. A defeat for one patient was a defeat for all. The patients who went home between courses of chemotherapy returned to visit the others who were not so lucky. That was the good part.

The bad part was that cancer is a slow, devastating, enigmatic illness that eventually catches up to one out of every four humans. "Is it contagious?" I asked Dr. Paul Gaumer while he was writing orders on Sister Margaret's chart. It was an idle question, for the sake of conversation.

"Could be!"

He must have heard my gasp as he finished the chart and pushed it back into the rack on the counter. He grinned and slipped his black horn-rimmed glasses into his suit pocket. Without his moustache, he might have looked like a mischievous little boy. "Handsome devil," Lynne called him.

"Some believe it is contagious, you know. Are you worried?"

Not until that moment! "You don't believe it is, do you?" I asked.

"Who knows?" he said. "I knew polio was contagious when I treated those patients. TB is contagious. Haven't you ever taken care of a pneumonia patient? That's contagious."

"Give me a cold, TB, pneumonia, whatever. Not cancer." I

couldn't imagine anyone voluntarily working all day with the risk of becoming infected by cancer. "Don't tease . . . I might have a heart attack before your very eyes."

"Please, no heart attacks! I'm crummy with hearts. Don't worry, when I find out if it's contagious, I'll tell you. Meantime, Sister Margaret needs some Compazine . . . give her a shot as soon as you can." It was a closed subject—the kind that went in that small steel vault of my mind marked "Do Not Open Ever!"

Sister Margaret did indeed need the Compazine. Everything that went into her stomach was returning as a result of the chemotherapy for cancer, yet she stoically drank gallons of water to stop the unquenchable thirst caused by the drugs. For any patient such a situation is pathetic; but her case was all the more poignant because she was a nun from the Philippines who could not speak a word of English. Even a muddled kind of sign language was becoming too much effort as the drugs decreased her strength.

"We can't send her home for treatment," Dr. Gaumer said. "They don't have the drugs there. We'll just have to do the best we can. Try to anticipate her needs . . . she'll get better soon." His brand of optimism was a great asset for an oncologist—a physician devoted to battling a disease fraught with mystery and more unanswered questions than answered.

It wasn't unusual to have nuns and priests at St. Joseph's, since it was the only Catholic hospital in a large area. And the Catholic affiliation meant an observance of Catholic rituals in addition to nursing more patients than seemed humanly possible.

Communion, the most time-consuming ritual, was a matter of making sure all the Catholic patients had clean sheets, cleared bedside tables, drawn curtains, spotless rooms and a special linen cloth spread across their chests—all by 6:30 A.M., which was just about the time all twenty patients were awakening and needing pain medication, help to the bathroom (which could take twenty minutes for very weak patients), and fresh water.

At the same time, there was only a half hour before the next shift to empty and measure all the urine-collection vessels, record the IV fluids, chart the events of the previous night for every patient, give the before-breakfast insulin injections, empty the trash in each room, count the narcotics, and prepare the shift-change report for the next group of nurses.

Except for the rooms where patients would be receiving Communion, every door on the unit had to be closed. Quiet doors might have been a partial solution. However, ours clanked and creaked so that all twenty patients were wide-awake and needing care just as the nurses were supposed to be disappearing into the woodwork when Sister Mary Theresa rang a little bell as she got off the elevator with Father Murphy. Together they would go from room to room, slipping from one open door to the next, trailing incense behind them, and be gone to the next floor within fifteen or twenty minutes.

"When you stop and think about it," Lynne commented, "there's something reassuring about the Communion ritual, even though it's not for me. It's as if maybe God really is watching over the tragedy on this floor . . . it's comforting."

Then one morning, when there was one crisis after another, it was not so comforting. Dr. Lawrence Stoddard, a chemistry professor from Oakmont University, was in his last few minutes of life, and I was trying desperately to comfort his family. At the same time, Sister Margaret was crying loudly in the next room, having finally given up on being stoic; a lung cancer patient whose brain was affected by the disease was shouting for everyone, anyone, to come help him; the blood transfusion on another patient was in its first ten minutes, the time when it must have careful attention in case the patient has a transfusion reaction; and I was running to the cart for some ammonia to revive Dr. Stoddard's wife, who had just fainted.

Holy Communion was the very last thing on my mind when

I heard the "tinkle-tinkle" of Sister's bell and the slam of the elevator doors. "Oh my God!" gasped Lynne. "Quick, get the Communion list . . . who's on it?" She was drawing up pain medication for Sister Margaret.

"God doesn't give a damn if the right doors are shut or if the patients have napkins on their chests," I hissed. "Tell Sister Terry and Father Murphy *they* can take care of the pomp and circumstance around here in the morning if it's so important to them!"

"God's gonna get you for that, Barbara!" It was Frank Bandini, in the room directly across from the nurses' station. "Shame on you . . . is that a mortal or a venial sin?"

Frank had been transferred to St. Joseph's from Oakmont County Hospital a week earlier for another exploratory laparotomy—this time with a new surgeon.

A hot flash crept up my neck, and my eyes stung. "You weren't supposed to hear that, Bandy," I called as I raced past his room. "And it's mortal!"

The next time I was in his room, he winked as if we were conspirators. "That incense makes me barfy! Don't you hate it?" He too had been raised Catholic and often talked about his altar boy days when he did such mischievous things as letting loose his pet white mouse from beneath his long surplice just as Mass was about to begin.

Taking care of Frank took every inch of my armor tightly cinched into place, with an extra coating of Teflon on top, to keep from drowning in sadness. "You'll be startled when you go in his room," Lynne told me the first day I worked at St. Joseph's, "but don't show it . . . it's a terrible tragedy . . . so pathetic."

It was a dark, sinister day, the kind that harbors a raging storm and then lets rain down in torrents that stop traffic and flood basements. Frank was stretched out on the bed, naked except for a small towel across his groin. The eerie glow from the fluorescent light just above his head turned the amber of his skin to a sickly, dark curry green. Large latex-covered clamps, each about two inches wide, zippered his abdomen together from chest to groin, and the iodine painted around each suture blended with the color of his skin, which was unlike any I had ever seen. His body was emaciated, like a bas-relief of a skeleton. My first impulse was to back out of the room.

Father Murphy was standing on the other side of the bed, his back to the door, looking out the window. Frank's eyes were closed, sunk deep in his cheeks, and his long, straight auburn hair was scattered on his pillow, looking as lifeless as he. I clenched a great gasp of horror behind my teeth as I remembered Lynne saying, "You'll be startled." Only the color of his hair matched the Frank I had been with during his first operation and the CAT scan that followed a few weeks later.

"You're new," he said, opening his eyes just a little. It seemed as if his voice came from the Other Side. I smiled, weakly no doubt, and began taking his blood pressure.

"Don't I know you?"

I told him where we had met, offered him fresh water and then hurried out to the nurses' lounge, lost in a confusion of nausea, dread and overwhelming sadness. After that first time, after I remembered to put on my armor, he never again looked so horrible to me.

"He was an open-and-close," Lynne told me, "slipping fast. We've never had a case like this ... too young ... too fast."

"He looks better today, don't you think?" Bonnie, his pregnant wife, knew he would never get well, but she was cheery and optimistic just the same.

"Hey, Frank, you're looking better," Dr. Gaumer would say. "Maybe next week we'll get you down to physical therapy for some exercise."

"Get me strong," Frank would whisper, almost too weak to speak. "Baby's coming ... gotta be strong ... kid's gonna play football with me."

"Happiness is the state of being well and artfully deceived,"

Lynne O'Malley told me. "They know Frank's dying, but they don't know it deep down."

When Dr. Gaumer spoke of Frank's disease, he never said "cancer." It was too harsh a word, but it was also too vague for a doctor who had great difficulty translating the academic way he thought about things into the jargon of the layman. "Cancer" is an umbrella over a hundred or more diseases that have only one thing in common—normal cells disconnect from the normal order of things and suddenly grow and grow. Frank's cancer was, specifically, renal cell carcinoma.

At the time, I knew renal referred to kidney and carcinoma referred to cancer, but the distinctions between one kind of cancer and another seemed inconsequential when compared with the distinction between life and death. Frank was dying. Nothing else really mattered.

"Death is nothing more than a part of life," the textbooks said, "a natural event." Mrs. Erin had quoted the text the first day at Oakmont when I had walked into Herman Otis's room and thought he was dead. "Are you afraid of death?" she had asked. Nursing Frank was forcing me to think about it, but only in short glimpses.

When I was with Frank and Bonnie in his room, we all pretended intense interest in the current incident; some change in the condition of Frank's incision, the latest news about Sister Margaret, a new doctor who had just joined the staff, the autumn wind that seemed to be starting earlier than most years, how Bonnie was outgrowing her maternity clothes—we talked of anything but what was ahead for both of them.

At night I would think about Frank and tell Dean, "I'm really surprised . . . nursing a dying person is not so bad as I thought it would be. I can do it. Maybe I'll be a great nurse after all."

Then in the middle of the night, when there was no way to hide from reality, I would think about what it would be like for Bonnie after Frank died. What would it be like for me if Dean died? What was Frank thinking, in the quiet, dark hours of the night? What would I be thinking if I knew I would be dead in just a few weeks? Was he as frightened as I thought I might have been?

Such thoughts were awesome, humbling—in the morning I would hurry to hold Frank's hand, send him messages of courage with my eyes. Always I expected he might say something like, "I'm dying ... God, that's scary!" I waited, with my armor all cinched into place, just in case, afraid to hear it. Each time I left his room, I thought, *Phew! Thank God he's not talking about death.*

When the four weeks of semester break were over, and the second year of nursing school about to begin, the thought of leaving St. Joseph's—Frank and Bonnie, Sister Margaret, Lynne O'Malley, even the ritual of Holy Communion—felt much like leaving home.

"I can't leave," I told Dean. "St. Joseph's is where I belong."

"It's insane, going to school full-time, working at the hospital and trying to run this household," Dean said. "We haven't entertained any of my clients, you fall asleep at the banquets ... what about *my* career?"

"But I'm almost not afraid of hospitals anymore," I protested, "and those patients *need* me."

"Your husband and children *need* you," Alan said in a voice I imagined must approximate someone like Socrates. "We've had more peanut butter and jelly meals around here than any other family in America!"

"The perfect meal," I quipped. "The nutrition expert at school says it's the perfect meal—grains, proteins, fruit, starch, all kinds of good vitamins. All families should eat so well."

"I'm a meat-and-potatoes man," he grumbled, "but that's okay ... we've learned to live without you."

Had I realized that I needed St. Joseph's more than any patient there needed me, perhaps I might have paid more attention to what Alan and Dean were really saying. But in the end, we struck a bargain. I would work two weekends a month at St. Joseph's, begin entertaining Dean's clients, stop falling asleep at banquets, and teach our girls to cook meat and potatoes for Alan.

How could any family short on hot meals and clean clothes argue with a mother's zeal for nursing patients short on days left to live? Hardly any profession for women is as socially sanctioned as nursing.

PART TWO

1 Capricious Life

At the beginning of our last year of school, Charlie was assigned to the burn center, while Lani and I went to Oakmont Hospital's intensive-care unit. We expected that Charlie would take care of Bill Goldsmith and we would take care of Jenny Tucker. We also expected Charlie to like the burn center much more than we had—such a monumental challenge was his cup of tea, we thought.

As it turned out, Bill Goldsmith was getting along so well, he had been transferred to the surgical unit, where he was being prepared for his sixth round of skin grafts. It had been almost a year since the fire—the hospital life seemed more real to him than his home life. Once he came to grips with his situation, he began taking it in stride, as though he had planned all along to spend his thirty-sixth and thirty-seventh years in the hospital.

Jenny Tucker was not the same good news. In her fifth month in the ICU, she was still struggling to go nowhere. The only thing that looked familiar about Jenny was the mass of blond curls and the array of tubes and equipment that were sustaining her life. Her face was bloated and chafed from the drugs, bruises from IVs and blood draws ran from one end to the other, the entire length of her arms and legs, and the braces holding her legs in proper alignment made her whole body look askew.

Ann Pruett, head nurse of the ICU, was changing the rate on Jenny's IV. "Where will all this end?" I asked her. "It can't go on forever."

Ann shrugged her shoulders and went about adjusting splints, pillows and tubes with a deftness I always admired. She had been nursing all the years I had been manicuring carrots. "Power pack," the other nurses called her. She was a small bundle of energy with only one speed—extra-quick.

"Who knows?" she said. "I've stopped thinking about it. That's the first thing you learn here . . . do what has to be done and don't stop to moralize." Ann was pragmatic always, but when she talked to patients almost in a whisper, the words were gentle—she cared, but she didn't let it get to her. She told Lani and me she would not assign us to Jenny. "Too involved," she said. "It's too late for you to be objective." We suspected she also thought we might not know enough about pediatric nursing to do a good job.

The changes in Jenny's mother were even more surprising than the way Jenny looked. She was twenty-six going on forty. One afternoon she was standing by Jenny's bed, so lost in thought she started when I put my arm across her shoulder.

She stepped back and nodded her head toward the bed. "This might never end." Her voice was so bitter. "I'm working now . . . it's hard to get here often." If anyone ever looked hopeless, it was she.

Lani squeezed her hand. "Remember Owen? His doctors couldn't explain his recovery . . . he'd been clinically dead for five minutes . . . remember?" Owen had been in the bed next to Jenny's for several weeks, the victim of a brutal stabbing which left him on a street corner with a shredded heart and blood swiftly pumping from his body.

"No one has ever been reported surviving such trauma," said his doctor, after eight hours of surgery, but Owen had survived. The morning after surgery, he opened his eyes and began speaking coherently while Jenny's mother was standing there.

The mother nodded her head slowly. "I remember . . . they called it a miracle." She snickered cynically. "There are only so many miracles. After all these months, how could there be one for Jenny?"

Later Ann Pruett told us Jenny's mother was there around

the clock, sitting in the waiting room or the cafeteria between hourly ten-minute visits with Jenny—but that was in the beginning, when she still had hope. At night the father came, laughing and joking with the nurses at first, cementing the pleasant relationship with the staff that he thought might be necessary to ensure proficient, compassionate care for Jenny.

He brought candy kisses, boxes of peanut brittle, platters of imported cheeses and crackers—he tried *so* hard to make it an innocuous tea party. Everyone in the hospital knew Jenny's mom and dad and would stop in the halls or the cafeteria to chat with them for a while, just to pass the long hours waiting for Jenny's condition to change.

"They put on cheery faces, at first," Ann told us. "Stiff upper lip . . . that lasted about five weeks."

Eventually anger and frustration began to set in. They had little tiffs about whether or not she could hear, which nurses were better than others, if she looked better today than yesterday . . . then Dr. Hastings referred the case to an internist and the little sparring became earnest combat.

"He squared with the Tuckers," Ann said. "Told them there was nothing to be done . . . gave them a choice . . . pulling the plug or not. It was horrible. Jenny's mom got hysterical . . . nothing was the same after that. She became suspicious, belligerent, wouldn't come in when the father was here, challenged everything Dr. Kohn said."

"The father wanted to pull the plug?" I asked.

"He never said, but it was after that day that they quit coming to see Jenny together. I think he was just trying to be realistic."

"What about the nurses?" I wanted to know. "Who would have pulled the plug if they had agreed? Could you?"

She smiled and said that was a bridge she hoped they would never have to cross. "Already I've lost two nurses over this case. The hopelessness gets to them . . . day after day of fighting one infection after another, looking for a vein that hasn't been already punctured full of holes, dreaming up new ways to splint and brace her, pulling and stretching muscles that resist more every day, suctioning her trachea fifteen or twenty times a day . . . then they sit and rock her like she's their own. It's easier when it isn't a little blond baby."

Lani and I talked about whether or not we could pull a plug. I suspect it was the kind of philosophizing scholars do about dying—it's easy to speculate when you're not the one involved.

When I thought about it in the dark hours of the night, I was glad Ann had decided she didn't want us taking care of Jenny. I would not have wanted to make pull-the-plug decisions that early in my career—maybe it would always be too early, for that matter.

When Ann assigned me to Barry Bauer, the patient in the bed next to Jenny's, my first thought was of the fright night movies Dean loved to watch on TV. Barry's head was swaddled in thick bandages, wrapped mummy fashion, with deep black holes where his eyes, ears, nose and mouth should have been. His tall, bodyguard build dwarfed the ICU bed and intensified the feeling that Dr. Frankenstein had left a monster in our midst.

"He's been here two weeks . . . still suicidal," Ann said. "Don't leave anything sharp near his bed."

The history on the chart was sketchy, but over the weeks we pieced together Barry's story. He had been working as a salesman for a pharmaceutical company when he met Beth, a receptionist in the office of one of the doctors he called on. Eventually they were married and had two children. Life was "okay," he told us later, fairly typical of young families except that his job kept him on the road a lot.

In his work he prepared proposals and reports, which was his least favorite part of the job, and eventually he relied more and more on one of the secretaries, Shari, to put the work together that he disliked. "She helped me," he said, "and I thought she had the inside track with the brass around there."

She would be typing his reports when everyone else went home, and sometimes they would have a drink together when she was finished. One thing led to another, and before long he was telling his wife he was going to be out of town when he really wasn't. Shari began traveling with him, and they were together most nights when they weren't traveling—eventually Barry left his wife and two children.

They lived a whirlwind life of dancing, sailing, hang-gliding—"All the things I'd never done before"—for about six months until Shari went out to the West Coast to spend the holidays with her family. It was the first time Barry had lived alone, and even though it was only for two weeks, the lonely holidays triggered depressing thoughts that mushroomed over the months following. By fall he had slipped into deep depression. Shari had become enchanted with an old boyfriend on the West Coast and was planning to return there as soon as she could arrange a transfer through the pharmaceutical company.

"There seemed no point to life," he said, "no reason to keep on truckin'." The night that Shari told him her plans, he sat up and drank all night. In the morning he swallowed twenty Doriden tablets—more than enough to finish life for most people. "I called my wife," he said, "just to apologize for what I'd done," but he didn't tell her he had swallowed the Doriden. She rebuffed his apology, and then his suicide was in earnest—he put his shotgun under his chin, pointing up toward his mouth, and pulled the trigger.

His slurred speech over the phone at that hour of the morning gave his plan away, and his wife called the paramedics even before she put the kids in the car and drove to his house. What he looked like when he arrived in the emergency room was hospital gossip for weeks. They pumped as much Doriden out of his stomach as they could get, and he hovered near death for days.

Peter Haynes had told me about the argument among the

139

doctors at the time. "Same stuff . . . right to live/right to die. It just seems to me that there's never been a patient who expressed more graphically his wish to die."

When the staff nurses talked about Barry during report, it was with the same expressions and words that people use to discuss the woman with whom the company president is having an affair—most of the discussion is with the eyes and a few sardonic innuendos.

"Why is he banging on the bed rail like that?" I asked. It was before I knew the story.

"Why do you think? What would *you* do?" The nurse hurried past me.

It was obvious I was supposed to know something I didn't. The first task of the day is to take a patient's temperature, pulse and blood pressure. Then get the patients to brush their teeth so they're ready for breakfast. The complex tasks bothered me, but the easy morning routine was one I did by rote, except with Barry. I took one look at him and thought about the thermometer, the toothbrush, the breakfast. Good grief . . . I had never encountered a patient without a mouth. At least I could take his pulse, but as I lifted his wrist he shoved me away from the bed and made a horrible guttural sound.

"Knock it off, Barry!" Ann Pruett shouted from the desk. "We're not going to take any of your bull today!"

He began banging on his rail again, with his fists, a pencil, a book, and the loud grunting noises were those of an enraged gorilla. I felt stupid, as if some text should have told me what was going on. Finally Ann told me the problem. He was angry that his life had been saved, and he didn't want anyone to come near him to try and perpetuate it. He wouldn't allow any IVs, no one could get near him to get his vital signs, and he wouldn't take any medications.

"He has only a partial jaw, no teeth, a fragment of a tongue—he can't tell us anything." The first few days, when he was coming out of the narcotized haze, he wrote on a Magic

Slate. But as he grew more alert, the slate was too slow and he became infuriated at being alive.

The general feeling among the nurses and doctors was— some gratitude! Save the guy's life and look what you get for it.

When I first began taking care of Barry, I would have been thrilled to trade him for any patient in the unit, probably because it seemed like we were on different planets. What do you say to someone who wants out of life so badly he shoots himself? How could I relate to a young man who could communicate only with grunts? To say the least, it was a challenge, but one I desperately needed at the time.

When we were ending the third week together, I went to the doctor for a routine physical exam that the school required every year. Our family doctor, Richard Magnum, usually did fairly cursory exams. He and I both believed that physicals were a waste of time if the patient didn't have symptoms.

He poked and probed while we talked about hospitals, how St. Joseph's and Oakmont stacked up in terms of innovative equipment and doctors. He was in the middle of a sentence when he said, "What the hell is this? How long have you had this?" He kept pressing on the right side of my upper abdomen. "Here . . . put your fingers there . . . feel it? Whatever that mass is, it has to come out."

I didn't feel the mass then and I never felt it later, but within an hour I was sitting in a surgeon's office. The surgeon poked around. "Probably nothing," he said. "We'll do some X-rays in a couple of weeks . . . just ignore it . . . probably nothing."

As I was leaving his office, his nurse handed me requisitions for X-rays. "Have them done whenever you like," she said. "When the doctor gets back from vacation in two weeks, you come in and he can give you the results."

Maybe other people don't panic when the doctor says, "You have a mass," but I have a mammoth aversion to the word "mass." It conjures up visions of drastic things, like long termi-

nal illness, hospitalization, orphaned kids, bereft husbands—
by the end of two weeks, overactive imagination was my middle name.

The doctor returned from vacation to tell me the X-rays had
been negative. "Probably nothing," he said again. "Why don't
you just wait and see . . . maybe it will go away."

"And if it doesn't go away?"

"We'll operate," he said, as if operations were like getting a
haircut.

At any other time in my life, I might have been content to
wait and see, but nursing school is the kind of project no one
would want to do just for fun. If there was any chance I
wouldn't be able to graduate, it seemed pointless to keep dragging out of bed at 4:30 in the morning to hassle through more
days which seemed endless.

"Go to another doctor . . . see what he says," Dean suggested.

The next doctor ordered more X-rays, a few blood tests, a
few more X-rays. Two more weeks passed. Finally, one Friday
afternoon I was sitting in the third doctor's office with a set of
X-rays. He took a cursory glance and said, "Look. You should
see a urologist . . . Dr. Harvey's a good one. Do you know
him?" I told him I didn't. "Well, it's almost five . . . I'll call him
. . . tell him you're coming. Will you go straight there now?"

Within ten minutes I walked into Dr. Harvey's waiting room
and was immediately shown to his office. The nurse put my X-
rays up on the panel beside his desk and said he would be right
with me. It was a long, narrow office, almost like a hall, with
the door and the bench on which I was sitting at one end and a
window at the other. Midway between the two was his desk,
facing me.

"Mrs. Huttmann? I'm Morton Harvey." He bustled into the
room and went straight to his desk as he was talking. He
flipped the light switch on the X-ray panel and stroked his
chin.

There wasn't much about him that wasn't ordinary—middle-aged, middle-sized, medium-brown hair that was getting sparse on top. He seated himself at the desk and looked at a sheet of paper before him. "Hmmm. You're a nurse. Who first found the mass?" The third doctor had told him a few details.

"Richard Magnum."

"Why so many doctors since then?"

"No one seemed able to identify the problem."

"Have you felt tired lately?"

I chuckled. "I think I'm starved for sleep because I'm much too old to be in nursing school."

"Lost weight lately?"

"No."

"Nauseated?"

"No."

"Well, look." It was the first time his eyes met mine, just for a fraction of a second. It was also the last time. "You're a nurse . . . you know what I'm talking about . . . I'll give it to you straight out—you have renal cell carcinoma." He leaned back in his chair, hands behind his head, stretching as though he had been solving complex math problems.

"I'm not really a nurse yet," I told him, as if that would change the diagnosis. "I'll graduate this June." There seemed a terrible confusion in my brain. *How is one supposed to respond in such circumstances*, I wondered.

"Renal cell carcinoma," I said, testing it for familiarity. "Is that cancer?" I asked him to spell it for me, as if I had never heard the term before—as if I had no idea that Frank Bandini had died of the same disease just three days earlier. As he spelled it, I wrote it on the calendar page of my checkbook.

The only sound in the room was the clicking of the digital clock on his desk. Every muscle in my body was taut, frozen, holding the stoic nurse composed.

"How long do I have?" The calm words were in a voice I hardly recognized as mine.

143

He glanced at the X-rays again on the lighted board beside his desk. "Well . . . you're a nurse . . . these cases are terminal, you know. Looks pretty far gone . . . I'd say a few weeks . . . maybe two months. You know about these cases."

It was embarrassing to know so much less than he assumed.

This can't be, I thought. This man cannot blurt out a death sentence so casually. He doesn't even know me. He has never even examined me. He should have learned in medical school that you choose a proper time and place for handing out a terminal diagnosis. You don't just blast it at the patient when she's sitting there all alone and defenseless.

I looked at the empty seat on the bench beside me. Couldn't he see that it was empty? "I'm alone . . . don't do this . . . take it back!" I wanted to shout.

"You're sure about this?"

Again he looked up at the X-rays. "It's obvious . . . a classic case."

I looked up at the X-rays, hoping to see whatever he saw that made him so sure. The outline of the kidneys was as I had seen them in school, except for an odd white blob suspended from the lower margin of the one on the right. To ask him about the blob seemed too direct, too much like mistrusting his observations.

"The kidney on the right," I said. "It's much lower in my abdomen, isn't it?"

"That's normal. Most women have a lower right kidney." Then it was not that white blob weighting down the one on the right.

"Are you sure about this?" I asked again.

"Well, of course, there's no way to be absolutely positive until surgery, but you're a nurse . . . you know what we're dealing with here. This is renal cell carcinoma."

Earlier that week at the hospital, another doctor had read my ID badge aloud: "Barbara Huttmann, SN. What does 'SN' mean?" Nurses my age are usually supervisors—he expected it meant "Supervising Nurse"—but I had asked a question a supervisor would be too smart to ask.

In a sudden burst of frivolity, I thought of answering, "Sensuous Nurse" or, how I really felt, "Stupid Nurse"; but I told him the truth—it meant "Student Nurse." Age was sometimes an advantage, but more often it was a disadvantage—I was assumed to be a far more knowledgeable nurse than I really was. Somehow I needed to make Dr. Harvey understand that I *didn't* know what we were dealing with.

"Well, you see," I said, searching for some natural order of words to get the message across, "I'm only a student nurse . . . that's all . . . just a student. I'm not sure what the next move is here."

"Surgery!" He straightened his chair, reached for the phone and looked up at the clock. "We'll do it tonight at eight. I'll see if we can get a room . . . shouldn't be any problem on a Friday night." It was 5:30 then—two-and-a-half hours was barely time enough to prepare for any surgery.

He was talking on the phone. "Right nephrectomy [kidney removal], tonight at eight, get the OR at St. Joseph's moving." He looked up at me. "Private or ward?" Without waiting for an answer, he told his nurse, "Get her a private room . . . tell them she'll be right over." He hung up the phone and stood as if to leave.

All the terrors from previous hospitalizations surfaced like oil from a wreck, as if I had never spent one day as a nurse. "Wait, Dr. Harvey! I can't have surgery tonight."

"Why not? The sooner the better."

What could I say, I don't have a toothbrush with me? My nightgowns are in the laundry hamper? My slippers have a hole in one toe? It would never do for a nurse to tell a physician she was terrified of cancer, terrified of hospitals, terrified of doctors, and three tiny millimeters away from hysteria.

I began talking fast, like someone who has had a magnificent brainstorm. "Dr. Harvey, we can't do this tonight. You see, I only have one semester of school left. There's a really important exam Monday, on the circulatory system. I can't miss it. They don't allow makeup exams in nursing school. I have to be there. I can't have surgery . . . this weekend I have to study." I put my checkbook back in my purse and got up to leave. "I'll call you Monday, after the exam. I really can't think about anything else till then."

"This can't wait, Mrs. Huttmann, you know that. Delay would be foolish."

My head was dancing to some frenzied internal beat. There must be something one should do in such a situation, but I couldn't think what it was. I felt apologetic, as if this poor man was being forced into a web with a frantic female who was spoiling his Friday night.

He sighed, like a parent who has tried to explain algebra logically and can't get through his kid's thick skull. Then he sat down at his desk. "You don't understand," he said. "Cancer grows by exponential leaps, Mrs. Huttmann. You know that. You need surgery and you need it fast."

The urge to burst into tears was stifled by the thought that I had a professional obligation. Nurses were stoics, and if it were not so, we certainly would never tell a doctor.

"Thank you, Dr. Harvey. I appreciate your concern, but nursing school and medical school are probably the same . . . you just have to put on blinders and trudge ahead. This weekend I must study for the exam."

"Well, all right. We'll postpone this until Monday. I'll get the nurse to take a catheterized urine sample before you leave." And he picked up the phone. His expression seemed to say, "What can you do with a fool?"

"Wait, Dr. Harvey." Even now, it is embarrassing to admit how I hated him by that time. He was a short, fat, vanilla-ice-cream-type person, bland, with no distinguishing characteristics except his obsolete military-crew-cut hair. We were probably about the same age, but I was thinking of him as

146

rather ancient. Anyone who hadn't heard how to tell a patient she was dying must have finished school in the days before physicians were taught that what goes on in a patient's mind is as significant as what goes on in a patient's body. In the mental state I was in, I would not have survived surgery. Even I, a second-year student nurse, knew that much.

"Why do you want a catheterized urine sample?" I asked. My modesty was against such indignity unless it would mean the difference between life and death.

"Well, you know," he said. "You're a nurse . . . sterile sample . . . clean-catch samples are contaminated. We take sterile samples from all our patients." Such a cavalier reason for catheterizing people!

In that instant I decided that I would crawl away from his doorstep even if I were dying and he were the last physician on earth. There were few human beings, let alone doctors, as insensitive as he.

"Let's do that Monday . . . I'll call you Monday, after the exam," I lied. "Thank you very much for your time." The sharp autumn wind startled me as I hurried out of his office. I was jumpy, having quick intestinal collapses, jerking parachute cords that wouldn't work. For the first time in my life, I had defied a doctor.

I sat in my car, feeling a precarious disorientation, as on New Year's Eve after too much champagne. No one on earth was left except Dean. Not only was it at least an hour before he would get home from the office, I felt that I no longer deserved what he had always freely given—protection from whatever pack of wolves happened to arrive at my door.

"You want to be independent?" he had said the week before. "Fine . . . you got it! You do your thing, I'll do mine." We had begun to argue about the division of labor. Why should I iron his shirts, pay his bills, shop for his shoes and figure out his income taxes? "For twenty years I've played maid. It's my turn now . . . you play maid for the next twenty years!" I said.

He had often joked that when I turned forty he would trade me in for two twenty-year-olds. "You're not wired for 220," I said, but he was "wired" for anything in life he wanted. All he really wanted was a wife who stayed home and played happy family with the kids.

My mother lived about a mile from Dr. Harvey's office. Going there to wait the hour for Dean to get home seemed a better option than going home where the kids would know, just from the electricity in the air, that an earthquake of crisis was about to take place.

"Good God, what's happened to you?" she asked, with no less perception than the kids might have had.

It was not a conscious decision to keep Dr. Harvey's opinion from her. Rather, it was a decision that what he said was indeed an "opinion," and who could ever place any value on the opinion of someone as blundering as he?

"I have to drop out of school," I cried. "Can you believe it? After all this . . . after getting so close to the finish line."

She thought it was God's way of sending me a message, that I had been making myself sick over getting through school, that mothers belonged home with their children, and that it might be the best thing that ever happened to me. The mass on my kidney was something that could be removed. I should find a good surgeon, and in six weeks it would all be over.

By the time I got to talk to Dean, I had lost sight of, or submerged, what the problem really was. I never mentioned cancer, renal cell carcinoma, or that I had only two months left to live. The tragedy was that I had to drop out of school and that I had narrowly escaped the scalpel of a knife-happy doctor. Anything else was simply unutterable.

And by the end of the evening, I had lost sight of, or submerged, everything except the narrow escape. I would spend the weekend studying for Monday's exam, and perhaps someday when I had more time, I would find another doctor.

"What about the mass?" Dean asked.

"What about it? I can't feel it. I've *never* been able to feel it. And anyway, if it were there, I'd feel sick. I've never felt better in my life!"

Though I must admit that concentrating on studying the circulatory system that weekend was like trying to scale glass walls; the slippery regions of my mind kept me from knowing *why* it was so difficult to concentrate . . . and kept me from associating myself with patients who did exactly as I was doing—denying the existence of crisis.

According to Dr. Elisabeth Kübler-Ross, the Swiss psychiatrist who wrote the classic book *On Death and Dying,* the first of many stages a terminally ill person faces is disbelief. We had studied these stages a year earlier in the first semester of nursing school. We even saw a videotape of Dr. Kübler-Ross discussing with her patients the phenomenon of the stages.

"Most patients can't cope with a terminal diagnosis," Mrs. Erin told us. "In the beginning, they seem to be unaware that they even heard it." It was only a textbook theory until the end of the first year when I met Marge Holden. Though I don't remember what brought Marge into the hospital in the first place, I do remember that the outcome of her surgery was a total surprise—she had a colostomy and a diagnosis of terminal cancer. Some cancers are curable, or at least they can be treated so that life is extended, but hers was apparently not. A colostomy forms an artificial anus from part of the bowel to the abdomen, where a soft plastic bag is affixed to collect feces. Marge's colostomy was simply for the purpose of diverting waste products because the normal route was blocked by a malignant tumor. Without the colostomy, she would eventually have been in excruciating pain.

Many people learn to live with colostomies, but it's not easy. The care of the skin is complex, diet must be carefully regulated, and it sometimes takes a lot of trial-and-error before anyone becomes adept at the whole process. A surprise colostomy would have been bad enough, but Marge had the dreaded diagnosis to deal with as well.

My job was to teach her the techniques of caring for the colostomy before she went home, but she couldn't even look at it, let alone care for it. "That's so sweet of you to want to help me," she would say, always as cheerful as any patient could be, "but I'm so tired just now. Perhaps tomorrow?"

She was a small, attractive, gracious lady with friends, relatives and neighbors who came to visit in an endless stream, always bearing gifts and flowers. They went into her room with long, sad faces and came out grinning and happy.

Greg Holden, Marge's husband, adored her and was a favorite of the nurses. He came and went, always with a stop at the nurses' station to thank someone for the care Marge was getting, and seemed as cheerful as she was.

Then one day he stopped by the medication cart in the hall and asked if he could speak with me in private. This was the first time he had ever looked troubled.

"Has Marge ever mentioned to you that she has cancer?" he asked.

"No. She's always bright and cheerful. I thought maybe you didn't want her to know, but Dr. Stewart says he told her himself."

Tears were pooling in his eyes. "Dr. Stewart *has* told her. I've told her, over and over. Our son has told her. Yet all our friends who visit her tell me they're sure she doesn't know. She keeps talking about next Christmas, and she won't even *be* here next Christmas!"

"The mind has a wonderful way of blocking out what it can't bear to hear," I told him. "When she's stronger, and can cope with it, she'll hear." At the time it was good advice I gave him, straight from the textbook, but there was no way I could apply it to myself when *my* turn came to cope with a terminal diagnosis. A terminal diagnosis didn't fit with my fantasy of nursing until my first patient, Mr. Otis, and it never fit with my fantasy of me. Terminal was for everyone else but me.

We talked about how isolated he felt, almost rejected by Marge, as if he had wished this horror on their life and was a bad person for believing she was terminally ill. Every day after that, he poured out his grief in brave words, which was the best thing he could have done—to deny his grief would have made him nonfunctional. "Still the same," he would say, shaking his head grimly. "She still can't face what's up ahead."

Eventually we decided it would be best if he learned how to care for her colostomy, since she was well enough to go home, and he attacked the project with the zeal of someone who desperately needs a reason for living. "Doing something at least keeps me from feeling so useless," he said, and he was an excellent student.

His enthusiasm infused her with interest, and she became involved in learning too, but it was the detached involvement of one who thinks the colostomy belongs to someone else. She went home still unaware that she had a colostomy and a terminal diagnosis.

Several months later, I almost passed by her in a department store.

"Barbara," she said, clutching my arm, "how *are* you?" She thought my stunned look meant I didn't recognize her. "Marge Holden," she reminded me. "Room 212? You remember?" Fortunately, I caught myself before I said what was on the tip of my tongue: "What are *you* doing alive?"

"You look wonderful, Marge"—which was true—"how have you been doing?" For over an hour, we stood in the aisle of the jewelry department while she told me about the day, two weeks after she got home, when it finally sank in.

"I was in my white Ultrasuede dress all ready to go out for lunch with my friend Beth. Without any warning, the colostomy bubbled over and stained the whole front of my dress . . . it was such a shock!" Her face was sad as she went on to recount the nightmare of the two weeks that followed. "I cried and cried . . . it was the most hopeless I've ever been." Finally she remembered a colostomy therapist who had tried to offer her help while she was in the hospital.

"She was young, in her early thirties, and she showed me her colostomy that day, but it didn't mean anything to me. Nothing meant anything to me when I was in the hospital." She shook her head in disbelief. "After two weeks of wallowing in self-pity, I got the therapist's phone number from the hospital and called her. She was *wonderful* . . . came to see me the next day . . . helped me find the right bags . . . showed me some tricks for taking care of the stoma [opening]. I've never had a problem since."

While we talked, I tried to orient myself to the notion that this lady who should have been dead, at least according to Dr. Stewart, was standing before me talking, looking perfectly happy and healthy. She doesn't know even yet, I thought. She's terminally ill and she still hasn't faced it.

She was all bright, cheery smiles as she told me Dr. Stewart intended to reconnect her intestine and seal off the wound in her abdomen. "Just when I've finally learned how to handle the thing," she laughed, "he's going to get rid of it." The only time I had ever heard of such an operation was when the patient had a temporary colostomy just to give the intestine time to heal.

"You mean the colostomy was only intended to be temporary?" I asked.

"I guess he thought it would have to be permanent," she said, "but whatever the problem was before, it's gone now."

I couldn't ask her if her case was still considered terminal, but it's doubtful she could have looked so healthy if death was near.

"Terminal is relative," Charlie remarked after hearing the story. "In a sense, we all have a terminal illness." Curbside philosophy like Charlie's was usually encouraging—he seldom missed the opportunity of using it to turn a puzzling and painful situation into something more positive—but there isn't any kind of philosophy that's effective when the doctor says, "You have a terminal disease."

Had I known that I would be condemned so early in life (forty suddenly seemed barely past adolescence), I would have made it a point to follow Marge's case. How could any physician give a wrong diagnosis if death was to be the outcome.

Like Marge, I became adept at disbelief.

"Not every dying person goes through all the stages at a predictable pace or in an exact sequence," Mrs. Erin had lectured long ago in first year. "Dr. Kübler-Ross hypothesizes that patients might make intermittent passes at one stage." This is exactly what I did. The disbelief stage stayed with me until the circulatory exam on Monday, three days after Dr. Harvey told me his diagnosis.

Lani and I were walking across campus to the parking lot after the exam was over. It was a gray, drizzly day, a few degrees from becoming soft snow, almost exactly like the day on which we had met a year earlier. Since then, the enduring, nourishing satisfactions of our friendship had grown swiftly without our even noticing.

"I need to find another doctor," I told her. "The X-ray of my kidney shows some weird thing attached." She listened to my explanation of what had happened with Dr. Harvey the previous Friday while I described it as if telling ball scores. "So now there are some things I must do . . . opting out of life is confusing. It's so disorienting . . . I can't think what to do next." We walked along a bit farther, settling into the delicacy of weakness like searching for a firm footing in thick grass.

"Well, Barb," she said, in the tone of voice she always used when we were jointly wrestling with some problem of logic, "let's go talk to Mrs. Harris. She always knows . . . ," and then she began to cry.

Crying was not really our style—but we wept for all the

times we would like to have wept together had it not been safer to "be strong." By the time we got to Mrs. Harris's office, the tears seemed to have straightened out my mind.

Mrs. Harris was a tall blonde in her late fifties who taught maternity nursing. Though she seemed totally impersonal most of the time, anyone who watched her in the labor and delivery rooms knew she cared more than many people and was more skilled than any of our other five instructors. She was sitting at her desk correcting the circulatory exam papers, when Lani and I walked in.

"I need the name of a good urologist," I told Mrs. Harris, "one who is not overly anxious to do surgery." After hearing the details of my plight, she recommended Dr. John Gary, who had taken excellent care of her mother a few years earlier. "He's on the staff at St. Joseph's," she said. "Brilliant man, mid-forties. I think you'd like his manner—earnest and compassionate.

"Now," she said, dipping her head and looking up at me through the top of her bifocals, "you're doing your ICU rotation at Oakmont, right?" I replied that I was. "Well, I'll inform them that you'll no longer be coming in." Her quick, objective analysis of every situation was a characteristic I had admired . . . until then!

"Oh, you don't have to do that," I stammered, panic twisting in my throat. "I'm not contagious. It's only a kidney . . . there's no reason to quit school . . . I don't feel sick."

"It isn't as if there's an escape from the mass in your abdomen. It's there and it has to come out. That's six weeks' recovery *minimum*, regardless of what the mass is. You know the rules—if you miss five clinical days in any one semester, you're disqualified from the program. I'm sorry . . . I know this meant a lot to you."

It seemed that dismissal from the program deserved more dramatic flair, a great orchestra of heartrending violins, some symbolic carving of a yawning gulf that would swallow me up.

"That's all? I'm out? You'll make a simple call to the ICU at Oakmont, and I'm out?" I asked softly, not wanting to suggest that her edicts were ones any student would question.

"I'm sorry. I wish I could tell you some alternative. Forget about school . . . you've enough to worry about now. Just call Dr. Gary and get yourself taken care of. We'll look in on you when you have surgery . . . maybe we'll even assign a student to take care of you." She smiled sympathetically while Lani nudged me toward the door.

I turned as we were about to leave the room. "Thank you, Mrs. Harris . . . thank you."

Later Judith said, "For that you would *thank* her?" As disastrous as it seemed to be dismissed from the program, there was much to thank Mrs. Harris for, which was difficult to explain. She was a *nurse,* in the strictest sense of the word, but "thank you" seemed the only words I could find to say how much that meant to me.

Lani and I had stopped to see Judith on the way home, Mondays being the only free afternoons we had that semester, and instinctively knew neither of us would mention my problem. Charlie had just brought her a snappy red and green wool lap robe to keep the cold from her one good leg, and was busy playing junior doctor. "You can't feel the cold . . . that's because your diabetes messes things up down there. Promise you'll always keep your good leg wrapped?" Charlie's gentle streak showed most around Judith.

"He treats me like a baby!" she said, always eager to claim independence, but she loved his affection.

Had we known it would be the last time all of us would be together, we might have each reached out to the others, but we prattled on about everything and nothing. I asked Charlie how things were going at the burn center. "Let's talk about something else," he said. He asked me why I hadn't shown up last Friday at the Pub. "Let's talk about something else," I said Lani asked Judith if she was able to sleep lying down, which it difficult for people with congestive heart failure. "Let's talk about something else," she said. We all had crawled into the safety of an emotional oasis, something we usually didn't have to do with each other.

While I sat there with them, in the warmth of their cocoon, my mind went about making plans without even consulting me. I would *not* drop out of school. We were in the midst of our ICU rotation, and I had a once-in-a-lifetime case I was assigned to—Barry Bauer—the young man whose thwarted suicide attempt had left him without a face. He needed me. It didn't occur to me that the need was as much mine as his.

"Mrs. Harris isn't the program director. She can't boot me out of the program," I told Lani during the drive home from Sunny Harbor. "I promised to teach Barry how to do his own tube feedings tomorrow. Besides, I haven't used up my five absent days. When I'm absent five days, I'll go to the college office and fill out withdrawal papers."

She could have said, "You have cancer" or "You only have two months left," but she knew instinctively when to resist confusing the issue with facts. "Right!" she said as we pulled into my driveway. "Then I'll see you tomorrow at seven?"

"Yep . . . I'll drive."

When I walked into the house I was sitting on a triple-layer life raft. The top layer was labeled "Student," the next layer "Surgery," and the bottom layer "Death." As long as I could cling to the student layer, I was free to deny any others.

2 Second Opinion

"So, did you find another doctor today?" Dean asked. My diagnosis still had not been mentioned, but he knew the mass would not disappear by itself.

I told him about my conversation with Mrs. Harris that day and that she had recommended I see Dr. John Gary. From what I had told him about her while she was our maternity teacher months before, he thought she was probably the ultimate authority.

"So make an appointment. What are you waiting for?"

Subconsciously I was probably waiting for the whole subject to dissolve. There were fleeting moments when I longed to tell him that Dr. Harvey had said I was dying, but then I couldn't imagine what words to use.

"I have to teach Barry Bauer to feed himself," I told Dean. "When that's done I'll find another doctor ... maybe John Gary ... by the end of the week I'll do it."

Teaching Barry Bauer to do his own feedings would be no small trick. A tube had to be inserted through a small hole in his bandages, in just the right spot so liquid could go down his throat without choking him. Sometimes when he was really angry, he would bat the tubing out of the nurse's hand so the formula sprayed all over the bed.

The day I was supposed to teach him feeding, I walked into the ICU with all my defenses down. I hadn't seen Barry since before Dr. Harvey dropped the death sentence on my head four days earlier, and I wasn't prepared for the impact his grotesque looks would have on me. Actually, it wasn't just Barry—it was the whole concept of intensive care.

Suddenly it was very personal. I could be the one in the bed next to Barry's. The only kidney-removal patient I had ever seen was one who went directly from the OR to ICU. Had Dr. Harvey operated, I might have been an ICU patient at that very moment. The sudden realization of what I was up against was smothering.

Lani was on her way past me to the linen room. "What? Barb, what happened?"

"I feel funny . . . like I'm going to faint." Then I chuckled. How stupid, I had never fainted in my life. "I think I'm scared. What if I end up in ICU?" The mass in my abdomen was beginning to seem like a balloon that was growing by the minute—maybe it was making me sick.

"C'mon, Barb. You're not going to end up in ICU. When are you going to Dr. Gary?"

"I'll talk to Peter Haynes. He knows all the surgeons . . . maybe there's someone better than Dr. Gary." Just making up my mind to do something, anything, felt better, but it didn't help the fact that I seemed to have a massive dose of crystal-clear vision about Barry's case.

Here was a man who had made the decision to end life, and there was no way he could do it. Even worse, everyone around him was acting like the enemy on the other side of the battle-field. He would get well if it was the last deed of their lives, dammit! How much less control could any human being have? He did not even have the basic right of deciding the course of his future. It seemed so incredible, almost like a crime I was compelled to investigate.

He could get out of bed and just walk out of the hospital. If the doctors and nurses stopped him, it would be assault and battery, technically, but how would he get a lawyer when he didn't have a mouth to use the phone? Well, he would have to write a letter. But who would mail it for him? He could give the letter to some other patient's visitor to mail. But if he went near a visitor, they would likely run in the other direction screaming—even the housekeepers and staff from other departments worked around him without looking at him, as if doing so might turn them to stone.

Any other patient who had made such a drastic attempt to end life would have had a strained relationship with his wife, but Barry's relationship with Beth was more than strained. Though her look of self-assurance matched the look of a model—tall, slim, high cheekbones—rejection was in her voice and eyes. She would walk into the ICU with quick, resolute steps that slowed and became more hesitant as she approached his bed. By the time she was with him for a few minutes, her confident "Everything's going to be okay, Barry" would be a pleading "We were meant to be together, Barry. Can't we go back to the way we were?" Barry would turn his head away and grunt.

Barry's ex-girlfriend, Shari, phoned the ICU daily, but Ann Pruett had decided not to tell Barry. "Let her find out from someone else how he's doing," Ann said, with a bit of spite. "Only his *wife* gets answers over our phones." The other nurses told me it wasn't uncommon for nurses to be put in the position of playing moral monitors. "Life's down to the short strokes when patients get here . . . anyone who ever loved the patient panics and wants to say one last word."

When I thought about Beth and Shari, I felt guilty for considering how I could help Barry decide his own future, but at the same time, I was the nurse, the patient's advocate—he had a legal right to be his own boss, no matter how the rest of us looked at his situation.

When I was through sleuthing, I concluded that Barry was indeed trapped. There was no way he could communicate with anyone outside the hospital, and there was no way he could leave. The security guards would tackle him to the ground and cart him off to the psychiatric ward if he attempted to run. Besides, he was really not strong enough to run.

Instead of seeing a Frankenstein monster peering at me with

eyes that seemed to look beyond into some T-zone the rest of us couldn't see, I began thinking of him as I should have from the beginning—a young man, trapped by his mind and body, in more desperate straits than anyone I had ever known. Maybe one of the worst things about being a nurse is the embarrassment of sometimes working with a patient for days or weeks before the lights all flash on and the situation becomes clear.

Of course, I couldn't say, "Hey, look. Just give us a chance to get you strong enough that you can walk out of here. Then I'll tackle the guard while you run. Once you hit the front door, you're free to do whatever you want—commit suicide, whatever."

In a sense he was in the same predicament as Bill Goldsmith in the burn center, facing months and months, maybe years, of reconstruction and rehabilitation, with really no alternative until the worst part was past. We cannot simply choose to die in such circumstances and be done with it.

That day I taught him to feed himself, but the significance was small in my mind. More important was setting him free. "Tomorrow I'll bring what you need to write letters. I'll mail them. Would you like me to make any phone calls for you?"

He was silent for a long time, and then he wrote "No" on the Magic Slate. He was consumed with the intricacies of feeding himself without splashing formula everywhere. Like a child with a new toy, he did it almost every hour, in place of banging on his rails and grunting like an animal. Learning to fly an airplane might have given someone else as much pleasure, but it is an axiom of hospitals that achievements that seem small outside may be monumental inside. Feeding himself was Barry's first step toward recovery.

Taking care of Barry demanded concentration on strategy, I guess because he couldn't respond with the usual cues in one's eyes and words. It felt like I was dealing with a time bomb without the advantage of knowing what time it was set to go off. It was exactly the challenge I needed—when I was with him, there wasn't a second to think of my own problem. When I was not with him, I went around caked with terror that only subsided at night when I curled against Dean's body.

But even my nighttime solace disappeared when at the end of the week, I still hadn't found a doctor—I hadn't even looked.

"Enough!" Dean said one night. "While you're out there playing fierce zealot nurse, God only knows what that mass is doing. Choose any day you want . . . I'll go to the doctor with you. Get this behind us!"

"But I don't know any good doctors," I said, which to him was inconceivable. Wasn't it logical to expect that nurses would be the first to know who the good doctors were?

"I know the bad ones, other nurses know more, but I can't ask them, and I can't ask other doctors."

"Ask, for Pete's sake. What's the worst possible thing that can happen?"

"Remember Janet Engels? Nobody needs the kind of fiasco that happened when she asked *me* to recommend a good surgeon."

The incident with Janet had happened on the surgical ward, about a year earlier, when I first discovered that there really is such a thing as a dangerous surgeon.

"They're talking about revoking Conrad Stewart's privileges," Lani whispered. "That means he can't operate here anymore."

Dr. Stewart was the surgeon with the beckoning eyes and a personality that was ten on the charisma scale. The infection control nurse had compiled statistics which showed the majority of the patients who had nosocomial (acquired in the hospital) infections were patients of Conrad Stewart.

"But he's so conscientious," I said. "I never saw him break sterile technique in the operating room . . . they're looking at the wrong doctor!"

"How many operations of his did you see?" Charlie asked, always more objective than I.

"So. I only saw one, the one he did on Herman Otis, but maybe he gets all the patients who have poor nutritional status and would be more susceptible to infection anyway. Maybe most of his surgeries are in the abdomen, where there's a higher risk of infection. Maybe his assistants use poor technique."

"Have you ever seen him change a wound dressing?" Charlie asked.

I had. He never washed his hands or bothered with sterile technique. Mrs. Erin had lectured in class, "If you see a physician or anyone else breaking sterile technique, you are responsible for doing something about it. *You* are the patient's advocate!"

"You are the patient's advocate" was the "Whiffenpoof Song" of nursing, but the consequences of being a zealot on the patient's behalf were never so clear as the time when Janet Engels was my patient.

Janet was an attractive girl, frail-boned, fair and blond, in her late twenties, undergoing diagnostic tests for stomach pain. We struck up an immediate friendship—at least *I* considered it friendship—because she was an RN. Having recently moved to Oakmont, she knew nothing about the hospital or the physicians who practiced there. In fact, she had chosen Dr. Dennis Gregory from the Yellow Pages the day she moved into her apartment.

Dennis Gregory was a gastroenterologist the students really liked. During our first year of school, he was in his last year of residency. Most of the doctors couldn't be bothered talking to nurses, but he went out of his way to be friendly. He waddled more than walked, probably because his height and width were about equal, but he had a big teddy-bear look about him that made him attractive.

"You can tell he's new," Charlie had said. "His writing is still legible."

A year later when Janet met him, his writing was no longer legible, he no longer bothered being friendly, and he was more gorilla than teddy bear. When he was angry (most of the time) Charlie would look at him and ask us, "Know what you feed a gorilla?"

"What?"

In a slow menacing drawl Charlie would say, "Any damned thing he wants!"

Janet wasn't skeptical about whether or not she needed the operation Dr. Gregory recommended—a cholecystectomy (gallbladder removal)—but she was worried about finding a good surgeon. "Who's good?" she asked me. "Who would you have do surgery on you?"

I stifled the urge to say there wasn't an operation or a surgeon on this planet that would transcend my fear of surgery. "Dr. Hastings is good . . . but he's half retired. It might be difficult to get him. Dr. Allen has a brilliant reputation . . . he's gruff . . . nasty sometimes, but who cares, if he's good. He's done dozens of cholecystectomies."

"What about Conrad Stewart? Dr. Gregory referred me to him this morning. Is he good?"

It was in my genes to keep silent if I had negative thoughts about any physician. In fact, I had been sure any evidence of incompetence or imperfection was a matter of my twisted perspective or ignorance. "Medical students flunk courses too," Charlie had said. "There are doctors who barely managed to get a degree, you know."

To tell Janet Engels the truth seemed a terrible breach of my contract with some Higher Power. On the other hand, if I was going to be a nurse, I was obligated to be the patient's advocate. Dr. Stewart's infection rate had gone beyond being grapevine gossip—the Medical Quality Assurance Board was looking into things.

"Dr. Stewart's patients love him," I told Janet. "For that matter, the nurses love him. You couldn't find a man more kind and gentle."

I closed the door to the hall, stood close to her bed and began having quick intestinal collapses. "His post-op infection rate is really bad," I said softly. "He probably wouldn't be your best choice." It felt almost like telling someone I had it on good authority that God and Satan were one and the same.

Then I went on to tell her about two of his patients who were in the hospital at the time, fighting post-op infections that had gone on for weeks and threatened their lives. She said she was grateful for the information and then asked again who I would recommend. Since I considered myself too new to be any authority, I suggested she ask the other nurses. "Faith Mason. She's been here forever, knows everyone, or Charlotte Topping. She'll be on duty tonight."

She said they had already declined to recommend another surgeon, since Dr. Stewart was listed on her chart. "It's unethical . . . you know how it is," she said with a shrug.

But she didn't think it unethical to tell Dr. Gregory that the student nurse, the tall one, had said Dr. Stewart was not a good choice.

Dennis Gregory did what no other physician has done before or since—phoned me at home. "You can't go around doing things like this," he sputtered. "Who do you think you are to judge a surgeon?"

I was naïve enough to be stunned at his reaction, and even more stunned that another nurse would tell him what I had said.

"It's not my place to judge physicians," I said meekly, "but Dr. Stewart's infection rate is no secret. You know about Mrs. Ranger . . . she might die before her wound can ever be healed."

"Dr. Stewart's infection rate is not the question!" I held the phone away from my ear and remembered Charlie saying feed him anything he wants. "I want to know who the hell you think you are, butting in on my patient's case? Do you know how that makes me look? You can't go around doing things like this!"

"She's a nurse," I told him. "To me, a nurse is a sister . . . maybe I wouldn't have done it otherwise. Besides, nurses are supposed to protect the patient. Isn't that my job?"

"Your job is to make the patient confident that she's getting good care. How do you think Janet Engels feels now?"

"Better to let her get rampant post-op infection and think it was an unlucky twist of fate?"

It was the wrong thing to say. He sputtered and fumed until I began to wonder what my role really was. When he hung up, he wasn't finished. He sputtered and fumed to Mrs. Erin; Rita Treece, the director of nurses; Faith Mason, the head nurse; and the hospital administrator.

The next day Rita Treece called me into her office. She looked very somber . . . but sympathetic. The one word that would characterize her is "subtle," but behind all the subtlety was a strong, compassionate, fierce advocate of patients and nurses. Most of what she said, she said with her deep dark eyes.

"Dr. Gregory has phoned me," she said softly, almost with apology. "I guess you know what he wants."

"He wants me out of here?"

"He does." There were actually tears in her eyes.

"Do you know his patient is a nurse? Could I really let a nurse unwittingly subject herself to Dr. Stewart's scalpel? Why doesn't someone *do* something about him? He's a wonderful man . . . maybe all he needs is another doctor to tell him what's so obvious to everyone else."

"That's being taken care of." She lowered her lashes. "Well, you know peer review of doctors doesn't really change things, but we have to deal with the problem at hand. Dennis Gregory brings in more patients than any other doctor these days. The hospital operates in the black because of him."

"You mean he's saying he won't bring his patients here anymore . . . just because of this incident?" Even then I had no conception of the power physicians hold over a hospital—you do it my way or I'll take my paying patients to some other hospital.

"This is what they call reality shock," Rita said. "There will be times when you must choose between keeping your job and protecting the patient."

"In school they tell us we are the patient's advocate. They never mention that we have to protect the patient without letting anyone discover it." Righteous indignation began seeping from my pores. "You want to know an even greater travesty? Janet Engels is a *nurse*. A *nurse* ratted on me for trying to protect her. You wouldn't catch a doctor ratting on someone in his profession. They all know about Dr. Stewart's infection rate and *still* they refer their patients to him."

"Dr. Stewart refers many patients to Dr. Gregory," she said. "Their incomes depend on one another."

"At the expense of the patient?"

She never answered. It was her sagging shoulders and sad look that made me realize what I had done—I, a lowly student, had jeopardized her reputation. Dr. Gregory wanted me out and it was her obligation to please him. In a way it was the philosophy of "the customer is always right," or "the boss may not always be right but he's still the boss."

"Dr. Gregory has talked to the administrator," Rita said. "I told him you're only a student . . . these things take time to learn."

"I told Dr. Gregory that."

She seemed to perk up, as if there might be hope yet. "What did he say?"

"I told him that I was sorry to be so insensitive to the consequences of telling Janet about Dr. Stewart. And I apologized profusely . . . told him I was just a student . . . grateful that he would help me learn the ropes. I made myself sick begging his forgiveness, if you want to know the truth. In the end, I promised never to do such a thing again. He said, 'Right! Make sure that you don't,' and hung up."

"Well, look," she said, "let's give him a day or two to cool off. Then I'll talk to him again."

For her sake, I felt extremely contrite. "If it will help, I'll ask

Mrs. Erin to transfer me to another hospital." For my sake, I felt enraged. "It seems incredible that I would be booted out of a hospital for trying to protect a patient, Mrs. Treece. This feels like it must be a joke."

Rita Treece never mentioned it again, but three days later Lani and I were walking down the hall when Dr. Gregory flippantly called, "Your friend is having her gallbladder out today."

"What friend?"

"Janet Engels . . . Dr. Stewart is doing the surgery." He gave me a cat-caught-the-canary grin and hurried off.

"What a creep Janet Engels must be. What nurse would be *fool* enough to take such a risk, knowing Dr. Stewart's infection rate?"

"Hey, turkey. You're the one who didn't want to believe it in the beginning. Janet Engels looked into those soft, blue inviting eyes and wasn't any more ready to believe Dr. Stewart could do anything bad than you were."

She was right. In fact, when I thought about having surgery to remove the mass in my abdomen, there was a fleeting moment when I considered going to Dr. Stewart for a second opinion. He was a comforting, soft-spoken person—the opposite of Dr. Harvey. It was a temptation.

Peter Haynes laughed when I suggested such idiocy to him. A year had passed since the Janet Engels incident. "Your memory is sure short!" Peter said. "Maybe you could get him to sign a promise that he won't cough over the sterile field when he does surgery on you?"

"Janet Engels didn't get a post-op infection. Maybe he stopped coughing."

"Go look up on the third floor. Read the chart of the patient in 311 . . . Dr. Stewart's latest testament to his breach in sterile technique. No, you don't want anything from Dr. Stewart, Barb."

"So who shall I go to for a second opinion?"

"Don't ask me ... I'm the one who wouldn't get on an operating table unless someone dragged me there unconscious."

"But you're a surgeon ... who better to ask? Maybe I could wait until your residency is finished. Would you do it then?"

He laughed, a cute, rumbling laugh, like a little boy's only much deeper. "Where have you been? Haven't you heard I'm in the family practice residency now? Surgery wasn't for me."

If the hospital grapevine was talking about Dr. Haynes, I had missed it, but he told me that during the summer, about two months earlier, he had "flipped out," as he put it. He had gone for days without sleep, operating when he could barely keep his eyes open, with Dr. Allen supervising. At night he was on duty in the emergency room, sewing up the victims of blade and bullet arguments, delivering babies, admitting critically ill patients.

"One night I admitted twelve patients, did a full workup on every one of them ... that's a hospital record. We've *never* admitted that many in one night," he told me.

The next morning all their charts were in order, the right therapy was in progress, and all the lab and X-ray results were on every chart. "I was never so confident that I had done an outstanding job," he said. "For once I had no doubt that I was a super doctor."

At the beginning of the day, Dr. Allen gathered a group of about ten medical students with him to make rounds on all the patients Peter had admitted. The group stood at each bedside while Peter reported on the patient's symptoms, history, plan for therapy and prognosis. Essentially it was a matter of Peter defending his reasoning behind what was being done for each patient.

"I didn't expect a compliment for the outstanding job," Peter said. "It wasn't Dr. Allen's way ever to compliment students."

Neither did he expect what he got—an abusive dressing

down in front of all the students and two patients because he had failed to memorize the values that resulted from each patient's lab work.

"It was on the chart . . . about ten or fifteen values for each patient . . . anyone could *read* the results." On top of all he had done that night, which was a fantastic achievement, he was supposed to memorize lab values.

"I could have taken that. So, I should have memorized, but the way he did it was too much . . . the last straw."

The incident was simply the trigger to all that had gone on in Peter's life, not the least of which was a malpractice suit by Mr. Otis's son Richard. Peter had been against operating on Mr. Otis from the beginning, and being sued was an emotional assault, even though intellectually Peter knew the suit was more a response to Richard's grief than anything. The suit was eventually dropped—"Richard was an intelligent man . . . he was just distraught at the time"—but it was more lava in the volcano that was about to erupt in Peter's world.

In the end, after a six-day stay on the psychiatric unit and hours and hours of soul-searching, Peter decided to change his priorities.

"The bottom line of it all was my military training and the Vietnam War. You can't believe the effect that had on the people who were there." He explained that all his moral values had been compromised—he was forced to do things he would never have done in peacetime, all in the name of patriotism.

Because the enemy placed so little value on life, the war was fought in strange ways. "It wasn't just men in combat, like every other war," he said. "Women would walk into a compound, or send their children in, carrying explosives, knowing their lives would end with ours. You can't image what it's like to be ordered to fight women and children." His descriptions of specific incidents were chilling horror stories that finally convinced me Charlie and Peter had indeed "seen it all."

"Fifty-six thousand soldiers were killed in combat," Peter

said, "and seventy-three thousand veterans have since attempted suicide. I was going to do it . . . jump off the top story of the parking building. Can you imagine?" He was chuckling, as if telling a joke on himself.

I didn't know anyone who had fought in the war, except Charlie, and there was no reason for me to suspect then that Charlie was headed down the same road Peter had traveled. Judith had commented that Charlie seemed different lately, but I thought it was something that would pass.

"I don't get it, Peter. What was so awful that you would want to opt out of life just because you were a Vietnam vet?"

"It's a matter of lost perspective," he told me. "We came home seething with anger and hatred . . . at the guys who commanded us to shoot and kill, at the guys who defected and walked out with white gloves, at the armchair politicians who perpetrated such idiocy . . . and we came home to what? Did anyone care that we had been months living like animals, defending a cause that was senseless? No one even wanted to talk about it! It was an embarrassment . . . a stigma to have been a Vietnam soldier."

He talked about the anguished nights after he came home from Vietnam, when all the battles replayed in living color through his nightmares. "If you can't talk about the war," he said, "there's no way to psychically process it, and if you can't process it, the anger and hatred just keep growing like a mushroom. How often does the patient's chart tell you he's a Vietnam vet? Next time you have a belligerent, aggressive, obnoxious patient fighting for control, ask about his military experience . . . you'll see what I'm talking about." I thought of Barry Bauer immediately.

"How do anger and hatred over a war that's long over cause mass suicide?" I asked.

"You've had psych nursing. What do people do with anger and hatred they're not allowed to express? What happens when they have to keep it all bottled up inside because no one wants to listen to the ghastly tales of combat?"

"Textbook theory?"

"Sure. What do the books say?"

"That unexpressed anger gets turned in on oneself?"

"Exactly! You begin to hate yourself . . . you project . . . assume you're only worthy of hate from everyone else . . . you lash out at everyone you care about because you think they hate you, and then you get depressed. Not just a little depressed! You simply have a total loss of perspective."

"So what's the solution?" I asked.

"It's a social problem . . . of major proportions. It even has a label now, 'posttraumatic stress syndrome of Vietnam vets.' The vets who are stifling and suppressing the war are psychically protecting themselves, but it shows up . . . they come in with ulcers, heart disease, colitis, all kinds of illnesses that won't be resolved if the doctor looks at nothing but the physical symptoms. It's a field that's desperate for doctors . . . doctors who know what went on in 'Nam and can help other vets process the whole thing."

He told me that he was leading groups, where vets gathered and talked about their anger and hatred, what had happened to them in Vietnam, how it was to return to a country that didn't care. "There are plenty of surgeons around," Peter said. "They don't need me. What I really want to do is help other Vietnam vets before they get where I got." He chuckled. "Can you imagine? Jumping off a rooftop? Boy was I out in left field . . . totally stressed out!"

"So now you're going to be a veteranologist . . . or a veteranarian?"

"I'll go into family practice . . . what happens to a Vietnam vet affects the whole family." Then he laughed. "A veteranologist? Maybe we should open up a new specialty. How about vietvetologist?"

By the time we were through talking, I had completely forgotten that the original purpose of our conversation was to find a doctor for my surgery.

"So now you know about Vietnam vets," Peter said, "but we still haven't found you a doctor. If I were you, I'd try Dr. Gary. Anyone who's been around the local hospitals as long as Mrs. Harris [about thirty-five years] should know more about doctors than anyone else." Then he grasped my chin and ordered, "Quit procrastinating, lady. Get yourself to a doctor before it's too late!"

3 No Way Out

Two days after Peter and I had talked, Dean and I were driving to Dr. Gary's office. Reality was crowding my mind. If Dr. Gary was going to substantiate what Dr. Harvey had said, Dean was about to hear that his wife of almost twenty years would be dead before Christmas. I tried to imagine how he would feel, sitting in a strange office, hearing that.

"There's something I probably should tell you," I said, suddenly feeling as if a can opener was wedged in my throat.

"What?"

"Well, this might not be very good news we're going to hear today."

"So? What's the worst possible thing that can happen? No one's going to *die,* for Pete's sake."

There was a long silence while I rummaged through my mind for the right response.

"Well ... what's the worst? Surgery, right?"

"You know how I am in hospitals." The tears began, almost in relief that he had averted a worse topic. "I'm afraid of surgery." Since then, I've always wondered how spouses tell each other the worst possible news.

"Whatever happens, we'll handle it," he said. He grasped my hand and transmitted courage as only he could do it. "If you have to have surgery, I'll be there ... Lani will be there."

"Neither of you can do anything about the fact that I've been known to wake up during surgery. I could do it again."

"But you won't. C'mon, stop stewing. Let's hear what Dr. Gary has to say. Maybe you don't even need surgery. Maybe you don't even have a mass. Have you ever felt it?"

"Never."

"Good. It's not there."

By the time we got to Dr. Gary's office, I was more than willing to absorb Dean's optimism. The office was in a low building with walls of glass—sunny, without the usual alcohol odor that makes medical offices seem so menacing. The nurse put X-rays on a panel—it seemed like a replay of the day in Dr. Harvey's office. But John Gary was much kinder. He might have seemed younger without the black-rimmed glasses that gave him a pinched look, but he was friendly—gave us both a healthy handshake. He was also quite vague, which, I confess, is just what I wanted.

When he looked at the X-rays, he said yes, he thought it was probably renal cell carcinoma, and yes, it did appear advanced, and yes, I probably would need surgery. But, first he would do some testing to see if he could get a handle on what he might find when he did surgery. He never used the word "terminal" or "cancer." He simply said *if* it truly was renal cell carcinoma, the prognosis was "not good."

I explained to him about Frank Bandini's case, that the disease seemed under control until after surgery, and that I wondered if Frank would have lived longer had they not operated and essentially added fuel to the smoldering brush fire that took over his body in just a few short weeks.

"We can't say that surgery makes it lethal faster—any more than we can say that surgery will cure it. What we *can* say is that the X-rays only help us make better guesses, and we won't know exactly what we're dealing with until we open you up and have a look."

We sat in silence, as if taking turns at a game—no one seemed to know whose turn was next. Was Dr. Gary waiting for a decision?

"What shall we do?" I asked Dean.

He squeezed my hand and cleared his throat, a familiar signal that he was taking control of the situation. All I had to do was sit back and play passenger. It seemed as if I wasn't there, while they sat and discussed my options.

When one is both a patient and a nurse, the obligation to be all-knowing before the physician is a tremendous strain. In a way, it's like the old adage "Better to keep your mouth closed and let everyone think you're a fool than open it and have it confirmed." But more than that, I could not think of what questions to ask.

In such a situation, there was no better person to have around than Dean. He could ask questions all day without ever being considered foolish. He could also ask questions all day and never hear the answers, except the ones that were tolerable—the mechanisms of the mind are such wonderful protective devices.

Since cancer is nourished by blood vessels that would not otherwise be present, Dr. Gary scheduled me for angiography at St. Joseph's the following week. If the radiologist saw blood vessels that shouldn't be there, renal cell carcinoma would be the culprit. I would be whisked off to surgery for a nephrectomy (removal of a kidney), and everything that followed would be "up for grabs" ("grabs" being a term for everything we could not bear to consider).

"You know what angiography is," Dr. Gary said. I replied, "Of course," since it would not do for a physician to think a nurse dumb. Actually, I had never seen angiography done, but I knew it was similar to heart catheterizations. And I had *almost* witnessed Albert Parks's heart catheterization during my rotation in ER about six months earlier.

Albert Parks was almost asleep, having been medicated with some of the drugs given to patients just before surgery, but he was alert enough to wisecrack the way people do who are accustomed to being strong but have suddenly been forced against a wall that makes them feel incredibly weak.

"Welcome to the igloo," the nurse said to him in response to his shivers, which probably had to do with the low temperatures at which X-ray rooms are maintained. "I'm going to slip an IV needle into your arm so we can inject drugs you'll be needing during this procedure." What she didn't tell him was that the IV is mainly to keep a vein open in case the procedure goes awry and emergency drugs have to be administered immediately.

"A few knockout drops would suit me fine," he said. "I'm not all that crazy about being awake for this!"

"Sorry . . . can't put you out," she said. "At one point, we'll need a hearty cough from you. When the doctor tells you to cough, give it all you've got!" Later she told me the cough is crucial to moving the dye and catheter safely through the heart.

The technicians scrubbed him, as if for surgery, and the physician was just beginning to insert the catheter in the femoral artery when I noticed a bubble in the patient's IV tubing. On campus the day before, Mrs. Harris had lectured about IVs and the danger of air going into the patient's vein. "Whatever you do, keep the tubing free of air bubbles," she said. "Flick it like this." She snapped her fingers against the tubing. "You'll have a patient dead from an air embolism if you don't get the bubbles out!" Like sterility in the operating room, air embolisms were everyone's responsibility. The bubble slowly traveling from the IV drip chamber toward the patient's arm, like a deadly bullet in slow motion, was *my* responsibility, or so I thought.

On the other hand, I had been sent to the lab simply to observe—who was I, a student, to be telling professionals how to do their job? It was not a particularly friendly crew, which was understandable considering the complexities of their jobs, and it didn't appear that they would take kindly to advice from a mere student.

By the time the bubble was halfway down the tubing, I was in the beginning stages of terror, envisioning Saint Peter barring the gates of heaven because I stood by silently while a bubble zapped life from a patient. A nurse was sitting beside the IV line charting the patient's vital signs. The only sound in the room was the patient's heartbeat on a monitor. This was a tricky procedure—one that demanded concentration from the physician and silence from everyone else. I tapped the nurse on the shoulder and pointed to the IV.

She gave me a quizzical look, adjusted the IV drip rate and resumed her charting. The bubble was just inches from the patient's arm when I tapped her shoulder again and pointed directly at it. She looked at it and then scowled at me, obviously wondering what I wanted. When she went back to her charting, I moved into the corner and waited in full-blown terror as the bubble drifted out of sight and into the patient's arm.

"I expected the alarm on the monitor to sound . . . I had even moved out of the way so they could get the crash cart to Albert Parks's side when they called a Code," I told Mrs. Harris later that day. "Nothing happened. The procedure went on as if there had been no bubble. The patient was just fine!"

"So, will you please describe the heart cath to the students at conference?" she said.

"I can't . . . I didn't see a heart cath. All I could see was the bubble. Why didn't the bubble kill the patient? How many ccs of air does it take to kill a patient?"

"You really must *deal* with your fears," she said and walked down the hall.

In the next semester, I researched the question of how much air in a vein is lethal to the patient and I discovered that the entire IV tubing could be empty without any harm. "Patients don't die of IV bubbles," I exclaimed to Lani. "Can you believe Mrs. Harris has terrorized hundreds of nursing students about a problem that is biologically impossible?" The pressure in a patient's vein is greater than the pressure in the IV tubing. To this day, the manufacturers of IV tubing sell their product by pointing out some gimmick that is guaranteed to keep the bubbles out of tubing; and hundreds of nurses believe what they were told in school despite the fact that logic might tell them otherwise.

Half a year had passed since that day with Albert Parks, and I still hadn't seen a heart catheterization or, for that matter, angiography. Maybe I should have told Dr. Gary I was too busy with bubbles. Instead of even thinking about it, after Dean and I left his office I went about the intervening week moving in zombie fashion through classes, working at St. Joseph's and taking care of Barry Bauer at Oakmont. Angiography seemed light years away, but I felt as if I were running away from a nightmare monster in pursuit. My mortality rushed in to cloak me in fear, and when I was completely enveloped, it momentarily subsided.

That week on campus I walked in hurried steps, my head bent as if in deep thought, embarrassed to face Mrs. Harris, but she would not be avoided.

"Barbara," she called. "How are you?" I was so grateful she didn't say, "What are you doing here?" but I rushed to explain, as if she had asked it anyway.

"I've only missed one clinical day . . . Dr. Gary is nice, thank you for telling me about him . . . I like him. I'm having angiography next Friday . . . I'll only be in the hospital two nights and back in school on Monday."

She said nothing and continued on her way. I cried, for feeling like a defiant brat, for knowing that any rational woman my age would not be so bullheaded, and I wept for the person I really was—the marshmallow with the tough, toasted skin which was slipping off in a charred piece, leaving the marshmallow core slithering in a sticky shivering puddle.

The next day, I was surprisingly subdued. I entered the hospital as a model patient—compliant, submissive, polite and uninquisitive. "Sign here." I signed without reading. "Put this on." I put it on. "Turn over." I turned over. "Hold still." I held still. To resist anything would have seemed so utterly futile. If six surgeons had entered my room and drawn long, sharp scalpels from scabbards, I would have watched wordlessly while they sliced and stitched to their hearts' content. It simply wouldn't have mattered—I had thoroughly investigated the outer limits of vulnerability.

In a freezing laboratory on the basement level of St. Joseph's Hospital, the technicians helped me onto a cold slab table. "You're a nurse," the radiologist said, "so I won't bother with the explanation." The thought that I was a nurse had escaped me.

I recognized the several stabs of the anesthetizing needle as he fished around the femoral artery in my groin, then felt the catheter as he threaded it through the vessels of my body. Tears slid down effortlessly as my last shred of composure vanished. "Hold absolutely still. One move and we'll have to do it again!" shouted the radiologist. Piggyback fireworks exploded thoughout my body as jolts of dye were forced through my veins. The technicians talked among themselves and decided to do it again. The catheter was removed, another one was threaded along, feeling as if it were a snagging crochet hook, and then the dye was forced through again, in huge, blinding, tissue-splattering jolts. It was a two-hour procedure that seemed to have taken six.

"Take her back to room 213," the radiologist instructed before I could ask if my body was still there.

Charlie was sitting in a chair by the window when they wheeled me back to my room. He moved as if to help them lift me into the bed, but stepped out in the hall instead. Noticing his white uniform, one of the nurses asked who he was. "A student in my class," I said. "We're both in nursing at Oakmont." She asked what I thought of male nurses, and before I could answer, told me what she thought of them—not much. "You should know Charlie," I protested. "Perhaps you would change your mind," but it seemed too much effort to explain. The other nurse checked the pressure dressing on my femoral artery—"Looks good—let me know if it bleeds or swells"—and they left.

Charlie came in, closing the door behind him, and suddenly the room shrank to closet size as he leaned his arms on the bed rail and bent over me. He clasped both my hands in his and murmured in a voice so gentle it frightened me, "Was it bad, Barb?"

"It's only that my whole body is splattered in bits and pieces on the ceiling of the lab, and I seem to have lost my courage. I call 'here, courage, come home to Mama, courage,' but all I can manage is tears." He kept staring into my eyes, with a soft, gentle look that made the air seem close. There was no way I could stop the endless river of tears.

"Sit down over there," I sobbed. "Tell me a joke . . . tell me about the burn center. I can't stop this whiny baby . . ."

"Shhhhh! I need to tell you something." He leaned down and kissed me gently on the forehead. "I love you," he whispered. I turned away, confused.

"Angiography is no big deal," I had told Dean the night before. "Don't bother coming to the hospital until after work." He came in the door just as Charlie backed away from my bed. They introduced themselves and were instantly at ease with the usual sports, weather, stock-market patter of men. Both had a unique ability to be comfortable, and make others feel comfortable, no matter the time or place.

"Say, have you heard about the guy who went to Sears for a vasectomy? . . ." It was like a tennis match—two professional joke tellers crossruffing each other's jokes. It helped lighten what could have been a morbid situation, and they were at their peak when Dr. Gary walked in. Charlie excused himself and brushed my hand as he went out the door.

"Well, I'm afraid I haven't got any good news, you two." Dr. Gary sat down in a chair by the window and sighed as he pulled out his pipe. I wanted him to take forever, fill it, tamp the shreds of tobacco down, fuss with it, fish in his pockets for

a lighter until the next century. "The grams didn't tell us anything."

"Nothing?" Dean looked incredulous.

"Nothing! We're right back where we started." From the
way he said it, I couldn't tell if it had been the machinery or
my body that didn't give him the information he needed.

"You can go home in the morning. Call my office next week
. . . maybe we'll do a sonogram then." He was in the hall before
we could ask questions, though I couldn't imagine what the
questions would be.

The Tuesday following angiography, I was back in the ICU
marking time for Friday's sonogram. Barry Bauer was in surgery for reconstruction of his palate, and as it seemed senseless
for me to take on a new patient of my own for just one day, I
was helping Lani take care of her patient, Jim Erickson. Jim
was a twenty-two-year-old with the body of a long-distance
runner.

A week earlier, Jim had walked into the emergency room
with a 105-degree temperature, complaining of a fierce headache. It was the middle of the night, and he explained that he
had driven himself in without waking his wife because she had
to work the next day. While standing at the admitting desk, he
had a seizure and stopped breathing. After the Code team
worked for a couple of hours to get him breathing on his own,
they had to give up and attach him to a respirator.

Jim's condition was considered "grave," in newspaper parlance—the worst. He had meningitis, an inflammation of the
brain tissues, which is often characterized by such sudden and
drastic changes as the 105-degree temperature.

Jim was over the initial crisis of meningitis the day I was
with him, but he had been weaned from the respirator twice,
only to Code and have to be put back on again. This was his
third day off, and his breathing seemed easy and rhythmical.
He was still in a coma, which, considering the maze of equip-

ment around his bed, might have been his brain's way to protect him from the sensory assault of the IVs in his arms, feeding tube in his stomach, chest tube in his lungs, drainage tube in his bladder, and the various bleeping, creaking monitoring machines. Just keeping all the tubes and wires untangled was a major project.

We had just finished bathing him when Ann Pruett beckoned me over to the desk to tell me that Penny Hammond, from the emergency room, was looking for Charlie. I called Penny and told her he was on the burn center rotation, but she knew that and had already called there. "We just got in that CHF case he clucks over . . . sent her to Two North . . . Charlie will want to know. The burn center says he's not there today."

"Judith Newman?" For all I knew, Charlie clucked over more than one person, but it was unlikely that anyone was as well known in the hospital as Judith.

"It's Judith. She's not as bad this time, though. We put in an IV and got the diuretics going . . . she'll be okay."

Lani still needed to stay with Jim until the shift ended, but I went down to Two North to visit Judith and couldn't believe how gray she looked. She was coughing and sputtering. "It's Barbara," I said. She lifted her hand toward me, and then it flopped back on the bed like a limb from a Raggedy Ann doll. She started to say something. Her head drooped and her whole body seemed to sag at once. I felt for her pulse, but my heart was in such a wild panic, I wasn't sure if I was feeling hers or mine.

"Help! Code!" I screamed and pushed the emergency button in the bathroom. I knew Judith's sleep look—she was not asleep. I put my mouth on hers and puffed two strong breaths in. Just as I started pumping on her chest, I heard the rumble of the crash cart and the room started filling with people. "CHF," I said. "Dr. Allen's patient."

"Barbara . . . blood's hanging in 209 . . . I just put it up . . . needs watching," one of the other nurses said. She waited while I finished my sequence of compressions, and then took over to continue CPR. Codes are not a place for students, as long as someone more experienced is around.

I stayed with the lady in room 209, watching for a transfusion reaction, and had just finished when the nurses were wheeling Judith to the ICU. Once again she was to be put on a respirator, which seemed little price to pay—she was alive.

I helped settle her in the ICU, and was at the elevator to return to her room on Two North for her belongings. Dr. Allen was waiting for the elevator with his usual impatient pacing. He nodded as I approached. That nod seemed to be the one thing doctors had in common, their way of greeting nurses without committing themselves. Neutered, aloof, benign, distancing, but still an acknowledgment. He examined the carpet as he paced, then stood still beside me, his hands clasped together behind him.

Looking at the "Up" and "Down" signs above the elevator, he muttered, "You're the sadistic kind . . . I'm surprised." I looked around, wondering who he was talking about. There was no one there but the two of us.

"Are you talking to me, Dr. Allen?"

Still muttering, he said, "It's inhuman, calling a Code on a patient like Judith."

Just then the elevator came, and I turned to walk down the hall, too stunned to chance riding down five floors with him, too confused to know what to say.

Later that day, I told Mrs. Erin about the incident. Did she say, "Don't worry—you did the right thing," or something about how Dr. Allen should have written "No Code" on Judith's chart if he didn't want her resuscitated? Heavens no! Instead, she looked over her chessboard of students on the clipboard. "No one's scheduled for the heart cath lab tomorrow. Would you like to spend the day there?"

"Sometimes I think I must be whacko. How the hell was I supposed to know not to call a Code? Erin just ignored the whole thing, like I was talking to the wall behind her." Lani and I were on our way to conference that afternoon.

"Don't try and figure it out. Who knows what we're supposed to do."

That I might really be sadistic and inhuman were thoughts too personal to be shared with intimates—even Dean. If Dr. Allen saw those characteristics in me, others might also, and what the world needs least is a sadistic, inhuman nurse.

The next morning, Judith was off the respirator. "Pulled the tube out herself, about three this morning," said Ann Pruett. "She's a tough little thing!" A piece of strong twill tape or twisted gauze is wrapped around the tube to the patient's lungs and tied behind the head. It would take desperate strength to undo it, and I was glad to hear Judith was still determined to control things herself.

Patients who have had open-heart surgery talk about the respirator as the worst part of the whole ordeal. "It feels like you're choking to death the whole time that tube's in . . . the damn machine pushes air in when you're trying to blow it out . . . nothing's worse." I never saw a patient take one out, but it happened often enough that I would say it was not uncommon. The nurses couldn't remove the tube without a doctor's order, even when it was obviously hurting the patient more than helping. They were usually happy when a patient managed to do it while no one was looking.

"If a patient has the strength, and they're alert enough to do it," Ann explained, "then they really don't need the respirator. They always survive."

Judith was sullen that day, for the first time. She had nothing to say about the Holocaust, no witticisms or proverbs, no warm strokes for the nurses—she seemed too defeated to bother.

"We need you, Judith," I pleaded. "Mr. Casper would never forgive us if we couldn't get you in shape for another gin rummy game." Somehow her silence was an indictment, a confirmation of Dr. Allen's statement. Would I have pushed the Code button if she had been any ordinary patient?

By the time I got to the sonogram lab at St. Joseph's on Friday morning, my heart was galloping like a spooked horse. Judith was in trouble, no one had seen Charlie for almost a week, and my apathy and resignation from the week before had somehow been whipped into heavy dollops of fear—everything seemed drastically out of kilter.

The sonogram lab, a room cluttered with overstock of IV solutions, looked as if it had been an afterthought, and the technician had forgotten my appointment. When he finally came running up the back stairs, looking tousled and sweaty, I was all the more jittery, wondering if this was something experimental. Our text didn't mention sonograms, there were no other patients waiting, and the skeptic in me was threatening to have a field day. Dr. Gary had told me he had a luncheon meeting at St. Joseph's that day and would meet me in the sonogram lab after my test. I was even skeptical about that. What doctor comes to the patient these days?

As it turned out, Brad, the technician, was not as scattered as he looked. He explained his machinery, what he would be doing and assured me it wouldn't be at all painful. "Put these pajamas on in there," he said, pointing to a room that had once been a small closet, "and then get up on the table and we'll get started."

After smoothing mineral oil on my abdomen, he rolled a transducer, which looks and feels much like a Ping-Pong ball, back and forth across my abdomen many times. The transducer produces a series of visual representations of the echoes sound waves produce when passing through the junction of tissues with differing densities. The result appears similar to a Polaroid picture, with tumors as solid areas and cysts translucent.

When Dr. Gary arrived, he spread the pictures out on a

counter and pondered them for what seemed like forever. "Not good news," he said, stroking his chin. "Brad, what do you think about this?" They shuffled them around, held them up to the window light, then away, and then Dr. Gary pointed out questionable areas to me.

The blob on my kidney was translucent for the most part (cyst), but the cyst was dark in the area adjoining the kidney (tumor). Statistical analyses of kidney tumors at that time said more than 95 percent of such tumors were malignant. "I can't tell what that dark shadow is," said Dr. Gary, and he kept twisting and turning the photo as if a certain beam of light might shift it into better focus.

Finally he put his arm across my shoulder in a fatherly gesture and told me we had run out of options. "I know you don't want to hear this, but there is no way out of surgery."

"Can it wait? Maybe until Christmas vacation?" It had already been six weeks since the mass was first found, and almost five weeks since Dr. Harvey had told me I had two months to live, but I was still grabbing for straws, hoping to stay in school.

"It can wait until Thanksgiving vacation [the next week], but no longer. Will that help?" His shoulders slumped, as if I was infecting him with my despair, which by that time I was sure had pervaded the room.

"This is no small surgery . . . an exploratory laparotomy. Even Christmas vacation isn't long enough. Six weeks minimum . . . and that's assuming all goes well!"

The "Student" layer of my life raft deflated with a big whoosh and left me clinging to the "Surgery" layer—not a safe place.

It didn't occur to me then—or even until years later—how willingly both Dean and I had closed the doors on our powers of reasoning and placed the brown-paper-wrapped problem in Dr. Gary's lap. Each minute was nothing more than a point in time—something beyond which we were too frightened to look. Dr. Gary could, *should,* look, but Dean and I were absolved from responsibility by virtue of the fact that we had engaged the services of a physician. Only eight months away from being a nurse and I *still* had not logically thought what I could do to avoid the horrors buried in the family tales of doctors and hospitalizations.

Surgery wasn't the *only* way to treat a malignant tumor. St. Joseph's sonogram technician wasn't the *only* one in the country doing sonograms. If the angiogram was questionable, and the sonogram was questionable, and if, for heaven's sake, it could have been the technicians or the machinery that prevented a definite diagnosis of my problem (which I now know it could have been), two, three, or even six more diagnostic tests would have been safer than surgery.

I should have asked how often Dr. Gary did exploratory laparotomies—perhaps I was his first. I should have asked about the anesthesiologist—who was he, how many operations had he done, what did the nurses think of him? How many people survived renal cell carcinoma? And if I had only two months, why spend them in the hospital, recovering from an operation, when I couldn't survive anyway? Who were the renal authorities in the nation? If Frank Bandini had gone to them, would his new baby be fatherless now? Those were questions we had never thought to ask.

4   The Worst Phobia

If scientists ever did a study of hospital phobia, I suspect they would find the disease is a common malady that manifests itself as panic over such innocuous things as the scent of alcohol and ether that pervades hospitals. The fear that comes from phobias is treated by exposing the patient to the worst possible phobic situation at maximum intensity for up to an hour, until the patient is no longer capable of experiencing fear.

This treatment method, called "implosion flooding," is an alternative to the method called "phobic desensitization," in which the patient is taught to relax while slowly entering the phobic situation, first in the imagination and then in real life.

"Nursing school has to be the ultimate implosion flooding and phobic desensitization," I told Dean, "which means I should be cured of hospital phobia!"

Nursing school had *not* cured the phobia, however, except when I was clad in my uniform, white stockings and pointy hat, and the anticipation of surgery gave me a sudden case of the old familiar terrors.

"Don't tell me it's all been for nothing," Dean said. "Remember you were going to save us all from hospital doom and gloom!"

The zealot nurse was still terrified, despite Dean's having sacrificed the comfort of a tranquil household. Still, he was the pillar of courage for both of us, and if the sacrifice was too much, he had not mentioned it lately.

In the four days between the sonogram and the surgery, it would have been appropriate to withdraw officially from school, but I was too busy being frightened to worry about such things. "There's a recipe for preparing for surgery," I told Lani. "First you worry a lot, then you think about the stories your friends and neighbors have told you about surgery, then you buy new nightgowns, then you worry a lot . . ."

"I'm on my way to Lord and Taylor for new nightgowns," I told Dean. He was standing at the mirror shaving, gave me a white-foamed kiss, and I headed down the hill for the shopping center, thinking about what I wanted to buy.

The right gown for the hospital had to be pretty but practical. No long skirt to fall into a bedpan. No buttons to pull loose and leave gaps. No sleeves to tangle the IV tubing. No sheer frillies, no granny flannels . . . I began seeing myself as I would look, as Frank had looked, with an abdomen zippered together with giant latex-covered clamps; as Frank had looked a month later, with his skin turning curry color; as Frank had looked near the end. I was relieved that I had not seen him the day he died, but my imagination filled in the missing visions.

I pictured Dean opening the bill from Lord & Taylor, some few days after "the end," and suddenly the nightgowns seemed like a dreadful act of narcissism. My "Surgery" life raft deflated with a whoosh and left me clinging to the last layer, the one labeled "Death." I would not need nightgowns.

I drove home, in a swirling haze of fear that was never greater before or since, and found Dean sitting on the bed, still with shaving cream on half his face, succumbing to the same thoughts that had been running through my head. His tears, the first I had seen in all our years together, were like the final seal on my fate. This was indeed the end.

We sat there, on the edge of the bed, hands clutched together. "What will we do?" he cried. "The kids . . . what will we tell them? I can't even remember life before you . . . it's like we've always been . . . we were born together . . . we were soul mates. Remember Grandma Huttmann telling us in the spirit world we were soul mates?"

We were laughing and crying at the same time, remembering

how she had called to tell us she had received that message from the spirit world. It was the month before we were married, and we were thrilled with the news at first. Then we cracked up laughing when we realized we did not believe in her spirit world; but we had placed so much value in her message from the spirits.

"This is so silly . . . this can't be happening," I cried. "We can't tell the kids . . . we can't let them see us like this." Shielding them from the spotted spurge in the grass of life was something we always worked at—too soon their fantasy world would give way to adult responsibilities. Perhaps that is not the right way to raise children, but the right way this year is the wrong way next year, and who ever knows before it no longer matters?

"We'll tell them what we know as gospel," he said. "You're having a bit of surgery . . . they can handle that . . . this isn't the first time."

"This is a graceful way of bowing out of nursing school," I said. "Let's look at it that way. Dropouts are such a disgrace . . . unless they have a really good excuse. This is a really good excuse, wouldn't you say?"

"Look, everything's going to turn out fine. Those doctors don't know it, but I talked to the Man Upstairs." He put on the happy face he used when teasing the kids out of pain, cast his eyes heavenward and said, "Hey, listen God! Forget all the bad things I've told You about her. Down deep she's okay, and You really wouldn't want her up there anyway—she's a lousy conversationalist. Besides, she's doing good work down here . . . there's a shortage of nurses . . . and who knows, she might even learn to cure the common cold!"

"Chicken soup," I laughed, "that's the cure for a cold. I'll get you some." On the way to the kitchen, I thought about God and how much sudden attention He must get from patients who face surgery. Could I call? Was He there?

"It's divine destiny," I told Lani that afternoon. "I don't have to struggle with the hocus-pocus of acid-base balance. I don't have to learn how to assist at arterial-line insertions. No one cares if I haven't learned to read the central venous pressure monitor, and the thousand-piece puzzle of Swan-Ganz catheters isn't mine anymore."

I began to soar on the euphoria of no more "shoulds," "have-tos," "musts"—it was wonderful. Did it really matter if taxes went up or the stock market took a dive? Did we care if the wrong person was just elected President? And so what if pollutants were destroying our air?

In her book on death and dying, Dr. Kübler-Ross identified euphoria such as mine—resignation to the inevitable, the last of the five stages that doomed people usually progress through. I'd already passed through the first stage, shock and disbelief, which is why I didn't believe Dr. Magnum when he found the mass. And I'd also accomplished denial, the second stage, by continuing nursing school in the face of a terminal diagnosis.

The third stage is anger, which might account for my urge to reduce Dr. Harvey to a pile of rubble. How dare he tell me I was going to die! In the fourth stage, the condemned person bargains for life, promising God a total body-and-mind shape-up program of goodness in return for another chance, another month, another year.

The fifth stage, resignation, I worked at during the three days before surgery, until I was *almost* convinced death was a more attractive option than life. "Mom, there's a slight problem with the car," Alan said. "Well, there was this concrete pillar I didn't see in the parking lot at the A and P . . . well, I hate to tell you this . . . the fender is really bad." His hands were trembling in the way of boys who have just jeopardized their chance at using the car to take a favorite girl to the Winter Ball on Saturday.

"Fenders are made to protect new drivers, Alan. I've done the same thing myself." Such unexpected tolerance rather boggled his mind—what was a smashed fender in the scheme of life and death after all?

Laurie pulled her brand-new jeans out of the washer,

splotched with holes that had white edges. "Doesn't bleach fade?" she wailed. "I just wanted them a little faded . . . now don't get mad, Mom!" Who? Me? The nastinesses of life were no longer mine.

"Mom, Scruffy chewed a hole in the couch," groaned Kim. "I only turned my back for a minute!"

"That's okay, sweetheart. Couches can be fixed . . . no big deal," I said. Nothing was any big deal anymore, which was a most unusual circumstance for someone who had previously held the East Coast franchise on worry.

More than once I had played the game of fantasy with friends: "What would you do if you inherited a million dollars?" Or "What would you do if you only had a month to live?" Friends would answer, "Oh, I'd spend the last month peaking out my credit cards . . . everything I ever wanted, I'd buy!" Others would travel to Europe, the Islands, wherever. What would I do with such a short time left to live?

When it's really *the end,* there is nothing so futile as anything one might think to do. Words of gratitude to a mother, poignant last conversations with brothers and sisters, a good-bye to Charlie and Judith, a last cup of coffee with my closest friends, Lani, Kip, Lou, Edie—they all seemed too futile. Until the last day before surgery I wandered about in a fog of irresponsibility.

Then I sat down to write last words of love to the kids—all the amusing, poignant incidents of their childhood that suddenly seemed so remarkable romped across the pages. As I sealed the letters and slipped them under a stack of old tattered piano music, Alan walked in from school.

"Hurry, Mom . . . I'll be late to work if we don't hurry. Aren't we supposed to be at the hospital by three?" He looked at the wads of Kleenex scattered around. "Hey, are you scared?" He wrapped his long, lanky arms around me and laughed in a teasing way. "You're a nurse . . . hospitals don't scare you anymore! C'mon . . . you can't cry . . . you're a nurse."

"I'm going to write a song, Alan. It'll be called 'Nurses Are Chicken Too.' In fact, nurses are probably more chicken than anyone else." He was kind enough not to remind me of all the meat and potatoes he had given up so I could be a nurse who would save everyone from being chicken.

While he went to start the car, I remembered something I had to tell Lani before I went to the hospital, where there might never be a chance to talk to her in private. Once I had her on the phone, I couldn't think how to put it into words:

"Well, I've been thinking . . . about Jenny . . . Frank . . . all those Codes . . ."

"You can trust me, Barb. Don't worry," Lani said. "I'll know what to do." Unutterable thoughts never had to be put into words for Lani.

"There's letters for the kids . . . under the piano music, just in case."

"Stop worrying, okay?"

For the hour it took to get to the hospital, register and get into a room, I might as well have been sleepwalking. It was the way I would like to have gone through the whole hospitalization—unseeing, unthinking, unfeeling.

My room, on the third floor at St. Joseph's, was in the oldest part of the building, but I liked it. Kim had been a patient in the same room, so nothing seemed unfamiliar. The floor was made of small hexagonal tiles, just the right size for counting when it's the safest thing to do. The ceiling was made of squares of acoustical tile, also wonderful for counting. In psychiatric nursing we learned that the urge to count is a symptom of some mental disturbance—perhaps it is the patient syndrome, something we do while waiting for the dentist or the doctor. Something to do to keep us from thinking.

I was standing at the window, my back to the door, as a nurses' aide came in for the third time. "You've still got your clothes on," she scolded. "Here. Put this on." She handed me the frayed, neutered hospital gown, with the knotted strings at the back, as if I had not seen it sitting there looking like an icon to lost identity.

"I'm sorry," I told her. "I know you've got P.M. care to do. Why don't you just ignore me until you have nothing else to do? . . . my surgery's not until one tomorrow."

She looked as if I had descended from another planet—but then it seemed everyone looked at me the same way, as if I had two heads and spoke some foreign language. "All rightee," she sang. "But I could get you some dinner. Would you like something to eat?" For the first time in my life, I no longer cared about food. It seemed too big a decision, too irrelevant, a waste of scarce brainpower.

"Whatever . . . if it's up here, fine . . . but don't bother going to the kitchen." The kitchen at St. Joseph's was about a mile from anywhere in the hospital. Too often I had gone there to get something for a patient, leaving all the others to fend for themselves.

Sometime later, she brought a dinner tray. I was still at the window watching, but not seeing, a tennis match in the courts across from the hospital. "Oh dear, you *still* haven't got that gown on," she said. "Do you need help?"

"Thank you. That's kind of you, but I don't need help. I'm not really sick. I don't have one single symptom." I knew that she probably had not seen my admitting papers and had no idea why I was there. It's like that in hospitals—too many patients, too little time—it was obvious I would survive until she got a chance to attend to me. I was certainly in no hurry for attention.

I sat on the bed and pulled the tray in front of me. The night before criminals were electrocuted, they were allowed to order anything they wanted to eat. I remembered when the newspapers made headlines out of one convict's menu—it was an elaborate conglomeration of the finest delicacies. I wondered if the convict had as little interest in that last meal as I had in this dinner I thought might well be *my* last! The thought was so

194

melodramatic, it made me laugh at myself. It also made me cry. Tears were dripping into the spinach when Dr. John Gary walked into the room.

"You've got your clothes on!" he exclaimed. "Are you going somewhere?" He sat beside me on the bed.

"Bak! Bak! Bak!" I was crying and giggling at the same time. "I think this chicken dinner is infecting me with a terminal case of chicken-ness." I told him I couldn't put the gown on, that I didn't feel sick and that I was waiting for Dean. "I'm not sure I'm staying. We haven't talked this out, he and I. When he gets here, we'll decide if I'm staying." There had to be some alternative, and whatever it was had to come dropping out of the sky soon—time was running out.

Later the lab tech came to draw a sample of blood. "You've got your clothes on. I'll get a nurse to find a gown for you." He was gone before I could tell him the gown was there, wadded up on the chair.

The anesthesiologist came to explain what he would do during surgery. "Oh, they haven't given you a gown yet? I'll tell the nurses on my way out."

The respiratory therapist came to teach me lung exercises so I wouldn't get pneumonia after surgery. "You're in street clothes! I'll come back after you're in the gown."

My husband, my savior, my knight-in-shining-armor, my Rock of Gibraltar (I only *thought* I was "liberated"), finally arrived. "For Pete's sake! Did you just get here? Why don't you have the gown on? What are you doing sitting on a hospital bed in your clothes? Get naked, woman!"

That he couldn't understand why I didn't have the gown on seemed the final insult. He could usually read my mind . . . now he couldn't. Now there was no doubt about it—in the darkest corners of our minds, there is no protective other—he couldn't save me from what was in my mind, any more than I could. He confirmed what I had already suspected—in this pitch-black place in my mind, there was no other living human. I was alone. The sense of isolation and alienation filled the breathing spaces of the room until it seemed I would suffocate.

"Life is what happens when you're expecting something else," I whimpered. "So I thought I'd stay dressed, as if I were expecting something else. Who knows? I might end up living."

"Get in your gown, for heaven's sake. How can I molest you if you've got all your clothes on?" He gave me a leering grin and began pawing at my clothes. Before long he was tickling me, we were both laughing, and we tussled on the bed and carried on a mock struggle with the gown. A chair fell over, and we collapsed in a heap in each other's arms on the bed. There had been other times when we played little kids like that, to vent the pressure from some obnoxious situation.

He was on top of me, our noses almost touching. "You're a dirty old man," I said, with all the punitive seduction I could muster.

"And you're a dirty old lady." He held me tighter than ever while we kissed. It seemed the world was empty except for the two of us lying there drowning in tears.

From across the hall, a grief-stricken wail, like a tenor saxophone investigating the upper regions of despair, sliced through the silence of our deserted island. The profound cry of one who has just lost a relative cannot be imitated by any other sound in the hospital—there is no greater sadness.

Dean left well past midnight, after finally convincing me to submit to the gown—that hideous, humiliating rag which strips away modesty, individuality, independence and control. "Help! I've been defrocked!" I squealed, trying to make the best of it, and we laughed about the designer's influence on hospital clothing.

In the halting gavotte of our twenty-year marriage, some times had been better than others. I intended to spend the night writing my last letter to him about those times. Instead, I shed my cloak of cynical despair and simply wrote the phrase I had had engraved in his wedding band—*love is eternal*—he knew the volumes of words and feelings that meant.

Watching families handle the surgery of a loved one had always interested me. The night before, some would say, "Well, I guess I won't see you again until after surgery . . . visiting hours don't begin until eleven A.M." Even though I would tell them visiting hours didn't matter, they stayed away and the patients spent the frightening hours before surgery trembling and alone. It was difficult not to resent those families, but it was not so difficult to understand their feelings—if they stayed away, they could pretend surgery wasn't happening.

Other families planned to be there to soothe the patient's last-minute jitters, but sometimes the hospital foiled such plans by changing the surgery schedule. Once I had tried to stop that from happening. A patient who had a slim chance of survival was having bladder surgery, which was relatively low risk, but his age and weakened heart condition were such that the hours before surgery might be the last he would be conscious.

"His wife's on her way . . . she wants to see him before he goes. Please wait," I told the operating room clerk.

"The clock ticks by the dollar bill," she replied. "Sorry, but there was an unexpected cancellation this morning, and Mr. Todd is next on the schedule . . . we can't hold things up . . . everyone down here is waiting. The orderly is coming for him now!"

I fiddled and fussed around his room, watching the clock, while the orderly waited with the gurney out in the hall. "We're running behind as it is," he called. "Let's get moving!" He paced nervously in the hall while I pretended to be completing the patient's chart.

The head nurse called from the operating room, and then the surgeon called my supervisor. "Get that patient down there," she hissed. "Hurry up!" In my head I was the patient's wife and would have wanted to whisper some last words of love to him.

Mrs. Erin poked her head into the patient's room. "Hutt-mann, you can't hold things up like this. What's the problem? Why are you so poky?" I whispered to her that the patient's wife was coming, that the surgery schedule had been changed, and that the patient's chances for survival were slim.

Such dilemmas must be difficult for instructors—they teach us to be the patient's advocate, yet their reputations depend on the students' pleasing the bureaucracy. "Just hurry," she said.

As the gurney was wheeled into the elevator, I clutched Mr. Todd's hand and wished him well. The elevator door closing was like the stamp on a notarized document—business first, patient later—"whomp!"

There was no change in the schedule for my surgery, and Dean was there with Lani for the long hours until 1:00 P.M. "No patient should have to lie around like this," I told Lani. "I should have stayed home until this morning!" It was difficult for the nurses when patients were admitted the morning of surgery, since they were so busy readying others for discharge at the same time—just one of many conflicts between patients' needs and "the system."

The orderly who came with the gurney to take me to surgery was a rare gem. "You can go downstairs with us ... to the doors of the surgical suite," he told Dean. I had the strong, protective grip of Dean's hand all the way. "I feel like I'm going to the gas chamber," I said, in the thick, fuzzy tongue of the sedated.

"This is it," said the orderly as we arrived at the huge double doors. He walked down the hall a way, knowing Dean and I would talk to each other with our eyes. "I love you, honey girl ... more than I've ever said," Dean whispered, and then the double doors swallowed me up.

They placed my gurney across from the scrub tubs, where I heard Dr. Dan Anderson talking about an orthopedic surgery he was going to do. "Barbara, what are you doing here?" he called. Two years earlier, he had advised surgery on my knees and I had declined. "I have hospital phobia," I had said. "Wild horses couldn't drag me into surgery again!" He remembered.

"About those wild horses . . . what are you doing here?" He laughed. The pre-op injection was turning the world hazy—I couldn't rise through the fuzz to answer him.

In a cold room that seemed to ripple and waver when I tried to get my bearings, a nurse began to shave my body, from neck to thighs. Were there windows, doors, a viewing gallery for residents and interns? How many people were looking at my naked blob of a body? "I'm cold," I said, but the hint passed her by. "Bend your right leg at the knee," she instructed, and it seemed a terrible effort to connect my brain with my knee.

"*I'll* do that," a male voice leered behind me.

"Greg, you're incorrigible." The nurse laughed. "I don't think this lady would like that."

I tried to smile, to show I was a good sport. "Thank you, no!" Thank you to her, no to him, and the tears poured out of me—for my own humiliation, and for the humiliation of all the patients who were ever wheeled into that operating room. The incident seemed symbolic of an overwhelming characteristic of hospitalization—human dignity is an obstacle to the smooth functioning of the institution. Resentment faded as I slipped into sedated oblivion.

5 | Rewards for a Zealot

"What's the worst possible thing that can happen?" Dean had asked me the night before surgery.

"I could wake up dead."

"Impossible, if you think about it."

"I'm not thinking about it. It's not the worst possible thing. The worst possible thing would be to wake up in ICU hooked up to a respirator, with my ribs cracked from a nephrectomy, a wound running from the middle of my back to the middle of my stomach, and tubes stuck in me everywhere. You couldn't stay with me . . . I'd be alone."

As I bobbed up from the thick sea of anesthesia the first time, Dean and Lani were bending over me. "ICU?" I asked, and I rolled down into the sea again before they could say more than "No."

It seemed an endless bobbing up and rolling down, always with a futile struggle to stay afloat long enough to hear what they were saying to me. Sometime later, when it was dark outside and I heard a crowd of people laughing and talking across the room, a nurse told me to turn on my side. As I turned, pain ripped up my middle in searing flashes, as though I had a xylophone of raw nerve endings with a sadist scraping metal up and down, up and down, with diabolical glee.

When the nurse left, Dean leaned over the rail of the bed and grasped my hand. "No cancer . . . none . . . not a speck," he said. I heard Lani and the kids laughing and chattering in the background—*they would not sound so happy if Dean were not telling the truth,* I thought. The next time I surfaced from the thick, fuming sea, Dean was leaning over me again. "No cancer, honey girl. How about that?"

"You wouldn't keep it from me, would you? You're telling the truth?" It seemed so incredible that Dr. Harvey could have been totally wrong.

"It's the truth . . . I talked to Dr. Gary."

"What did he say?"

"No cancer."

"Do I still have both kidneys?"

Dean thought I had two kidneys, but he said the only thing he could remember was that I did not have cancer—that was certainly enough.

In the middle of the night, when the room seemed to swirl and tip from side to side a bit less, a nurse came to change the IV bottle. "Do you know what happened when I was in surgery?" I asked.

"Exploratory laparotomy," she said.

"Did they take anything out?"

She patted my hand. "Don't worry, dear. The doctor will be in to tell you in the morning."

"Do I have cancer?"

"We're really swamped tonight . . . no time to read charts. Besides, the report of your surgery won't come up from medical records until tomorrow or the next day. You'll have to ask the doctor what he found."

I knew a recovery room nurse would have reported the important points of my operation to one of the staff nurses when I was brought back from surgery. *Was she withholding bad news, or was she just not willing to say anything at all,* I wondered.

In the morning I tried again. "Dr. Gary will be here any minute," another nurse told me. At noon he walked in, all smiles.

"I took you all apart . . . looked at everything," he said. "It all looks okay."

"I still have two kidneys?"

"Yep."

"No cancer?"

"I don't think so . . . no . . . well, you know we can't be sure about that until the biopsy reports come back in a few days, but I think everything's just fine." He was vaguely reassuring, but the anesthesia fog was still fragmenting my thoughts and keeping me asleep much of the time.

The IV bottle ran empty, though I had promised that I would watch it. "Not to worry," said one of the nurses as she irrigated the tubing with a syringe of saline. The next few bottles of fluid seeped under the tissues rather than in the vein, swelling my arm to a tight, hot balloon. The swelling would disappear eventually, I knew—it was such overwhelming comfort to *know*. My surgical scar, looking exactly the same as Frank Bandini's, would not split, eviscerate, spill its gross contents into the sheets; I *knew*. For all the times I had wallowed in the guilt of zealot nurse, I had finally reaped the reward. I *knew* and was no longer afraid.

On the second day I awakened to find Lani sitting beside my head, her chin resting on her folded arms. Like a sentry, she was always there, warding off menacing shadows—such a friend cannot be found by looking or by passionately wishing.

"Have you heard from Charlie?" For days I had wanted to ask. She shook her head.

"Mrs. Erin said she sends good wishes. The class sent that." She pointed to an enormous houseplant suspended from the ceiling. She opened the card—each student had written a message—and I realized what a close family we had all become. What happened to one of us, happened to all of us. There was no message from Charlie.

"Was Charlie in class?" Again she shook her head.

"Remember you were worried you wouldn't get your Christmas shopping done? Now you'll have time to do it." Lani was the queen of optimism, always holding a bouquet of bright thoughts. It sounded enticing—I *loved* to Christmas shop—but optimism was not my strong suit. "When the biopsy reports come back," I told her, "then I'll know if there's going to be a Christmas this year."

In the next day's mail there was a card from Mrs. Harris, saying she was happy everything had turned out well. Like the other instructors, some of whom had read my hospital chart, she questioned how it could be that *everything* was fine. The mass was a cyst, but one does not have a terminal diagnosis, two months to live, for something as benign as a cyst. She hoped I would review the biopsy reports carefully, she said, which worried me only until I read the last sentence of her note: "Perhaps you should apply soon for entry into next year's nursing class."

"Apply?" I shrieked to Lani. "Go through the whole process again? She must be crazy!" I had been rejected the first year I applied, because of my age. "I'm three years older. They'll never let me in again. Besides, I'm too tired . . . I'd never survive."

"You have until next September to rest," Lani said. "You'll be ready by then."

"It's not in the cards for me to be a nurse," I told her. "I couldn't stand all that ego slaughtering that goes on at conferences, the endless days and nights without sleep . . . no, enough's enough." Actually, I was still thinking Someone Up There was sending a message that I should go home and cook meat and potatoes for the rest of my life. At that moment, nursing school was a thing of the past—something I never wanted to think about again.

On the fourth day, hospitalization was smothering me. "Be patient," said Dr. Gary. "Perhaps tomorrow you can have a cup of tea." Still, my digestive system was sleeping, too lazy to digest food, which is the case after all abdominal surgery. If only such matters could be explained to a dry, furry mouth that would have sold out to the devil for a sip of tea.

Since the beginning, I had been ambling down the halls, steadying myself with the IV pole I dragged along beside me. The floor would swirl up to me with messages that I might faint, but the messages from the nurse in my head were more compelling: Walking cures almost everything that ails a surgical patient, including clogged lungs, painful abdominal gas, creaking muscles and rank disorientation, and so I walked. It was such comfort *knowing* that there were no secrets in the medical wizards' own vast ocean of mystery that weren't available to me.

That night, I talked to Lani about the business of *knowing* like a new convert from the Church of Ignorance. "It's like having a pot of gold with an infinite bottom," I told her. "Think what I can do for patients with all this gold!"

She never said, "You can't do a thing for patients because you're not going to be a nurse." She just sat there and let me ramble about how I was going to cure the world of hospital phobia. After she left that night, I began thinking how unfair it seemed that I was a measly six months away from being a nurse and was never going to make it. The more I thought about it, the more it chewed at me. I was not dead, I probably did not have cancer, I was merely inconveniently incapacitated.

Lani barely had time to get home before I called her. "Listen. I've got an idea. I never officially withdrew from school. If my biopsy reports come back negative, why shouldn't I keep going?"

There was a long silence, which was Lani's way—she didn't always agree with me, but she never *dis*agreed when I was as enthusiastic about something as I was that night.

"Will you tell Mrs. Harris I haven't withdrawn yet?" I asked. Lani would see Mrs. Harris on campus the next day. "Tell her I can't wait until next year to get back in school . . . my motors will never get started again if I wait that long."

The next morning, the fifth postoperative day, my belongings were all packed, sitting on the bed, when Dr. Gary arrived. "Where are you going?" he asked.

"Home. I can't sit around here. Hospitals bug me."

He pulled on his chin, at the beard that wasn't there. "It's too early . . . well, will you have to climb stairs?"

"No."

"Cook?"

"No."

"All right, then . . . as soon as we get the biopsy reports. If they're good, you can go this afternoon."

While I was waiting to leave, Lani came with the news about her talk with Mrs. Harris. "Sorry, Barb. She says miss five clinical days and you're out. How many have you missed?" I had missed exactly five, and there were still five weeks of recovery stretching before me.

"Did she sound final . . . the end . . . no discussion?"

"What's to discuss? This program moves too fast to miss so much time. How would you ever catch up?"

I was so busy trying to think what to do next, I hardly noticed the nurse who came in and said Dr. Gary had phoned a discharge order. "Just let us know when you're ready to go," she said.

Lani pulled some papers out of her purse. "Here, Barb. This is the application for next year's class. You need to turn it in by December first."

"Mrs. Harris doesn't understand the problem. I can't apply next year. Already there's talk about Dean being transferred again. We probably won't even *be* here next year. Besides, if I went home and played Mrs. Brady for the year's wait to get back to school, Dean and the kids would get used to it again . . . they liked life that way . . . then it would be the same old struggle over what *good* mothers do and what I'm doing."

"Do you really think you'll be transferred before next year?"

"If we are, I not only have to start over from the very beginning; all the schools have different prerequisites for nursing. God only knows what courses I would have to take before I could apply. If we got transferred in June, I couldn't get into a university until spring the next year, just because of the time application takes. Then I couldn't apply for nursing until the next fall. If I were lucky enough to get in, it would be the following fall. There isn't a nursing school in the world that would let a forty-four-year-old woman in. I'd be almost forty-six before I could start practice . . . that's insane . . . no way . . . it's now or never."

"Maybe you could talk to Mrs. Bills, the director of the program. Mrs. Harris doesn't really have the final say."

"It's no use. Mrs. Harris is right, there's no way I could make up five weeks."

That night, when I was safely stowed away in my own bed at home, I complained to Dean about what Mrs. Harris had said. "Hey, look," he said. "You don't have cancer. The biopsies were all clear. What more could you want? Nursing did what you wanted it to do . . . got you over hospital phobia. You don't have to be a nurse."

"What shall I be?"

"Do volunteer work at a hospital. Don't all hospitals have volunteers?"

It seemed useless to try and explain what nursing was to me—as useless as defining love. Had he known patients like Herman Otis, Judith Newman, Bill Goldsmith and dozens of others that made nursing seem so compelling, he might have understood. It might have made a difference had he been a bit less rational too.

The next day I decided to call Mrs. Bills and plead my case. She told me that I would be surprised how long recovery would take, that strength was transitory and would wax and wane for quite some weeks, that the probe of all my organs was more assaultive than less complicated operations, and no, she could not change the rules, and yes, she was very sorry but, "There's always next year, you know!"

"I'm approaching antiquity and gray hair on a greased slide," I protested. "Do you know what will happen if I get off the treadmill now? My motors will rust and freeze up!"

"So sorry," she said, and she advised that I write to the admissions office and inform them I was withdrawing so my grades would be W instead of F.

The next day I phoned again with a plan of how I could make up the lost clinical days, take the final examinations for the semester currently in progress, and finish all the work in time to graduate with my class. She said she appreciated my optimism, but the tone of her voice said she was far more appreciative of college rules. Again she said she was sorry, but that I had the right to appeal her edicts if I cared to appear before the board.

"I'll do it! When do they meet?"

They were meeting in three days, my ninth postoperative day, and she postulated that I was too weak to drive to campus and walk the long distance to the room where the meeting would be held. "I'll be there," I said.

Washing my hair, painting my face and dressing were major efforts, with pulling and tugging on the ugly incision down my middle, but I doubt I've ever been so highly motivated to do anything.

The room on campus seemed stifling, jammed with people, in the midst of their monthly meeting. All the nursing instructors were there, listening to a speaker I didn't recognize. Mrs. Erin smiled at me, which gave me a new burst of courage, but my body was protesting and the room kept swirling in dizzy circles. When the speaker was finished, Mrs. Bills informed the group of the campus rules disqualifying me from the nursing program. She said that I had been informed of my disqualification, but that I was not willing to accept her decision and had come to appeal.

"No hysterics," Dean had advised. "Make your plea so logical they can't refuse. Be calm, matter-of-fact and submissive as hell."

They stared at me with poker faces while I told them that during my recovery period I would write the term project, study the curriculum for the finals, and conduct interviews for the Crippled Children's Society. I would miss eight class lectures and twelve clinical days. The twelve days I would make up the next semester by doubling the time I spent in the hospital. The class lectures I would "make up" by passing final exams without them. If I did not get at least a B on all final exams, I would willingly withdraw from the program.

Mrs. Bills asked if anyone had any questions, and I think it was Mrs. Harris who commented that one does not defy the laws of nature, but she and Mrs. Erin both sent me eye messages that I interpreted as positive, which helped a little to counteract the negative messages from the other instructors. Mrs. Bills never liked to have her decisions appealed, even if they were only about the weather. Neither of us would have cared to be stranded on a desert island together. She dismissed me from the meeting, saying she would call me with a decision in a week.

"To suggest that you could pass final exams without their lectures is to say their lectures are of no value," Dean said.

If one of them had walked outside the room after I collapsed as the door closed behind me, they would have heard me say, "Uncle! I give up! You win!" The starch that had sustained me—the imperative of finishing nursing school—was entirely gone. Subdued once again, at home I sank into the sanctuary of sickness as though I might never come out, and slept through the wait for Mrs. Bills's phone call.

"We'll give you one chance," she said. "If you fail to pass final exams, this semester or next, with at least a B, there will be no appeals, you understand." She made it clear that this was not a matter of the faculty's best judgment, that it wasn't a relaxation of the rules for anything but my own stubbornness. She conveyed the feeling, though it might have been just my own paranoia, that I would never be able to keep my end of the bargain—within a few weeks it would be clear what folly I was pursuing.

Mrs. Bills wasn't the type students would hug, but had she been there, I would have done it. "Thank you . . . thank you, Mrs. Bills . . . you can't imagine what this means to me."

She chuckled at my enthusiasm. "Oh, you're welcome. Good luck. We'll see you at the final exam in two weeks."

I hung up and went skipping down the hall like a three-year-old, grinning and laughing out loud. As I passed the mirror over the table in the hall, I said, "Hey you! You're going to be a nurse . . . a *great* nurse, in six measly months."

While I was dialing Dean to tell him, it suddenly occurred to me that I was not dying. For eight weeks I had been living with no future. Suddenly I had one. "Hey! Guess what . . . I'm not dying." There was a long pause on Dean's end of the phone.

"Well? Aren't you going to say anything? Aren't you glad I'm not dying?"

He laughed. "Of course, silly goose. We've known for a week that you're not dying. Is that what you called to tell me?"

"Well, maybe *you* knew, but I didn't know. Not only that . . . are you ready for this?"

"What?"

"You're talking to a living, breathing nurse . . minus six months."

"Terrific! Mrs. Bills called?"

"She did. How incredible . . . eight weeks ago I was told I would be dead by now. Today life snaps back like a rubber-band, right to where I was before I went to Dr. Harvey. If any-body ever asks me what were the most incredible eight weeks of my life, I'll sure know how to answer."

As before surgery, my one goal in life became graduation day, which is probably why thoughts about what had happened over the preceding two months were little more than lurking shadows. Why had I been told I would die? Why had I been given an invasive angiogram when the painless, no-risk sonogram gave the doctor all the information he needed? How would we ever pay the bills for such needless diagnostics? Why hadn't Dr. Gary simply aspirated the mass with a needle, rather than cutting me open from stem to stern? Such questions were vague naggings I thought would be answered later when I became a "smart nurse."

When Dr. Gary removed the sutures from my abdomen on the tenth day after surgery, I asked to read my chart. "What are you looking for?" he asked. There was something—I wasn't sure what—that I wanted to see. "There's not much on it," he said, and indeed there wasn't. Less than a page of scribble seemed a great deal of minimizing to me, but there was some satisfaction in having read my own medical chart for the first time ever.

That same day I complained to him of a disoriented feeling that was hampering my concentration, making it difficult to study for finals. If I put my hand out to reach for something, the object was a little farther to the left, or to the right, than anticipated. "Common," he said. "A doctor friend recently had surgery and complained about the same thing. It probably has something to do with the anesthesia." Whatever it was, it took almost six months to pass.

The only long-term effect of surgery was one that couldn't have been anticipated—the scar was an ugly long earthworm crawling down my middle. Many people form such scars (keloids) for unknown reasons.

And in the end I renewed my vow that wild horses could not drag me into surgery again.

During the six weeks following surgery, I did what I could never do again—worked at a school for disabled children, wrote my term project and passed final exams. Though such achievements might imply a bulldog determination that defies the laws of nature, the vagaries of recovery from major surgery—the waxing and waning of strength—were concealed by my unique situation. I was alive when I had expected to be dead.

Outside our bedroom there was a faulty drainpipe. For two winters the melting snow had clattered down the pipe like nickels and dimes being thrown against a metal tunnel. "I'll have to repair that damned pipe," Dean would say when I complained that the din made it difficult to sleep. That winter the clattering was comforting, a soothing reminder that I was alive, nestled in my own warm bed, safe from the clutches of a far worse fate than noisy drainpipes.

The dent in the fender gave the car character; the pomegranate stain on the kitchen wallpaper was an interesting design; hardly anything was really worth stewing about if put in its proper perspective. Months earlier Judith Newman had said, "I never really saw until I was blind." At the time, I thought it was odd that she could look upon blindness as a special gift that enhanced the quality of life.

Though I wouldn't assert that we should all go out and harvest a calamity so life can be put in proper perspective, the shimmer that had replaced the greasy sheen of hopelessness in my life fueled the motors that kept me running long past when my body would rather have stayed in bed.

Sometimes the shimmer was a bit misplaced, like when one of the kids should have been reprimanded. "Why did you let Kim get away with that?" Dean would ask. That everyone seemed to be wearing a new halo was simply part of the shimmer. In time it would be tempered, but there is that special delight in the newness of things that I intended to savor as long as I could.

Shimmer turned to glitter on Christmas Eve—it was such a magnificent surprise to be alive for another Christmas—and then it turned to full-blown dazzle. Dean and I were with Lani and Lee at the wedding of Lynne O'Malley (the nurse from St. Joseph's oncology unit) and Dr. Loren Mulwards. Because Charlie had worked with Loren in Oakmont Hospital's emergency room, there was a chance Charlie would show up at the wedding. It just seemed to me that no one would miss a wedding that had been the talk of both hospitals for so long.

"Heaven help the patients of this county," I whispered to Lani. "Who do you suppose is minding the store?" In the congregation of several hundred people, we recognized more doctors and nurses than most hospitals would need for a full-time staff.

I was busy scanning the pews, looking for Charlie, when Lynne and Loren knelt at the altar and the organ began the introduction to "The Lord's Prayer." The profound blend of romance and divinity, cast in the glow of hundreds of candles, might have been enough, but when the introduction was finished and a magnificent tenor voice filled the cathedral, the ethereal effect was overwhelming. "Bill Goldsmith," Lani whispered.

"Bill? The burn center?" It was a redundant question answered by the tears of every doctor and nurse there. That Bill had survived burns which covered 80 percent of his body was miraculous—that he was singing again was more than a miracle.

Loren Mulwards had been the physician on duty when Bill was brought to the emergency room the day of the fire. Later, Bill's wife, Harriet, told us how Loren had teased, coaxed, raged and pleaded with Bill during the year and a half that followed. Though he wasn't the primary physician on Bill's case, he had decided to make Bill's rehabilitation his own personal crusade. "Listen, Crispy Critter . . . ," Harriet laughed when she told us how Loren had used such graphic words to incite riot in Bill—the riot that fueled his determination to survive through all the skin grafting and the agonies of retraining wasted muscles.

Bill was still in a wheelchair that Christmas Eve, and he was far from the end of the skin grafting, but there was certainly no flaw in his voice—Luciano Pavarotti might have been jealous had he been there. The wedding of Lynne and Loren, as spectacular as it was, was definitely upstaged by Bill Goldsmith.

And Charlie? Harriet knew him. Everyone who spent any time at all at Oakmont knew Charlie. But no one had seen him since the last time I did, the day of my sonogram, just before Thanksgiving. "There's plenty of gossip going around the hospital," Lani told me.

The strange thing about his disappearance was that he never officially quit his job in the emergency room—he simply never showed up for work.

"Chelsee said he made a drastic medication error in the burn center," Lani told me. "He split rather than face the music."

For no other reason than that she looked unkempt, with bleached hair that looked similar to a broom, I never thought of Chelsee Jones as a credible source for any information. When I saw her in the auditorium on orientation day, with inch-long, bright-red fingernails, bare feet and jeans that looked as if they had been buttered on, I wondered how she ever got into a nursing program.

"How could Charlie make a drastic med error?" I asked Lani. "There isn't any drug we use that's lethal except insulin. Insulin doses have to be checked by a second nurse. He wouldn't have made a mistake on that."

"I didn't say he made an error . . . Chelsee said it."

"What does she know? She doesn't even know Charlie. He's too conscientious to make med errors."

The more we talked about it, the more we realized Charlie had seemed out of place in all of our rotations but the emergency room. Often he thought he was smarter than some of the doctors, and most of the time he was right. In that respect, it was no surprise that he would leave without saying anything.

Someone at the hospital thought he had gone to work for one of the pharmaceutical companies, and someone else thought he had run off with a married blonde from the X-ray department at Oakmont.

"You'd think Judith would know," Lani said. "He might just duck out on us, but not on Judith." We might have asked her, except that she was on Three North at Oakmont again, being spoiled by Faith Mason and Charlotte Topping, out of it much of the time from the insufficient supply of oxygen to her brain. If she wasn't missing Charlie, we weren't going to tell her he was gone.

PART THREE

1 Picking Up Pieces of Life

Doctors advise patients not to push recovery—in its own good time, the body repairs itself. If I had been able to give my body the time, perhaps I would not have been in such a state the January morning I dressed to return to the hospital for the first time. It had been six weeks since surgery—time enough for any recovery—still I felt, and looked, rather like a patient with some wasting disease.

Dean was watching me in the mirror and started chuckling. "Sorry to laugh, but talk about the walking wounded! You look like you need a nurse."

The back injury from lifting Violet Fraser waxed and waned. That morning it was waxing—shoelace tying was a major project. Then I was trying to get into the hooks, laces and elastic of the back brace without destroying my supersensitive scar from surgery. I might have cried if I hadn't looked so comical to myself.

"Six months and it'll all be over," Dean said. "Just hang in there . . . you'll make it."

When I walked into the kitchen in my uniform, Alan said, "Hey, world! Watch out . . . here comes Florence Nightingale." He draped his lanky arms around me in a hug. "My momma the nurse . . . you're gonna be a nurse if it *kills* ya. Right?"

"Right!" I laughed. "It may kill you guys, but it isn't going to kill me."

"Hey, we're gonna be okay . . . don't worry about us . . . just keep that meat and potatoes comin' once in a while."

"Shoot! I meant to teach you how to cook your own meat and potatoes during Christmas vacation."

"Women's work!"

The feud over the division of labor had been diluted by my brush with calamity—I found out I needed "the enemy," and they had been more than willing to feel sympathy for my plight. At the same time that I was vowing to be more sensitive to what they wanted from a mother, they were beginning to think maybe they didn't need what they wanted. We never openly talked about it, but that morning they all cheered like relatives on a station platform sending the favorite son off to war. Graduation day had become as much their goal as mine.

"They're acting like I'm Joan of Arc and they're fighting off the dragons so I can win the crusade," I told Lani. We were driving to the hospital through dark, icy streets.

"You mean they've finally discovered there is no Brady Bunch or Partridge Family?"

"Or Cinderella, Santa Claus, or Easter Bunny. What a disappointing thing, giving up such pleasure."

We drove along in silence, preoccupied with dodging the deep swaths of snow the plow had missed. I felt jittery—not as jittery as I had on other first days in a new rotation, but there was a special dread about starting pediatrics.

As usual, Lani's thoughts mirrored mine. "Let's skip this day," she said. "I don't think I'm ready for nursing kids."

"What do you do to get ready?"

"That's what I'd like to know . . . I just know I don't want to do it. The first time a little kid cries for his mother, it'll probably shred my heart. How could you stand giving a little kid a shot?"

"If that's *all* we have to do, we'll be okay."

The jitters faded as we drove into the hospital parking lot. It was such an incredible thrill to see that enormous sturdy building, all its lights reflected in the snow, contrasting with the surrounding dark of a neighborhood that was still asleep—a symbol of such magnitude that it defied description.

"I'm an incurable romantic." I laughed. "That hospital

building gives me goose bumps, flutters my heart. Do you believe in reincarnation?"

"I'm not coming back as a student nurse, that's for sure!"

"I think I must have been a nurse in a past life. Why else would it always feel like coming home, every time I look at that building?"

Dean and the kids would say it was because I spent more time in that building than I ever spent in any of the houses we had lived in, but it wasn't the same kind of "coming home." Standing in my uniform in the hall, any hall, of Oakmont County Hospital was the ultimate satisfaction, a high almost equal to the first day in the operating room. I was *myself*, Barbara the nurse, home at last.

As Lani and I got out of the elevator on the seventh floor, a little boy came screeching around the corner on a Hot Wheels. "Beep-beep, hooga-hooga!" he shrieked as he went speeding by.

"Good grief, it's a playground." I laughed.

The elevators were a square island in the center of the seventh floor, and we had barely turned the corner before the Hot Wheels came heading straight for us again. In less than a minute he had gone all the way around the square. Then he stopped right in front of us.

He got off the bike and held up a Pooh bear that had been riding with him. "Hey, who are you?" he asked us, all the while swinging the bear over and over itself until the short, pudgy arms were twisted strands. He cast down his long, spidery eyelashes in a flash of shyness that we never saw again after the first meeting. "This is my bear."

Lani crouched down to his size (motherhood *is* instinct, at least for her). "I'm Lani . . . this is Barbara. Who are you?"

"Rocky."

"What's your bear's name?"

"Pooh," he said, as if she had asked a silly question—*doesn't* everyone *know Pooh bear?* he seemed to say. Then he hopped on the Hot Wheels as if he suddenly remembered he was on his way to an important birthday party. We didn't know then that the "party" was an urgent need to get to his oxygen mask.

Later we saw him making morning rounds with Liz Andrews, skipping from room to room as if he were the hired court jester out to entertain the other children.

"He's our mascot," Liz said. Liz was a deep-bosomed, grandmotherly nurse with a perpetually mischievous face. When she tried to look stern, it seemed like a bluff. "We make sure we only try and recruit nurses on days when he's here . . . gets 'em every time."

When Rocky came into the hospital, which was about once every two months, he arrived gasping for air, as close to death as a child could get.

"He was only three months old the first time," Liz told us. "We never expected him to make it." She was so crazy about him, it was hard to imagine how she could let him go home when he got well. "By the time he was a year old, he had us all figured out. He got attention by stripping off his clothes, shoving the bed linens through the bars of the crib, and chasing back and forth in the crib, naked."

When he got a little older, he added net swinging to his act, and he would make gorilla sounds while he swung from the net that covered the top of the crib. He kept his clothes on only when no one was looking, which might have been fine in his own house, but was not so fine with some of the nurses.

The walls of the ward, which faced the halls, were all glass. "Other little kids would stand in the hall, pointing and snickering, which of course he just loved," Liz said. "Some of the nurses said, 'So what?' but others thought his nakedness was offensive."

Similar problems occurred with other children. Behavior modification was the biggest conflict on that unit, which shouldn't be surprising, since even two parents living in the same household have conflicts about raising children. Considering the number of nurses each patient might have, consistent treatment was almost impossible.

Liz was discussing behavior as she took our group of twelve students on a tour of the floor, stopping now and then to point out some special feature about a patient or a section of the ward. "This is our isolation room," she said. "You've probably heard about this case . . . a drowning . . . almost a year ago."

"Same thing here," she said, pointing to the next door. "This one's only been here a few days."

I was lagging at the end of the group and stopped to look through the windows of the isolation room. "She's off the respirator," I whispered to Lani. "Look, it's Jenny! My God, how'd they get her off the respirator?"

"Didn't I tell you about that?"

Liz gave us a withering glance.

"I'll tell you about it later," Lani whispered.

It was the kind of story that newspapers wrote about, a Karen Ann Quinlan story—a court battle over whether or not mechanically maintained life was really life, whether anyone had the right to pull the plug of the respirator, and who would pull it if they did have the right. Jenny's story was unique, however. Her parents were in the process of divorce when the battle first started. The father wanted the plug pulled, the mother didn't.

When Jenny's father argued that it was cruel, inhuman and financially devastating to keep her alive when there was no hope, her mother was well prepared with her side. The National Science Foundation had recently reported the results of a ten-year study on the price society is willing to pay to avert one premature death.

According to the Foundation's 1975 figures, the cost of saving one life through improved median road barriers was $230,-000; through upgraded coal-mine safety, $22 million; and through safer radioactive waste disposal, $100 million. The fifteen hundred dollars a day it was costing to keep Jenny alive on a respirator in the intensive-care unit was a cost the mother thought should be considered in the same light. After all, if society would pay the tab for one coal miner, why not for her Jenny?

The problem was that the family's insurance had run out and the amount Medicaid would pay each day didn't even come close to covering Jenny's bills. Society wasn't about to pass some instant legislation to finance Jenny's hospitalization, of course; the hospital could hardly afford to run in the red; and the physicians could not be expected to continue working for free, especially since Jenny was only one of several such cases.

In the end there was a compromise, and the doctors decided to try weaning her from the respirator, slowly withdrawing the oxygen to see if she would breathe on her own. If she had not been able to do so, the court battle would have gone into full swing again. As soon as she was off the respirator, there was no need to stay in the ICU. When I saw her on the pediatric unit, she had been there about a month, at almost five hundred dollars a day, and there was no more hope for her then than there had been in the emergency room almost a year earlier.

Cost was only one part of the moral and ethical dilemma which is the price we must pay for the scientific advances that have given us the ability to retrieve and sustain lives that can't be saved. Jenny had been retrieved by a Code, but she could never be saved.

When we went home the day that Lani told me the story about Jenny, I forgot to leave my patients at the hospital. At the dinner table I started telling Dean and the kids the story.

"Pass the salt, please," Alan said.

"So anyway, the mother would stand there at the bedside . . ."

Kim asked to be excused. "Math test tomorrow, Mom."

". . . and that tiny little blond body looked so helpless . . ."

"S'cuse me, Mom. It's not that I'm not interested. I told Jim I'd help fix his motorcycle . . . see ya later."

Tears were streaming down Laurie's face—there is no more compassionate heart in this world than hers.

"I'm really sorry, you guys," I said. "I'm getting to the good part. Jenny's going to be okay. These cases do fine sometimes, and her mom and dad are getting back together again."

Laurie giggled, an embarrassed kind of giggle like when one is discovered crying over a movie. "You tell such sad stories, Mom. Doesn't *anything* happen in a hospital that's not sad?"

Later when the kids were all asleep, I told Dean the real story. "I'm going to have 'No Code' tattooed on my chest," I said, just in case I'm ever taken to the emergency room.

"Swell! Tattoo on your chest, an earthworm scar all the way up your middle, and a great big corset just to hold you all together. You know the beauty of getting old?"

"What?"

"My vision's getting poor and I won't be able to see you anyway."

The next day I made a pact with Lani, the one I had intended to make before I had surgery. "Please, don't ever let anyone Code me."

"I won't," she said, "if you promise to never let anyone Code me."

"It's a deal." Then I laughed. "We'll have to walk around like Siamese twins to protect each other. Watch out ... the paramedics will get ya."

It seemed to me that advances in technology had robbed us of the right to a sudden death. Only a long, drawn-out financially and emotionally devastating death was legitimate. I couldn't even dream of a "quick death on the golf course." Someone would be sure to call the paramedics ... unless Lani were there to protect me.

Of all our rotations, pediatrics was the least depressing—the natural resilience of children seemed a stunning contrast to the way adults were affected by hospitalization. Even the sickest children used their IV stands like scooters and went careering through the halls. One minute they might look as if recovery would take a miracle—the next minute they wanted to be in the playroom with other children.

And then there was Jenny. In terms of technical skills Jenny needed everything a nurse had to offer, which is why Mrs. Erin assigned her case to students. Though she was no longer on the respirator, all her body functions were supported by tubes, equipment and machinery. All the supports needed constant maintenance.

The challenge was to coordinate things so the IVs never ran dry, the tube feedings were done on time, the dressings around all the tubes were changed before they became saturated, medications were constantly coursing through her bloodstream, catheters were kept irrigated so they didn't clog, and the oxygen was dispensed in the correct quantity with the proper humidity. The most important task was to keep moving her so her skin stayed intact. All patients are in danger of getting bedsores, but patients like Jenny, who have every body system severely compromised, are at higher risk than most.

The first week I was assigned to her, mastering all the technical tasks on time kept my mind occupied. If I stopped to think about her situation—the hopelessness—I quickly whisked it from my mind. Mrs. Erin would pass by the window now and then to watch how I did the tube feedings or to make sure I was using sterile technique for the dressing changes. Perfect technique was my goal.

At the same time, I was finishing my ICU rotation, working with Jim Erickson and Barry Bauer. Then there were the campus classes, surprise quizzes, lengthy projects that demanded hours and hours of lecture review, weekly written examinations, daily care plans—poor-meism would have seemed legitimate, if I had stopped to think about it. As it was, I was so grateful that graduation was only six months away, no obstacle seemed anything more than another hurdle to be jumped—quickly.

When Dean came home one night and announced that we

were being transferred again, I was busy trying to make a
schedule of all the tasks that had to be done for Jenny so the
nurses who followed me would not have to reinvent the wheel
each day. "No kidding," I said to Dean. "Well, we've moved
enough. Seems to me we decided we wouldn't move anymore
the last time this happened."

"Yeah," he said. "You're right." The undulating of his left
jawbone was barely perceptible—twenty years of marriage had
trained me to use the jawbone as a weather vane for trouble.
He was a man of few words, but his muscles often betrayed
what he might have said. When the jawbone was still undulating the next night, I knew the transfer was serious.

"This is the last," he said. "The last stop on the ladder. This
is an opportunity we can't pass up."

"Where?"

He smiled. "Guess."

"New York?" I shrieked. It would have been my first
choice—worth the hassles of moving.

He was grinning. "Better."

"Home?" We had both been raised in the San Francisco Bay
area. When we began all the transfers, leaving home had been
a monumental trauma. "We'll go back when I retire," he had
promised, but through the years it had become less and less of
an imperative.

"Home . . . I'm leaving Friday."

"This Friday?"

"This Friday. I'll get an apartment, come back here once a
month. You put the house on the market, get stuff packed, finish school. During Easter vacation, you can come out to San
Francisco, and we'll look for a house."

Suddenly I felt the most exhausted I'd ever felt in my life—
not because there weren't enough hours in a day to sleep, let
alone get ready for a move, but because I needed the thud of
the garage door when he came home every night; I needed the
warm spoon of his body to curl against when I crawled into
bed at one or two in the morning.

"I'm not so brave anymore," I said. "Whither thou goest . . . I'm no libber, you know. Can't you wait until June?"

It was a rhetorical question. When the corporation asks, "Would you like to go to . . . ?" that's also rhetorical. Corporate families know the only response is, "Yes, sir. When must I be there? Thank you very much, sir."

Although for Dean and me it would be returning to our roots, it wasn't the same for the kids.

"Count me out," Alan said. "I'm staying here."

"You can't do this," Kim cried. "I've gone to eleven different schools. I'm tired of being the outsider. I'm not going!"

Laurie suffered in silence. "No sense making Dad feel worse," she said. Only she realized how each transfer made him feel more like a victimizer—something I rarely considered.

By the time Dean left for San Francisco, there was a house full of undulating jawbones. "The kids will get over this," I said cheerily. "By June they'll be used to the idea of moving."

"Of course," he said, but we both suspected what was ahead —silent, brooding, tearful rebellion, with a burst of aggression here and there—broken curfews, dented fenders, slipping school grades, cut fingers, shattered ashtrays. Three Huttmann poltergeists making their angry statements in silence.

With Dean gone, and the kids acting as if I'd damn well better solve this mess we were in, my armor began to slip. In fact, I was at the hospital without any armor at all, by the second week after he left, when Jenny's mom, Mrs. Tucker, came to visit while I was changing her bed.

Because Jenny was in isolation to keep the other children from getting her infections, Mrs. Tucker and I were both dressed in operating room scrub clothes, including masks and booties. When we left the room, we would shed the clothes so the infection would not be taken into the halls. Isolation rooms have an anteroom, just like in the burn center, and then a door into Jenny's room, which is to say that being in the room with Jenny, all swathed in scrubs, often felt eerie. There was never a sound except the hissing and gurgling of all the equipment. The double doors muffled the activity outside her room, no one came and went, the lights were dimmed so the room would stay cool, and Jenny was there, but not there.

I was grateful for some sign of life when Mrs. Tucker walked in. She began tucking in the sheets, helping me move Jenny from side to side, adjusting all the tubes and equipment—but she was silent. We finished the bed, and she sat down in the chair by the window. The day was gray, morose—she looked wistfully at the playground of the grammar school across the street.

"A year from now, I might have watched Jenny in that playground," she said quietly.

I went on adjusting the dials on the equipment. She watched me for a few seconds. "Are you afraid of dying?" she asked. Her voice was strong, like a challenge.

Mrs. Erin had asked me the same question. "Yes, I'm afraid," I said. "It seems so impossible . . . so hard to fathom not being here."

"I used to be afraid, for as long as I can remember." She looked out the window again. "But I don't think I'm afraid anymore. Some things are worse than death."

We both stood at the window watching the children across the street while she told me, for the first time, about the day she looked from an upstairs window and saw Jenny at the bottom of the pool.

"Each time I walked into the ICU, I thought she'd magically awaken."

When she finally gave up hope, it angered her. "We picked at each other unmercifully without ever knowing it had anything to do with Jenny." Her husband had moved out, and for a time she thought of it as good riddance. Sometimes they happened to come to see Jenny at the same time. Anything they said to each other was biting and sarcastic.

Eventually they decided to reconcile, after admitting to each other the reality of Jenny's condition. "It was so foolish to deny death," she said. "Pretending as if it would never happen was such a waste of time."

For almost an hour, she talked about religion, how she had bargained with God for Jenny's life, about the hereafter and the phases she had gone through to resignation. There was no despair in her voice. If anything, she sounded hopeful, but it was not a hope for Jenny's future. She and Mr. Tucker would have more children, she said, and whatever happened, whenever it happened, they would be able to handle it.

There was no magical instant after she left when Jenny's room no longer seemed eerie, nor was there some epiphany that stopped my shrinking from the sight of a dying patient. When Mr. Tucker came a few days later, he too talked about death and what it was like to face up to his own mortality. For the first time, I was not looking for some sudden excuse to leave the room when anything related to death was mentioned. "Whatever happens, we can handle it," he said. "There are some things worse than death."

One day when Lani and I were eating lunch in the hospital cafeteria, I told her about my conversations with the Tuckers. "Death's not the worst possible thing that can happen," I said.

"For doctors, it's the worst possible guilt," she said. "Peter Haynes and I talked about it a few months ago. He said most doctors come out of school believing that death is a symbol of their failure as doctors—no matter the patient's age or condition—if they didn't save the patient, it was their fault."

Lani and I had hashed over the same topic time and time again, but the Tuckers had added a new ingredient—during the year of Jenny's struggle, they had gathered courage to face the inevitable. There is one benefit of prolonged terminal illness—when the end comes, most people will say, "It is a blessing."

Admitting to Mrs. Tucker that I was afraid of dying was admitting it to myself as well, for the first time. The cards were on the table. Though I'm still not sure why that should have made a difference, it seemed that I had jumped the highest hurdle to being a good nurse. I would never again have to dodge the nursing tasks that had terrified me in the past.

"I could take a patient down to the basement if I had to," I told Lani. It was *such* a relief to stop walking around all caked with terror. I chuckled to myself, remembering the first time I had gone to the basement—the ultimate terror—with Charlie about a year earlier.

"Sometimes people die in hospitals . . . it's a well-known fact," Charlie said. "So why are we trying to hide it?"

We were sitting in the noisy, clattering cafeteria, having lunch and talking about my fear of seeing a dead patient. It constantly worried me that I could never be a good nurse as long as I harbored the fear. Charlie didn't seem to share the fear.

"It must be wonderful to have your objectivity, Charlie, like death is just an everyday natural event." I was being sarcastic, but I also envied him.

"When you've seen what I've seen, you get tough. I was in 'Nam . . . you only survived if you were tough. Jeezuz, you should see some of the results of the murders that go on. I see them in the emergency room. What's to be afraid of?"

"Murder's different, Charlie. 'Nam's different."

"Sure! I've got it. The hospital is Barbara's fantasy land where she runs around in a funny little white cap fending off the hungry clutches of the grimy-grim-reaper. Is that it?"

"Got it. Can you imagine one of us doing postmortem care for Judith, covering her with a white sheet from one end of the gurney to the other, pulling the gurney in the elevator, and then riding down to the morgue with any Tom, Dick or Harry who happens to be riding in the same direction?"

Charlie laughed, the little disjointed chuckle he used when a topic was too close to his heart. "Hey, that reminds me, have you seen the new morgue chariot?" He was always crazy about being the first one to know something new, to shout down the sheltered tunnel of my existence with a tidbit for the "old lady," the uninitiated. "I'll show it to you this afternoon . . . it's a real credit to some Rube Goldberg out on the West Coast, where they have nothing to do but think up ways of gilding lilies."

"What's different about it?" I wanted to know. "How many ways can you transport dead bodies?"

"It's terrific." He explained how it looked like an empty gurney, once the body was concealed in a lowered platform. "You could wheel it down Main Street and no one would ever know you're pushing a body."

"Oh bless you, Charlie! I've had such a craving for pushing bodies down Main Street." I ignored his suggestion that this could be a novel relay race for the hospital picnic coming up in a few weeks.

We rode the elevator down to the basement after conference that day, and hurried along a dark corridor that had the familiar smell of the hospital where I had been a patient during my early childhood years. It was a blend of canned carrots, stale urine and freshly laundered linens, similar to the odor of liquid baby vitamins. Broken wheelchairs and gurneys were scattered about the corridor along with parts of hospital beds awaiting repairs.

Huge ducts and pipes hung from the ceiling, suspended just inches above our heads by wires that looked too slim to bear the weight. I had the feeling that someone might jump on us from the dark tops of the pipes, or that a pipe might come crashing down and no one would ever find us again.

"It's spooky as heck down here," I told him.

He bared his teeth, rolled his eyes in opposite directions and growled at me through clenched teeth. "I am a vampire . . . and I'm going to suck the last drops of blood from your body." He lunged at me, with his arms held high over his head in monster fashion, and stalked around me until I was backed against the wall. He gave one last giant growl and pretended to choke me while he pulled me away from the wall and into his arms.

"Knock it off, Charlie ... I'm a bundle of nerves ... I've never been in the morgue before!" His antics half terrified me but also embarrassed me.

It seemed forever that we walked from one corridor to the next, past the carpenter's shop, the freight delivery dock, the physical therapy equipment room, and gigantic boilers and heaters. Charlie unlocked the morgue door—I was almost hoping he had forgotten the key—and I walked in timidly, as if I were about to step into the outer limits.

In the center of the room was a long metal table with a deep sink at one end and a scale and a microphone suspended over the sink. I kept my vision narrowed, not wanting to see anything beyond such familiar sights as the table.

"What's the microphone for?" I asked.

"The one who's doing the autopsy dictates his report as he goes. Say he's examining the liver. He weighs it, then reports the weight and what he finds ... infarcts, fat, whatever."

There was one window, across the room from the door, and shelves lined the walls on either side. Jars of every shape and size filled the shelves. Up close I probably could have identified the contents, but I stayed just inside the door in case I needed to make a hurried exit.

"Look." Charlie went to the jars and began reading the labels. "C. Moffitt, liver ... caudate lobe ... August 19, 1953." The jar was a murky amber, covered with dust. "Don't ask me what they're storing these things for ... maybe it's still an open coroner's case."

Out of the corner of my eye, I had seen the essential part of the room when we walked in, filling the wall on our left. "Is this where the bodies go?" I asked, just to draw his attention from the jars. Looking at the refrigerators together would be like holding someone else's hand in a pitch-dark room.

Six metal doors, stacked in two rows, faced flush on the wall, each with a small handle and a place for a label. The wall could have been mistaken for a giant file cabinet with each drawer about three feet square. One drawer above eye level had a label on it—"Shirley Jefferson." It seemed incredible. Shirley in a drawer. She was a hospital regular, a ninety-two-year-old black lady who was to many nurses as Judith was to us.

"Shall I open her drawer?" he asked. I *wanted* to view a dead body, especially with Charlie there to see me through another of the traumatic mysteries of life, but I did not want to see Shirley. A familiar face would be too much.

"Let's open that one." I pointed to the one bottom left with a white sticker that read "Arthur Ben Bailey—age 98." I stood there, clasping my hands under my chin, my knees about to pucker, as Charlie opened the door. All I could see was a thick mat of gray hair, a sheeted body tucked into the long, thin metal box, and suddenly a sea of emotions washed over me.

How sad his family must be. Did he even have a family? I shouldn't be staring at him like this, like an intruder butting in on a transaction between him and God. And was God watching?

Charlie closed the door. "Well, Barb, you've seen your first."

"Yeah . . . let's go." It was something I would always want to escape.

"What about the chariot? Don't you want to see that?"

"No . . . thanks . . . not today." I waited outside while he locked up, grateful that he had been with me, relieved that I had finally seen a dead body, but overwhelmed with the idea of death.

Charlie put his arm across my shoulders as we walked back through the corridors of the basement. "Got to ya, Barb?"

"Got to me . . . I'm just tired . . . it's been a long day." Mostly I was embarrassed that something so ordinary to him was so dreadful to me—"good" nurses thought of death as something very ordinary, an all-in-a-day's-work part of living.

"Are you afraid of dying?" I asked Lani.

"Isn't everybody?"

"Not Jenny's parents."

"If you look at it from their perspective, maybe it isn't so scary. Until I met Judith Newman, I thought blindness would be worse than death. But whoever knows until you're there?"

"Mrs. Erin says it's just another stage in life—that we can't help patients through that stage until we have faced our own mortality. We're supposed to accept death."

Lani chuckled. "What does 'facing' it mean? I doubt that Mrs. Erin likes the idea of dying any more than we do."

In the end we decided that we could accept death to the extent that we could listen to patients and their families talk about it, even though we might never think of death as something very ordinary—another stage in life.

For Mrs. Tucker listening was all she had wanted. "It's such a relief to talk about it," she had said. "You can't imagine how awful it is to go around thinking such frightening thoughts, feeling so guilty about that swimming pool, hating God for what was happening . . . there's nothing so lonely as not being able to talk to someone about all that."

"In a way, I guess talking about death to patients and families is like talking about the war to Vietnam vets," I said to Lani. "Talking about it with someone who seems to understand takes away the mystery and the vague ghastly images in your mind."

"Nothing's half so scary if someone's there to share it," Lani said.

"When I think about it, that's all hospital phobia really is . fear of death, unknowns, all that big clanking machinery, people in white rushing around with their lethal-looking equipment, about to do heaven only knows what."

That night I told Dean a smattering of my conversations with the Tuckers and Lani. His end of the phone was very quiet, with a distracted "um-humm" now and then. Finally he said, "Look, do we have to talk about it? I'm too busy living to worry about dying . . . at least today. Can we talk about it another time?"

"Yeah . . . sure," I said, feeling slightly rejected, forgetting that it had not been long since someone mentioning death to me could send me into a frenzy. There was always one gigantic problem with being a nurse—very few people wanted to discuss the kinds of experiences that crossed my path each day.

Jenny's condition never changed while Lani and I were on the pediatric rotation. In fact, it never changed during the rest of that year, but the nurses, the doctors, the Tuckers—we all changed. Perhaps if there is a meaning to everything that happens in this life, if there is ever anything at all justifiable in a case like Jenny's, perhaps it was the vehicle for change to those of us who cared for her.

"Not all drownings end like this," Liz Andrews told me. "Kids are tough . . . look at the one in the next room. It would have been the simplest thing in the world to compare that case to Jenny's and throw in the towel. Never give up hope! That's my advice. Just keep on pretending that a miracle will happen and maybe it will."

It was the last day of the pediatric rotation and Liz was buzzing around Jenny's room, humming cheerily, when I walked in. It was her nature to be cheery, but the only times I heard her hum were the times when she was in a room of a patient who was considered hopeless by some of the nurses. "Music is good for the soul . . . therapeutic," she would say. It was part of the therapy she used for the child in the room next to Jenny's—the one who had drowned, been placed on a respirator, given up as hopeless, and had awakened three months later. In fact, Liz had tape-recorded music that she left on in the child's room at night. "Let them wake up to music," she said, as though waking up was only a matter of time. "Hope! That's the key . . . ya gotta have hope, miles and miles and miles of hope." The way she sang the song was almost as convincing as the words.

2 *That's* Nursing

During the three months Lani and I were on the pediatric rotation, I was also finishing time I had missed in the intensive-care unit. Piggybacking the two rotations would have seemed an impossible feat except that Mrs. Bills had fueled my engines by suggesting it would be impossible—zealots thrive on adversity perhaps.

Though better days were yet to come, the first day in the ICU had me just about ready to concede to Mrs. Bills. Ann Pruett, the head nurse, was going through the Kardex, reporting to the nurses on our shift about all the important points on each patient.

"Bed one . . . Marilyn Scott. Forty-three years old, suicide precautions. She's a Seconal and ETOH [alcohol] overdose. Dr. Allen thinks she'll make it. Vital signs are stable, urine output's good, neuro signs okay."

"Intentional?" I asked.

Ann shrugged. "Probably. It takes too much for an overdose to be accidental."

Bed two was Michael Dawson, also in his forties. He had parked his car on the railroad tracks and waited for a train to come along, counting on the snow-covered tracks to keep the train sliding even if the engineer tried to stop it.

The next bed was Barry Bauer, the thirtyish man who had taken Doriden and then tried to finish it off with a shotgun blast under his chin. Next was Jim Erickson, but we knew his meningitis wasn't attempted suicide, and then there was a seventeen-year-old girl who had jumped from the window of her third-story apartment. In the last bed was an elderly lady, so thin she looked as if she had tried to starve to death, who had taken an undetermined amount of Valium. All the patients except Jim Erickson and Barry Bauer were on respirators.

As Ann finished the report, she scanned the room and, in a rare burst of gallows humor, said, "Will any patient here who wants to be alive please stand up?"

I was so busy thinking about what it would be like for those people who thought they had escaped life to wake up and find themselves captive in an ICU, I missed the humor.

"No offense intended," Ann said. "This place could drag you under on days like this." She attributed the rash of suicide attempts to the full moon. "But we've never had more than two at the same time before." The "whoosh-whoosh" of the respirators, all going at different speeds, sounded like a poorly timed chorus of doors being pushed shut against a great vacuum.

Michael Dawson, the man who had parked his car in front of the train, was lying on the X-ray table when I arrived at the hospital the night before. It was so unusual to have any activity in the X-ray department at night, I stopped to see if they needed an extra pair of hands.

"I'm not on duty for an hour yet, can I help in the meantime?"

Kent, the X-ray technician, was standing behind some equipment. "You bet! Penny Hammond is supposed to come from the emergency room to help, but they've got a Code Three coming in over there." I had heard the Code announced over the intercom and thought of stopping there to help, but I still felt too chicken to get caught in there without Charlie to bail me out.

Had the lights been less dim in the X-ray room, I might have noticed the patient. As it was, I only saw a large body on the table covered with a white sheet, until he spoke. "Let me die . . . don't do anything . . . let me die." His voice was a muttering monotone, and he was obviously being careful not to move his mouth a fraction of an inch more than necessary to be understood.

I moved to the side of the X-ray table, intending to take his hand in mine, smooth my hand across his forehead and say something soft and comforting. As I looked down, I instantly turned away and walked out of the room. I leaned against the wall in the hall, trying to comprehend what I had seen.

"Hey!" Kent called. "I thought you were going to help me. This patient needs turning . . . might need some oxygen. Huttmann?"

"I'm here . . . in the hall. Could you come here a moment, please?" He huffed out to the hall, obviously frustrated. He'd been called to the hospital just as he had gotten into bed, and wasn't all that happy with fighting the snowstorm to get here.

"I'm really sorry, Kent, but the light's so dim in there, I can't tell what's going on. Where's the patient's head?"

"I can't turn the lights on . . . too bright. His head is at the end of the table, dummy, where'd you think? Oh, that's right, you weren't here when he came in . . . suicide . . . train hit him. Hang on to your guts and come help me."

Michael's face looked like pulverized meat with jagged edges of bone sticking out and rivulets of blood oozing slowly onto the tabletop. If he had eyes, I couldn't look long enough to see them, and I was grateful that Kent had thought to keep the lights dim, if not to protect the patient's eyes, then to protect my own.

Michael was a huge man—not just fat, but huge—with a thick neck and a very large head. How he had sustained no head injury, I can't imagine, but I suppose the train must have shattered the windshield and thrown him face first into the splinters. Whether he passed out from shock or from the alcohol that he had obviously been drinking (the room smelled like a bar), he sank into an oblivion that made me grateful for the marvelous mechanisms of the body that allow us to retreat when consciousness would be too overwhelming. Still, Kent and I worked silently, not knowing what Michael might be able to hear.

We got him to surgery just as a doctor arrived, and the operating room crew, who had also been called from their warm beds, were setting up for the reconstruction, which took the entire night. Dr. Okamoto was an ear, nose and throat specialist newly out of his residency, and I must admit to having been skeptical—how could a neophyte doctor make anything human of such a pulverized mass?

Michael was wheeled into the intensive-care unit seven hours after I left him in the operating room, and Dr. Okamoto's work had been nothing short of miraculous. Michael's face looked like a series of zippers laid side by side, with the tops of the zippers at his forehead and the bottoms at his chin. It wasn't ugly so much as an astounding work of art.

He couldn't talk, his face was so swollen and stitched together, but I always wondered what was going on behind his troubled eyes—if he was glad to be alive, hostile about being "half saved," or uncaring either way.

Before Michael ever talked, he was transferred out of the ICU to the alcohol-abuse center, and I was assigned to Jim Erickson and Barry Bauer. Some weeks after Michael Dawson left, one of the nurses who took care of him told me he looked terrific—"as terrific as you can look when you've been smashed by a train"—and that the psychologist thought Michael's life would be worked out. He was embarrassed over the suicide attempt and had joined Alcoholics Anonymous because he was convinced drinking was the bottom line of his problem. Whether or not he was grateful that he had been Coded was a question that would never be answered.

Jim Erickson was alive only because he had been Coded, but his case was different—there was no time lapse between when his breathing stopped and the Code. Since he was standing right at the admitting desk in the emergency room when it happened, resuscitation was immediate. Still, it was questionable that we had done him any favors. He was out of the coma and progressing as well as could be expected, but no one knew how many of his brain cells had been destroyed by the high fevers of meningitis. By the time he was assigned to me, in February of my last year in nursing school, his future was anything but predictable.

Barry Bauer was another case of questionable favors. The reconstruction of his face was painfully slow, he still wasn't able to talk, and there were many times he had absolutely no will to live. As Dr. Peter Haynes had suggested, Barry was a Vietnam War vet, and though his suicide attempt may have had nothing to do with the war, it frustrated me that Charlie or Peter would not be there to help. If there were some special methods of nursing people like Barry, I would surely like to have known them.

Because he was so full of energy in between the operations on his face, he paced the ICU from one end to the other, frightening patients and their families. Sometimes we thought he derived pleasure from frightening them—other times we thought he had no idea how he looked. "Don't let him see himself, whatever you do," his wife, Beth, instructed. Before he got up to walk for the first time, she covered all the shiny paper towel cabinets with typing paper and made sure there was no place where he could see his reflection.

During Barry's reconstructions, our job was to keep his surgical wounds free of infection. Sometimes this involved painful dressing changes every three hours, with treatment similar to that used on patients who have skin grafts for burns. At first, he would make animal-like guttural yelps as we removed the bandages. More than once he shoved a nurse away with enough force that she landed against the wall. Then we were back to the same old problem that I had encountered with him months earlier, before my surgery. How could we give him control over what was happening unless we let him look in the mirror and do his own dressing changes?

Getting shoved against the wall once myself inspired me to suggest that he try removing the outer wrappings around his head, by touch. "You set the schedule," I told him, "and we'll help you unwrap whenever you want. The closer to every three hours you do it, the faster you'll get well."

I was surprised that he never suggested he do it while looking in a mirror so he could have even more control; but he was content with doing it by touch and using my instructions, which seemed like guiding an airplane in from the ground: "There's a half-inch piece just below your left ear . . . pull up . . . not too fast . . . good. Now it goes in a figure eight." It was slow going—much too slow for staff nurses, who had a multitude of other patients' concerns—but one of the benefits of student nursing is sometimes having only one or two patients.

Progress with Jim Erickson was equally as slow since he had awakened from the coma. When he finally began to talk in full sentences, he was lost in a time fifteen years earlier, when he had worked for the telephone company in Pittsburgh. Fortunately, his parents could fill in some gaps for us, since he was talking about incidents that had happened even before he met his wife, Kathy.

When his parents first came from the West Coast to his bedside three months earlier, it was the day after he had walked into the emergency room, and they fully expected to arrive just in time for his funeral. As each day passed they grew more hopeful, and when he finally awakened they were the only people he recognized. He would stare at his wife blankly, as though he didn't understand the term "wife." She acted untouched as long as she was with him—then she would crumble in the waiting room.

It took about six weeks after he awakened for Jim's mind to progress through the years. It was like reliving his life in fast motion from the age of seventeen to thirty-two. It was agony for Kathy until he reached the mental age when they had first met. Then she rather enjoyed filling us in on the details of their past so we could talk to Jim in whatever time period was current for him.

One day he was twenty years old, which was about a three-year progression since the day before, when Kathy last visited. He looked at her with a puzzled expression as she walked up to his bed, and then he talked to her in rather seductive tones. "You're cute. You know ... cute, perked-up nose." Still, he didn't recognize her as his wife, but Kathy was beside herself with excitement that he was at least paying attention to the fact that she came and went each day.

A few days later he told us, "That girl that comes in here ... the one with the stuck-up nose ... I used to date her. She's a snob ... thinks she's hot stuff." For days she came in every hour, and he would turn his back and pretend to be asleep. "Can't you keep her out of here?" he asked. "She bugs me!"

Kathy told us they had dated for almost a year when he went off to one of the national parks to work for the summer. He met a "blond bombshell" who was a cocktail waitress at the lodge, and Kathy stopped getting letters and phone calls from him. Kathy was no "bombshell," but she was attractive in a wholesome sense, with enormous blue-green eyes and a chic precision-cut hairstyle.

But while Jim was in this phase, poor Kathy was a bereft waif who looked as if she had given up on life, even though she hoped it was just a time warp he was stuck in for a while. "What if he stays at this mental age?" she asked. "What's to say he won't be stuck with rejecting me forever?"

It was something the doctors worried about behind her back. "We have no way of knowing how much brain damage there is, or how it will be manifested," the neurologist told us, but there was no point in telling Kathy. She had hovered over him for weeks, shampooing his hair, exercising his muscles, bringing him milkshakes and goodies from home—then suddenly he refused to speak to her.

For every two steps forward, it seemed Jim went one step back, which was probably more noticeable to Lani and me because we weren't with him every day. After having had so many infections from all the tubes that were in his body during the coma, he was insensitive to many antibiotics, and new infections that were side effects of past antibiotic therapy were often resistant to therapy. In addition, the whole left side of his body was almost useless, as though he had had a stroke, and he was still having periods of erratic heartbeats.

"We don't know if he'll ever walk again," the neurologist said, "or if he'll be able to use his hands for fine motor skills. He might never think clearly again, for that matter. We'll have to wait and see."

The waiting was easier for Kathy after the day he said to her, "Ronnie was just a flash in the pan, you know. She wasn't really my type. I was just flattered such a hot number would pay attention to me, that's all." He fumbled to clutch her hand, smiled weakly, then flushed in embarrassment. "I didn't really stop loving you. I was just mixed up." Ronnie was the "blond bombshell" he had met the summer he worked at the national park.

"He's twenty-two now," Kathy told us. "We got married six months after he came back from the park."

"A wedding in the ICU." Ann laughed. "That's what this place needs. Let us know when Jim asks you to marry him again, Kathy."

Like a teenager in love, Jim began courting Kathy as best he could. By that time, she had started back to work and was coming in around 5:30 every day. By 5:00 he was frantic, wanting his hair to be just perfect, his face cleanly shaven and everyone out of the way.

"Someday I'm going to marry that girl," he told us. "What do you think? Would she make a good wife?"

Every patient in Jim's physical condition should have such a motivator. He was convinced he had to walk so he could marry her. "Can't I go down to physical therapy?" he asked the doctor. "While I'm sitting here being a cripple, God only knows who might come along and sweep her off her feet!"

Because of his erratic heartbeats, he couldn't go down to the physical therapy department, but the nurses were only too happy to work at getting him on his feet. It was slow—such things are always painfully slow—but he not only had the nurses, Barry Bauer made it his own special project to teach Jim to walk. At the same time, Barry was working with the speech therapist, who had been running out of patience with him. "You can't use that Magic Slate anymore," she would scold. "You can talk if you'll only try!"

His palate and tongue reconstruction was hardly an approximation of how his mouth had been before the shotgun blast, but it was the best that could be done. "He'll never talk as clearly as he could before," the doctor told us, "but we'll be able to understand him in time."

His wife, Beth, was the first to understand him, but like a mother with a newly talking baby, she understood more from his gestures and tone than from his words. She watched carefully while the speech therapist tried to teach him, and then she would reinforce it over and over when the therapist wasn't there. Her patience was limitless, which was admirable but not in Barry's best interest.

He was grunting at Jim one day, trying to tell him to put his left foot forward, when Jim said, "Christ sake, man! I don't know what you're saying. Why don't you stop the damned grunting? It bugs me!" Both of them were short on tolerance that day, mainly because Jim was so close to walking and Barry was so close to talking—they were both fed up with the struggle. Barry had his left arm around Jim's waist, bracing him, and was supporting his right side with his own right arm as Jim faltered and appeared about to tumble.

"Lefth! Lefth! Lefth one!" Barry shouted, sounding enraged. Everyone in the unit looked up, stunned, while Jim moved his left foot, stood wavering, then moved his right foot, in painfully slow, tiny steps.

There wasn't a sound from anyone—nor was there a dry eye—as the two of them acted as if they were all alone and went on with the struggle. "Lefth . . . riiigh . . . lefth . . . riiigh." After about eight steps, they both realized what was happening and tumbled into each other's arms. I quickly slid a chair behind Jim, and he plopped down gratefully, like a long-distance runner who has just exceeded the world's record.

"That's nursing," I told Lani later. "For all the pain, horror and godawful tragedy that goes on, it's worth it when a day like this happens now and then."

Everyone agreed not to mention the incident to Kathy—Jim was going to surprise her. "Give me a week," he said. "I'll walk out to the elevator and surprise her when she gets off."

He couldn't wait a week. In fact, he could barely wait through the day, and he was so agitated his heart monitor kept bleeping, signaling trouble. "Slow down," Ann would call, "you're making the machine go crazy." The problem with bleeping heart monitors is that they signal trouble with the same insistence as they do when the patient is moving around a lot, loosening the sticky pads that keep the monitor wires affixed to the body. We could only tell what the bleeps meant by watching Jim.

Around 5:20 that night he said, "Hey, Barbara. Do me a favor . . . will you draw the curtain around my bed?"

"You're going to sleep at *this* hour? Isn't Kathy coming tonight?"

"She's coming . . . what's the big deal? Do I have to sleep just to get my curtain closed?"

"I'll close it, but only if you lie perfectly still so we know whether the monitor bleeps are because your heart's acting up or because you're jumpy and moving around too much."

"Can't lie still. You win . . . here, help me get my robe on, would you?" If I had only known what was going to happen, I might have borrowed a rosebud from one of the vases in the chapel to pin on his lapel.

He sat on the edge of the bed in his robe and started grinning when Kathy walked into the unit. When she was about twenty feet from his bed, he called, "Hold it . . . wait right there!" She stopped and looked on worriedly while he heaved himself to an upright position by bracing himself on the bedside table. When he was up straight, he stood there like a soldier for a second or two, drew in a deep breath, put the widest grin on his face I had ever seen, and started walking toward Kathy, in slow, steady steps that just barely lifted his feet from the floor.

He took only five steps before she couldn't contain herself any longer and raced up just close enough so he had one more step to go before he could touch her. He reached out his hand, almost like a ballet dancer who barely touches his partner's hand before sweeping into a final dazzling swirl, and then he took both her hands in his. "Kathy, will you marry me," he said, almost in a whisper, "as soon as I can walk down the aisle?"

We never heard her answer, because they buried their faces in each other's shoulders, but it was only a few days later that Jim caught up to the present.

"New love," said Ann wistfully. "I'm jealous." We were all jealous in a sense, but not one of us would have wanted to pay the price they had paid for that moment.

The next day Jim's doctor said, "Send him down to the medical floor. If he can make it through a marriage proposal without stirring up the heart monitor, he's over the hump. He doesn't need to be here anymore."

"You're all alike," Ann grumbled at him, playfully. "You give us the tough part, wait till we get them over the hump. Then just when it gets to the good part, you transfer them out."

"Gripe, gripe, gripe!" He laughed. "You were the one who griped when we brought him in here. Remember? You said you were tired of me sending you dead bodies ... that he'd never survive."

"So I was wrong once ... sometimes there's a miracle . is that any excuse for Coding everybody?"

Her questions were the same as mine—maybe the same ones every nurse asks—and the answer was the same, "There is no answer, that is the answer!"

"What if I had been the Code Blue nurse and refused to resuscitate him the last time all the systems of his body were failing?" Ann mused.

"Do you have a choice?" I asked. "If you're an RN, you're a Code Blue nurse, right?"

"Right," she answered, "but sometimes I dream that I have a choice. For patients like Jenny Tucker, I'd like to have a choice ... then someone like Jim comes along."

Had Jim been much older, and a little less healthy when his illness started, the high fever he had when he was admitted, and the subsequent ones he spiked during the parade of infections that came one on top of another, would have permanently injured him had he been lucky enough to survive at all.

As it was, three months after Jim left the ICU the nurses were all gathered for the afternoon report when a couple came in looking as if they were dressed for the Easter Parade—he in a three-piece gray flannel suit with the chain of a gold pocketwatch adding the perfect touch of glitter, and she in a stunning blue-green silk dress that exactly matched her eyes. Ann Pruett looked up from the Kardex on her lap. "Yes? May we help you?" The tone of her voice said, "What are you doing here?"

Then suddenly she recognized Jim's proud grin, the Kardex went clattering to the floor, and Jim and Kathy were caught up in a flock of nurses hugging and laughing. "A walking, talking miracle," Ann exclaimed. "Why didn't you tell us you had a ten for a husband, Kathy?" They both looked spectacular.

Later Ann told me that one of the drawbacks of ICU nursing was that they rarely saw a patient after recovery. "They go out of here barely surviving," she said, "and that's usually the last we see of them." Many times patients never even remembered that they had been in the ICU, which, in a way, was at least an advantage—the sights, sounds and smells in an ICU are tolerable only in very small doses, and best endured through a narcotized haze.

Patients helping each other recover is a catch-22, which is why most hospitals try not to put patients with the same diagnosis in the same room. Though it sometimes helps a resistant patient to have a roommate who keeps saying, "C'mon . . . you can do it . . . look at me," it can be very depressing for someone who lags behind and is truly unable to recover as fast.

Barry Bauer's helping Jim Erickson was of enormous benefit to Jim, but after Jim was transferred out of the ICU, Barry took six steps back for every step forward. From the day they helped each other walk and talk, it was a competition for perfection that Jim easily won. He would walk perfectly within a few days—Barry would *never* talk perfectly, no matter how hard he tried.

Finally the day came when Barry's reconstructions were complete enough to leave the bandages off, but a far cry from the way anyone would want to look. His new nose was almost flat because of the scarcity of skin and bone, and his mouth had no lips except for a small, poor facsimile that gathered his face skin around the hole where his mouth should have been.

"We'll keep working at it," the plastic surgeon told Beth. "A little grafting here, a little grafting there . . . but it's going to take time . . . lots of time."

If Beth ever wearied of coaxing Barry along, working with his speech, or encouraging him to pull himself out of depression, she never mentioned it. "She's one in a million," he would say proudly, when he was in one of his rare up moods.

The turning point in Barry's recovery came one day in early March when the plastic surgeon wanted X-rays of Barry's nose.

Before, a portable X-ray machine had always been brought to the ICU, but the clarity of those X-rays wasn't really good enough. Wheeling patients to the X-ray department is so routine, we would never have anticipated what happened.

Barry's youngest child, Christopher, was having his fourth birthday that day, and Beth had arranged to bring the children to see Barry for the first time. Because of the divorce, Barry had not seen them for several weeks before his hospitalization. Since then, six months had passed before Beth thought it might be not too traumatizing for them to see how he looked.

"There has to be a first time when they see a face they will never recognize as his," she said.

Some nurses thought it was a bad idea—others thought it was like squaring with death. The sooner you do it, the better. In a sense, it resembled the question of whether or not children should be taken to funerals. Once Beth made the decision to go ahead, the nurses decided to make the most of it by turning it into a birthday party for Christopher.

Ann Pruett made a birthday cake in the shape of a rabbit, with fluffy white frosting and coconut sprinkled on top. We cleared the bulletin boards in the nurses' lounge and hung Lani's weird version of a donkey. She never claimed to be an artist, but it was good enough for playing Pin the Tail on the Donkey. While we were tying balloons to the IV stands and gathering the ice cream and punch from the kitchen, Barry was down in X-ray.

A few minutes after he left, Ann Pruett poked her head in the nurses' lounge. "Barbara, run some Valium down to X-ray . . . they left Barry alone . . . damned fools. He saw himself." It had been so long since Beth went around covering all the shiny towel cabinets in the ICU, we had forgotten to worry about such a thing.

The person who wheeled him into the X-ray room left him sitting there alone. There was a mirror in the little cubicle where outpatients changed from their clothes to a gown. When

Barry saw the mirror, he decided to have a look. Perhaps he would have been able to cope if it had been any other day, but all he could think was how that face would look to his children.

"Hysterical," the X-ray technician said as I rushed into the X-ray department. "The guy's gone ape."

It was one of the many situations when I missed Charlie the most. You turkey, I thought, you would know exactly what to say.

Sometimes the only right thing to say is nothing, which is how it was with Barry. It seemed like forever that he sat in the wheelchair in the dimly lit X-ray room, a sobbing heap, begging to know why we had not let him die. Sometimes I held his hand, or put my arm across his shoulders, hoping that would convey, "I feel your anguish."

Probably a half hour had passed when Beth came in the room with Ann Pruett. "Betsy and Chris are waiting," she said. "This is something we have to do, Barry . . . we're tough, you and I." She stood before him like a soldier who intends to be tough while crying inside.

I whispered to Ann that I still had not given him the Valium. There are some situations when dulling the senses only delays the inevitable—this seemed to be one of them.

"You can have some Valium if you want," Ann told him.

He shook his head. Beth crouched in front of the wheelchair, holding his hands in hers. "We can be a family again, starting today, Barry." The pause before she said the rest was far more threatening than her voice. "Or we can go back to the way we were . . . the kids and I will have to learn to go it alone." She stood up resolutely, waiting. Barry stared at the floor.

It was a moment too personal to share—Ann and I slipped out of the room and closed the door behind us. "Beth can bring him back to the unit," Ann said. "Lani's entertaining the kids in the waiting room." If there had been more than two other patients in the ICU we might have been worried that the only patient getting care that day was Barry.

A few minutes after Ann and I returned to the ICU, Beth wheeled Barry into the nurses' lounge, got their children from the waiting room and closed the door to the lounge as she took them to see Barry for the first time. To be honest, we expected to hear frightened shrieks from the children, sobbing from Barry, some terrible heartwrenching sounds. For ten or fifteen minutes, we heard nothing. Then there was laughing, singing of "Happy Birthday," the fast chatter of children, bumping of furniture.

"*That's* nursing!" Ann said. "We're finally over the hump."

Only a few days later Barry was transferred to the second floor where he would stay for a few more skin grafts. Then he would go home and return for short stays throughout the year or so it would take to do the best that could be done. He would never look like you or me, but Beth and the children couldn't have cared less.

"We'll take him any way we can get him," Beth said. "Mean and nasty, cute and lovable, however ... just so long as he comes home to *us!*"

At the end of the semester, I finally caught up to my class. Piggybacking the ICU and pediatric rotations wasn't something I could ever do again, but the gross exhaustion was worth the scent of success in the air—graduation day was only one semester away.

Lani and I were crossing the campus to the parking lot. It was the last day, last final exam—always the best day of every semester. Lilacs were just beginning to burst, tiny new leaves covered the trees, and dozens of birds flitted around gathering bits and pieces for their nests.

"For one whole week we can do what we want," Lani said. "Sleep or to the mountains for some skiing?"

I had yet to tell her what I couldn't bear to think of myself—by graduation day I had to be packed and ready to leave. Leaving friends had been a way of life, but leaving Lani would be like leaving part of myself.

"Ski? Are you kidding? Thanks . . . I'll sleep."

It was Easter vacation, for the kids as well, and the four of us did what we have learned to do best—packed *A* boxes with things we will want for sure, and *B* boxes with things we could do without in a pinch. There might be days, weeks or months, camping in hotels, motels or whatever, until we could settle in a house.

Dean had been home twice since the start of that semester. One weekend I had flown to San Francisco to sign papers on a house that was under construction. Though we knew the house would not be completed until September, neither of us coped well with separation. He intended to come home the day before graduation, and we would all leave for San Francisco the day after.

Coping with separation would have been far more practical than leaving one house before we could move into the next, but each of us had a problem we had never solved—he would rather starve than cook a meal, and I have chronic imagination that turns strange sounds into dangerous unknowns at the door. He needed a cook—I needed an interpreter of strange sounds.

Feminists might assert that there are no wolves at the door, that women have exchanged their individuality and independence for the privilege of having a man protect them from wolves that don't even exist. But there were *always* wolves at our door, just ask any police department in the cities where we have lived. They usually know when the head of the Huttmann household is out of town.

Sure enough, Dean had been gone a month when I heard a noise just as I was dropping off to sleep. It was the sound of a dresser drawer closing—familiar, but wrong.

"Mo-o-o-om?" Laurie had a very special way of calling when she was half choked with terror.

"Yeah, Lor." Already I was sleuthing to figure what the next move should be. Alan's bedroom was on the first floor, but he was at his part-time job at a gas station. *Anyone* could at that moment be down there, about to come up here.

"What are you doing, Mom?"

"Have you been asleep, Lor?"

"Mo-o-o-o-om?" Kim's terror call was twice as eerie as Laurie's.

Within seconds we had called the police from Laurie's bedroom, locked her door that led to the hall, and were huddled together outside on the balcony of her room. When the police drew up in front of the house (two cars in all), I wished I could have been Rapunzel and slid down my hair to safety.

It seemed forever that they were on the first floor of the house, opening and closing doors, and then there was rapping on Laurie's door.

"Don't open it!" Kim hissed.

"Why not?" I whispered.

"It might be HIM!"

Oh my God . . . she was right. While the police were fooling around downstairs, we were about to get it. "What's the worst thing that can possibly happen?"

"We can get raped, shot, stabbed," Laurie whispered.

"Where's your purse?" Kim whispered. "Give him your purse, Lor."

"All that's in it is makeup, a can of hair spray."

"That's it . . . get ready. When I open the door, you squirt the hair spray."

A deep voice said, "This is the police . . . open the door."

Laurie was standing with the can of hair spray poised at what we thought should be eye level. "Don't squirt, Lor. Not until I tell you," I said.

When we opened the door, a massive, gorgeous, blond Adonis stood there grinning, in the uniform that I had come to love the most (when Dean was out of town), with thirty pounds of wonderful attack equipment hanging from his belt. Never have I appreciated the sight of guns and clubs so much as on nights like that one.

When they had assured us we were safe, that the sound we heard must have been the echo of a neighbor closing a door, and that they would patrol now and then until we moved, we offered them a cup of coffee. There was still a long, dark night to go, without a culprit in custody! They were busy and had to leave.

"Look at us," Laurie said as the last policeman walked out the door. "We had a houseful of tens and just look at us!"

Curlers and Clearasil were not their most attractive features. We were the most motley-looking group of people who had ever dragged clothes out of a dark closet just before running out onto an ice-covered balcony. "Nude sleepers should keep something at the bedside in case the police come," Kim said laughing.

It wasn't just missing Dean, or trying to control three teenagers who were using passive-aggressive behavior to resist the move, or packing endless boxes of belongings for the move, that made the last few months of nursing school seem very nearly impossible. It was the nights of someone calling "Mo-o-o-om!" that sent me off to the hospital each day, feeling like I couldn't drag one foot in front of another, much less look like I had good sense.

3   The Longest Mile

Dr. Allen happened to be with Judith when Lani and I went to visit her on the first day of Easter vacation. "She's rummy these days," he said, "maybe has hospital fever. Let's get her back to Sunny Harbor and see if she does better there." Getting "rummy" often happens to elderly patients who are hospitalized for a long time. They also get grouchy, resistant to therapy and are sometimes very paranoid. "Stop! Stop! You're killing me" means trouble to most people. To nurses it means someone with hospital fever is objecting to something as innocuous as having their face washed.

Judith wasn't causing trouble, but she wasn't getting better either. The toes on her good foot had become infected, as is so often the case when diabetes and congestive heart failure compromise circulation to the toes, and it was looking like she might eventually have to have another amputation. Each day she sank into the sanctuary of sleep a little longer, moved about less, and gave infection a good chance to increase.

"We'll take her home . . . look in on her every day," Lani told Dr. Allen. "We can show the Sunny Harbor nurses how you want her dressings done."

When Lani and I wheeled Judith into her room at Sunny Harbor that afternoon, she immediately smelled the scent of roses and knew they were from Jules Casper. "Everyone else thinks because I'm blind I wouldn't see flowers," she said, "but I see them better than I ever saw them when I could see." Mr. Casper was standing discreetly across the hall, with a grin from ear to ear, waiting for us to get her settled into bed so he could come in.

"Mr. Casper's waiting to see you," I whispered. "We'll leave you two alone . . . Lani and I will come back tomorrow."

"Oh bosh! You don't have to leave us alone." She turned toward the door and called, "Mr. Casper . . . how have you been? What perfectly lovely roses!"

He shuffled in, with blushing cheeks, obviously overcome. "You look very well, my dear"—which she didn't—"and I've been practicing gin while you've been gone."

She laughed and told him he could practice forever but he still wouldn't beat her. Tears filled his eyes when he first started talking to her but he was smiling with joy, and then his shoulders began to droop. She had grown weak and thin, wrinkled, sallow, and just the effort of talking to him a little so exhausted her that she gasped and wheezed. By the time he left the room, he was having difficulty stopping the flood of tears and sorrow.

During the week, we visited her every day, struggling to get her toes to heal. Sometimes her mind wandered, and she would take up the subject of the Holocaust, and other times she seemed more lucid. She told us about her time in the ICU, that she had told Dr. Allen she wanted no heroics (no Code), and she told us she had a Living Will. "It's in the top drawer there, girls, and he has a copy." She asked us to put it on file at the hospital. We hadn't the heart to tell her it might not do any good—no one has to honor a Living Will, especially if it happens to be someone who sees her stop breathing and calls a Code without knowing the Living Will is on the chart. Telling her that would not have changed anything.

"Mr. Kelly," she said. My cheeks flushed in embarrassment for him. "Has he been angry with me?"

"I don't think so. Why would he be angry with you?" This was a game that didn't have a clear rule book.

"It seems so long since I've seen him. Is he well?" We assured her that he was well, he was busy, and he probably was visiting her when she was sleeping . . . or perhaps she didn't remember his visits. Her memory was slipping, and she didn't have the blessed ability of so many others who lose their memory to forget that they can't remember. She knew it and it bugged her.

"I'll wring his neck if I ever see him again," I told Lani.

By the end of the week, Judith was having less difficulty breathing and was more willing to eat than she had been in the hospital, mostly because Jules Casper was taking over where Charlie had left off. "Eat this little bit of pudding, my dear . . . now you take a little nap, my dear, and I'll sit right here and read." Though his eyesight was little better than hers, and he hadn't been able to read for years, he wasn't going to mention that he didn't have whatever it took to keep himself entertained while she slept.

"Oceans and oceans of lotions and potions couldn't do a thing for her that Mr. Casper can't do," remarked Lani. "If every patient had someone like Mr. Casper around we would be out of business . . . so would the doctors."

When we began our last semester, on the third floor at Oakmont County Hospital, my patient could have used a Mrs. Casper. No one came to visit him, there were never any cards or flowers, and even the brother and sister-in-law with whom he had lived seemed to ignore the fact that he was in the hospital. Ed Mackey was the kind who is easily lost in a crowd—even the hospital staff barely noticed he was there.

With no facial expression, a graying crewcut and an out-of-shape, overweight, forty-seven-year-old body, he would need conversation to give him personality, but he was said to be "unresponsive."

When Charlotte Topping, Ed's night nurse, was reporting off, she told me that he was having a craniotomy (brain surgery) the next week, after medications had lowered the pressure in his brain. "There's nothing to do except bathe and feed him," she said. "I've put the new IV tubing in there . . .

you should change that today." Charlotte was the kind who would do favors for other nurses, like passing out the fresh tubing so we wouldn't have to bother going to the utility cart for it.

She had been at Oakmont, on the same shift and unit, for eight years. She was in her forties, had lived alone all of her life and liked the slow pace of the nights. "You can have all the pandemonium of doctors running around the unit in the day," she said. "Just let me do my thing at night." Her thing was a rigidly organized pattern of tasks that she had perfected over the years. You could set the clock by the intervals when she took a flashlight and made her rounds through all the rooms to see if any patient needed something.

On the Friday morning that she passed out the IV tubing, I was sorry that she had been so considerate. Changing the tubing is a matter of disconnecting the old tube from the needle in the patient's arm at one end, and the solution bottle at the other end, then replacing it with a fresh one. This is done on all IVs every day or so. That day, I intended to do it in the afternoon, so I put the box of tubing on the large metal rectangle above Ed's bed, just to keep it out of the way while I did other things.

I was just getting out the thermometer to take Ed's temperature when Mrs. Erin called and said I was to go with Lani to help transfer another patient from the emergency room. "They're short staffed down there today," she said. "Just leave your·patients sleeping . . . you can take their vital signs when you come back."

Lani and I were hurrying into the emergency room when bells began clanging in the hall and the hospital operator announced a Code Red, the signal for fire in the building. "Code Red, Three West! . . . Code Red, Three West! . . . Code Red, Three West!"

When I sorted out which direction was west, I realized my patient's room was on that hall. "That's me," I told Lani. "See you later." The first rule for fire is that nurses return to their patients and make sure that all the doors are closed.

Though I wasn't particularly worried—fire drills were common, and false fire alarms were as common as false alarms for Codes—I ran up the three flights of stairs as fast as I could and almost knocked over a fireman dragging a hose across the doorway. "Watch it, lady!" he called, as I bolted through the door.

Just then, the elevator emptied out the big brass band—Rita Treece (director of nurses), Faith Mason (head nurse), Mr. Martin (hospital administrator), the fire marshal, and Mrs. Erin, our instructor. I leaned against the wall as they passed, then followed them halfway down the hall.

Thinking it was another false alarm, I went along the hall, poking my head in each room to tell the patient everything was just fine. "We'll have this cleared up in no time," I said, flashing my most reassuring smile.

Mrs. Erin was almost at the end of the hall. "What happened?" I asked her. "Who did it? Who did it? Who did it?" echoed up and down the hall like soft background music. "Did what?" I whispered to Mrs. Erin.

The only open door was the one directly in front of her—Ed Mackey's. "That's my patient," I said innocently. "What happened?" Her silence was so irritating, I thought telling her he was my patient would make her open her mouth and let out a secret.

"Oh no!" I said, just as the last flames of a charred bedspread flickered out in my patient's washbasin. Ed was lying there looking as he had when I left earlier—bored, staring straight ahead, oblivious to what was going on around him.

Suddenly Mrs. Erin looked tired, to the point of hysteria. "No . . . no. Please say that isn't your patient." The pleading was so pathetic as she looked down at her clipboard to be sure a student was assigned to that room. "Not a student. Anyone, but not a student. That really is your patient." She, the parent,

I, the child. I had broken her wealthy neighbor's Steuben glass vase.

"The light," she said. "Did you put a box of tubing on top of the light?" No one ever used the lights during the day, but I had no idea there was a high-intensity bulb at either end of the fixture that was used when the doctor needed strong light to examine a patient.

When the doctor switched the light on that morning, the cellophane package exploded. As he threw it across the room to the sink, flaming pieces dropped on Ed's bed and the spread caught on fire.

"I did it," I said. "I was going to change the tubing later." The look on Mrs. Erin's face told me my very best move would be to walk straight to the elevator and pretend the whole two years had been a Fig Newton of my imagination—back to washing clothes and waxing floors.

Mrs. Erin clutched her clipboard tighter, straightened her spine as if to prepare for battle and announced, "We've found the source . . . we know who did it." Her voice approximated that of a narrator at the horse races—using a megaphone.

Everyone stopped moving and looked as if waiting for the punchline of an unfunny joke. She turned on her heel and headed down the hall in her usual rushing-to-a-meeting walk.

And I? I stood there feeling as if I had made a very large puddle at my feet and everyone could see the nasty dribbles on my white stockings. "You did it?" asked Faith Mason, grinning like the mother who has just discovered it was not *her* child who broke that irreplaceable glass vase.

"You did *what?*" Dean shouted when I phoned him that night. "Do you realize what this does to the reputation of the school? Do you realize this could cost Mrs. Erin her job? She'll be blamed for not teaching you fire safety, you know. So?"

"So what?" By that time I was in tears.

"So what happened to the patient?"

"Nothing . . . he's out of it . . . probably had no idea what

259

was happening." Then it was more than tears. "He probably does know, but he can't say anything ... he's dying ... it's really sad ... no one comes to see him ... no one cares."

His voice was very sympathetic. "Look, honey. Maybe you weren't meant to be a nurse. You've learned a lot ... you aren't afraid of hospitals anymore ... this isn't the worst thing that could possibly happen. No one was hurt. A bedspread costs hardly anything. Why don't you fly out here and spend a few days with me?"

"You think they'll kick me out of the program?"

"Well, haven't they?"

"Not yet."

"You're kidding! They've already had enough problems with you ... wrecked back ... surgery ... now a fire." Then he laughed. "Maybe they'll keep you in just to see what can happen next." By the time we were through talking, it did seem rather like a joke—one that could not be improved by dwelling on it.

Narrow escapes have a way of creeping into memory, leaving a flash of what might have been, then creeping back out again. Every time I looked at Ed Mackey after the fire, I stifled the narrow-escape memory, but something gave me a sense that we had been thrown together in a twist of fate that had to do with divine destiny.

Ed had never been sick or hospitalized, never complained of feeling poorly and "never made a fuss about anything," according to his brother. "My wife and I were away for Christmas," he told me. "When we came home, it was like Ed was gone. He never talked much anyway, but it wasn't like him to stay home from work." He said Ed could only answer "Yes" or "No," and after waiting two weeks for him to "snap out of it," they had him hospitalized for diagnostic testing.

Of all the invasive, obnoxious, risky tests there were, Ed was subjected to the top three. Eventually he had a brain scan, the least of the evils, but only after a whole string of unnecessary diagnostics. "This patient has been exploited," I raged to Mrs. Erin. "The brain tumor was obvious without any of those tests, and the scan told them everything they needed to know for treatment and prognosis."

"Barbara, have you turned in your care plans?" she asked, clutching her clipboard to her chest. Did I think she had purposely changed the subject, or that she didn't agree with my raging? Certainly not. "She never listens to me!" I had ranted to Dean. "I can't get through to her." Exploited patients were nothing new to her, I realize now, and I forgive her for appearing dense, but she was a real crazy-maker back then. What could she do about the hidden agenda of the medical community? She did what most nurses do—the only thing they *can* do—ignored it.

The first morning, while feeding Ed a breakfast of frightful-looking, watery scrambled eggs, I wondered how on earth I was going to communicate with him. "He's aphasic," Charlotte Topping had told me. "Totally unable to communicate."

I sat there with him feeding him the ugly eggs, giving him sips of coffee now and then, and there probably was some sort of fruit and cereal on his tray. The weather was dull gray, as it had been for days, the hall outside his room was silent, and the food looked cold and tasteless. Breakfast is such a personal thing, and I was feeling sad that he had to take what he could get, whether he liked it or not. Maybe he would have loved to have a cup of tea, a piece of toast—maybe there was a fixed way he started every day, and maybe a day without that routine seemed awry.

If he didn't want a certain food, he grimaced and rolled it around in his mouth as if to say, "Yuck! No more of that!" but he couldn't say what he *did* want. The textbooks said brain tumors cause severe headaches that usually bring the patient in for treatment, so I was trying to figure a way to find out if he needed pain medication. "Ed, I know you can't talk to me," I said, "but I'll do the best I can." There was something so sad about him just sitting there lifeless that I was determined to talk to him even if he couldn't respond.

"I need to know if you're in pain. Can you raise your hand if you hurt anywhere?" He just stared at me, looking blank, but I felt that he could hear. "Ed, do you hurt anywhere, are you in pain?" I tried again.

His eyes moved, looked directly into mine as if sending me an ESP message, and then he moved his lips around, dragging an answer from somewhere deep inside him. In a booming monotone he said, "More than that!" If God had spoken, it wouldn't have startled me more, but I pretended I expected him to talk. "Where is the pain? Where do you hurt?" I waited. He said nothing.

"Is it your head? Do you have a headache?"

"No!" There was no expression on his face or in his words, but he wasn't the aphasic or unresponsive patient I'd been told he was.

"Does your chest hurt?" To every body part mentioned, he said, "No," but I decided to get him medication anyway in the hope that it would touch the right place. On the way down the hall I started thinking about his saying, "More than that!" Was that his way of describing the intensity of the physical pain, or did he mean he was in psychological pain? I went back to his room with some kind of general pain-reliever.

"Ed, are you still in pain?"

"Yes."

"Is it your back?" He answered, "No," and there were no more body parts left. I took his hand in mine, sent him all the warmth and sympathy I could with my eyes, and then said, "Ed, is it a heartache?"

He still looked blank, said nothing for a long time, then he squeezed my hand, very gently, and said, "Yes," as tears began to roll down his cheeks. He never spoke again.

At the end of the week he had a craniotomy and was sent to the ICU with his head all swaddled in bandages. "You look like a Hindu in that headgear." I laughed, hoping he would chuckle right along, but he gave me the same blank stare as before surgery. "Grade III astrocytoma," his chart said. "Inoperable tumor—life expectancy six months."

How terribly alone he was became brutally clear when I telephoned his brother to say he would need to select a nursing home where Ed could spend the remainder of his life. "I'll give you a list of good ones near your home," I said, but he had essentially crossed Ed off his list and wanted nothing to do with worrying about how he would spend the last six months.

"Just keep him there till he dies," the brother said. "The insurance doesn't cover nursing homes."

I told him insurance companies did not allow hospitalization for custodial care, which is what Ed needed, and they would no longer pay for his hospitalization. Finally he agreed to ask the state to give him Medicaid, and the insurance company agreed to cover Ed's costs until the state paper work could be completed.

The next morning I arrived to find Ed covered with urine and feces. With no way to ask for a bedpan, that was understandable, but he also couldn't ask for water, a blanket, something to eat, or pain medication—he was a prisoner manacled to the whims of technicians and nurses.

When a student is assigned to a patient, there is also a staff nurse who supervises the care the student gives. Ed's nurse was Esther, a middle-aged lady who had been nursing cancer patients for years. "He's covered with feces," I told her. "What if he's cold? Does anyone bother to try and find out what kind of food he likes? How do you know if he's in pain? And for God's sake, why doesn't anyone ever offer him a bedpan?" It was obvious that he had been a low priority during the night. "Forty-seven years old and he has to end up like this, no one really caring. Not one single person cares if he lives or dies."

She looked at me as if I had struck her—I expected rage in return. Instead, icicles began dripping with each word, her eyes narrowed and bored frozen holes in me. "How many patients do you have assigned to you today?" She was almost whispering, and she was so calm I wanted to smack her.

"Two. Ed and Mrs. Ames," I huffed.

"Well, I have twelve. Twelve today, twelve yesterday, twelve tomorrow. You couldn't even bathe twelve in one day, let alone sit around long enough to figure out which one of them wants to eat, whether they're cold, if they're in pain, or when they might have a bowel movement. Talk to me about who is really caring when you've figured out how you would bathe twelve patients if they were assigned to you today."

"You have an aide," I countered.

"Yeah, well, let me tell you about that aide I have today, Mrs. Huttmann." She said "Huttmann" as if she were spitting bullets. "She was sent from the registry [a temporary nursing agency] today and hasn't the slightest notion what she's doing. She can't work the blood-pressure cuff and doesn't even know which end of the thermometer gets pushed in. My big project for the day is to make sure no one dies of neglect while she's here. You've got a rough road ahead, lady . . . you really don't know what's going on!"

She lumbered off down the hall in a nonchalant walk that had irked me from the day I met her. A year earlier when I had remarked to Charlie how unconcerned Esther seemed with everything, he said, "So what's the rush? She's been here forever, knows she can't rescue anyone, what's to get steamed up about? If she got as steamed up as you, she'd be burned out in a month."

I miss you, Charlie, there's no one here to make me laugh anymore, I thought.

It was a pivotal point that day, the beginnings of reality, the sneaking suspicions, all in tarnished trappings. Esther, incompetent aides, intractable dying, feces-covered beds, faceless patients, a flock of nurses with too much to do and no time to do it—they were the band, all marching in one direction, and I was marching in the other.

Cleaning Ed and his bed was the mindless task I needed right then. "By tomorrow I'll have figured out how to keep you out of messes like this," I promised him and put my mind on cruise for the day.

"Phew! Get some air freshener sprayed in here." Mrs. Erin stood in the doorway with the clipboard clutched to her chest. I smiled, grateful that she couldn't see the vision of herself passing through my mind—she as an infant in the newborn nursery, arriving in the world with the clipboard attached to her chest like an extra appendage.

With my mind on cruise, I worked most of the day with Ed, but Charlie's absence was crowding in. The little jolts of sadness were like a fly that buzzes and then flits away, then comes back and buzzes again. Eventually the sadness turned to anger, and I thought what I would say to him if I ever saw him again: that deep in my smoking heart I would despise him, that he was like a bowl of curdled custard, a vacuum cleaner of life, a chicken-hearted turncoat, a frigging, failing flop out.

Rage and resentment infused me with energy. I couldn't take care of twelve patients at once? I don't know what's going on? Hogwash! I'll show you.

I went to the campus library and asked for everything they had on aphasia and astrocytomas. Florence Nightingale was going to rescue Ed . . . or at least she was going to find a way to communicate with him.

"Hamburgers again?" Alan complained that night. "I'm a growing kid. I need a decent meal . . . meat and potatoes." He was growing all right—a six-foot seven-inch spider, all hollow arms and legs, a 160-pound food processor that seemed never to switch off.

"Don't worry, we won't starve to death because you've abdicated, again," Kim said, with the special playful emphasis on "again" that let me know they would all dip into the well of tolerance for at least the hundredth time.

"Arghhh! I'm starving. Help me . . . nurse, nurse . . . I need a nurse to feed me!" Alan sprawled on the floor writhing.

"Look, you guys, this is important. There's a patient who's dying. He can't even tell anyone if he needs a glass of water. When I figure out how to help him, you'll be glad . . . then I'll know how to help you. If you ever get a brain tumor, call on me!" I said it flippantly, as though brain tumors were little patches of poison oak that could be easily treated by savvy nurses. "Tonight I have to hit the books, tomorrow may be too late. I'll fix roast and mashed potatoes tomorrow night." Once again they ate at the blessed Golden Arches—the savior of middle-aged zealot nurses.

I was lost in the books on aphasia when they got home, and when they went to bed, and when they got up in the morning. The simplest definition of aphasia is that it is a loss or an impairment of language due to brain injury. Messages that arise in the brain have difficulty getting to the mouth, but that doesn't mean asphasic patients can't understand what's being said to them. Some can't, some can—and I was counting on being able to teach Ed all the tricks in the book that day.

"Quick, Lor, get a Sears catalogue. Kim, find paste and scissors. I need you guys to make flash cards—a blanket, food, a glass, a toilet, and get a picture of pills out of one of the nursing magazines." I had an hour to get to the hospital, and I was lucky enough to have daughters whose hearts bled like mine when they heard about Ed's situation.

I arrived at the hospital late for report. "Huttmann, you have 311, 312 and 313, and before you do anything, get 311 ready for transfer to St. Joseph's." Mrs. Erin hated students to be late—she would be abrupt all day. "The ambulance will be here at nine." She hurried off to the elevators while I went to get report from Esther.

Suddenly it dawned on me that Ed was in room 311. There must be some mistake. Why would they transfer him so suddenly?

"Get moving on 311," Esther told me. "The ambulance company doesn't like to wait." She handed me the papers to fill out for transfer, the instructions for the nurses who would be taking care of him next.

"Wait," I said, "he can't be transferred today. Today I have to teach him how to tell us what he wants. They can't just take him out of here."

"Wonderful! You're going to teach an aphasic to talk? All in one day? Wonderful." She looked down at the diet lists she was checking and silently dismissed me.

"I made flash cards, with pictures on them. He can show us what he wants. I can teach him to signal with his hands. He won't be able to say words, but . . ."

"Marvelous, Huttmann. Tell Mrs. Erin about your marvelous feats. I'm sure she'll really be impressed."

"I don't give a damn about what Mrs. Erin thinks. How would you like to be dying of thirst and not be able to ask for a glass of water?" Her total lack of interest in the situation had triggered my anger button.

"You're really idealistic, aren't you? New nurses are like that." She chuckled in a blend of sarcasm and admiration. "You'll find out soon enough that people come, and people go, and all your wonderful plans will not save them."

"Saving him wasn't what I was after."

"What would you like to do?"

"Maybe no one knows the straits he's in. Can I call the doctor?"

She explained that Ed's neurosurgeon was going on vacation, that he had transferred the case to a Dr. Wade at St. Joseph's and that Dr. Wade was planning to do chemotherapy.

Very calmly I told her that Ed had no one, that I could help him, that I would need only one day, two days at the most, and then I would have a solution the nurses at St. Joseph's could use with him.

"Nobody said you couldn't call a doctor . . . go ahead. Strum his heartstrings if you think you can."

I called the neurosurgeon, and the answering service told me he was gone. Then I called Ed's brother, and he said he didn't really care where Ed was transferred, so then I called Dr. Wade and explained the situation.

"That's very nice, Mrs. Huttmann, but I'm sure the nurses at St. Joseph's will take very good care of him. Don't worry." The nurses didn't have the time that students had, but I couldn't explain that to a doctor.

When I wrestled down all my anger and thought of all the information I had read the night before, the bottom line looked very ugly. Ed's inoperable cancer was not susceptible to chemotherapy and, if left to progress, would eventually encroach on his respiratory center. He would slip into a coma and die of respiratory failure.

Ed was being transferred to St. Joseph's because Dr. Wade was not on the staff at Oakmont Hospital. And he was to undergo chemotherapy with devastating side effects because that was the choice of Dr. Wade. Ed had nothing to say about it. No one had anything to say about it—except Dr. Wade. Would it prolong Ed's life? Not according to the text. Would it make him more comfortable? On the contrary, according to the text—chemotherapy is never comfortable. Did he have any choice? No. The week before, he would have been sent to a nursing home where he would receive palliative care, lapse into a coma and end life without any trauma. Sneaking mistrust, exploitation of patients, unnecessary diagnostics, now this—useless chemotherapy. These dark thoughts rustled through my mind while I prepared him for transfer.

I walked beside the gurney while they wheeled him to the ambulance, squeezed his hand, told him he would be getting good care, promised to visit him as soon as I could, and felt as if part of me would be carried away in the ambulance. I had promised I would find a way to keep him out of feces and urine messes—there was no way now.

No one ever mentioned him again—it was as if he had never existed. It was not professional to visit him at another hospital—he was their "property," and meddling nurses are frowned upon, but I had promised. The nurses at St. Joseph's told me he was unresponsive, on his way out, with a raging pulmonary infection and a 104-degree temperature. Meddling or not, I had to go see him.

There he was, with the same blank stare, his hands folded in the middle of his abdomen and his head swaddled in gauze. A huge rubber hypothermia blanket gurgled noisily, chilling the fever from his body. He shivered and grimaced.

"Hi, Ed, it's Barbara." I put my hand in his, and he turned to look at me, still with a blank expression. He squeezed my hand, ever so gently, and tears slipped down his cheeks. "They're going to make you better here," I lied. "They have some brand-new drugs." I felt like a very bad actor, reciting lines with no feeling, babbling to fill empty spaces.

The next day he was dead. "Pulmonary embolism," the nurses told me, a blood clot in his lungs. He never got the chemotherapy, but he did get Coded three times the day he died. The news of his death infused me with a euphoria I hadn't expected to feel. He had cheated the medical community out of six months of experimentation.

"Somebody has to be the one to try investigational drugs," Esther said. I was too irrational to think what that six months might have done for some other patient someday in the far distant future.

Lani and I were sitting in the cafeteria the next day, discussing Ed Mackey and our views on the use of investigational drugs and experimental therapies, when Barry Bauer strolled into the cafeteria, dressed in khaki pants and a plaid shirt. One quick glance at him and my mind shrank like a turtle pulling in its head. I looked down at the table, my chest hurting, as I imagined how he must feel when he watched people's reactions to seeing him.

"My God!" Lani exclaimed, and she too looked down at the table. It was one thing to see Barry often in the ICU and be fairly desensitized to his looks, but it was quite another to experience the surprise shock when he had been gone a few weeks.

After standing in line for a cup of coffee, he came and sat at our table. "How's it going?" he asked, in the slurring kind of speech that can't clearly enunciate sounds requiring contact between tongue and palate.

He had been for an appointment with the plastic surgeon in the medical building next to the hospital, and was to meet his wife in the cafeteria at Oakmont when he was finished with his appointment and she with her appointment with an obstetrician.

"Is she pregnant?" I asked.

"We'll see ... thath's what she's there for." He seemed pleased.

"Everything's going okay?" I was thinking about his secretary friend, Shari, and the triangle that had existed when he first came to us.

"Greath! I'm really lucky ... Beth's a trooper." I thought he would want to bury the past and never mention it again, but he was surprisingly anxious to tell us in great detail about the events leading up to his suicide attempt. It was so difficult to understand his speech, we might not have known what he was saying except that we already knew most of the story.

Beth came along just as he was finishing the tale about Shari and their affair, and she gave us her version of the day he shot himself and how she got help so fast. "It was meant to be," she said. "There's a purpose to our lives now."

As we had suspected, part of Barry's problem was the psychological impact of the Vietnam War. "We're in a group," Beth told us, "of other people fighting the war again in their sleep. When they look at Barry and hear what he's been through, all things are possible."

She told us about the group leader, and how he also had attempted suicide—almost. "Is he a doctor?" I asked.

"Dr. Peter Haynes ... and he has an assistant, a clown,

Charlie Kelly . . . he's not a doctor yet, but it's what he's going to do when he gets his feet on the ground." She chuckled and stared with a faraway look, remembering. "He was about to try the quick way out too. Would you believe the Ferris wheel at Aquatic Park? Now c'mon," she said incredulously, "have you ever heard of anyone attempting suicide by jumping off the Ferris wheel when it's at the highest spot?"

I wanted to laugh, but I also wanted to cry, and I was more than a little angry. "He didn't jump?"

"At the last minute, he phoned Peter . . . I guess they knew each other before. Peter stayed with him a couple of days while he ranted and raved. Barry did the same thing, got really violent . . . and on Thanksgiving Day, Charlie finally gave in and admitted himself to a psych hospital."

"How is he now?" Lani asked, without giving any indication we knew him.

"Great, I guess . . . he's such a clown when we have parties. Barry owes him a lot. Charlie helped him sort things out . . . taught him how to take care of the ear that was grafted. Underneath the clown, there's a gifted doctor. He's going to be a great one."

They never talked about Beth's visit to the obstetrician, but later we found out she was indeed pregnant and was saving the news to tell Barry in private.

When they left, Lani and I sat there looking at each other like two investigators at the end of a *Quincy* show when they've come back to the office after solving some complex mystery. "I'm so incredibly tired," I sighed, "more drained than I've ever been in my life."

"I'm ticked!" she said.

"Me too. He could have let us play mother hen. What are friends for if you can't go to them when you're in trouble?" When Charlie wasn't around during my surgery, it hurt. Now it hurt that he hadn't wanted us around when *he* was in bad straits.

"What would we have done with the both of you in crisis at the same time?"

"Punt! Lucky thing there's one of this trio that wasn't in a pickle then. I wouldn't have survived without you."

"All things work together for good," she said. "Charlie will be a sensational doctor . . . but I'm still ticked. Why hasn't he called us?"

"Maybe we're part of a life he needed to shed . . . who knows?"

At the time, just knowing he was helping and being helped seemed enough.

4 Winding Down

By the end of the week, Lani and I had turned in all our term projects, passed the preliminary exams for the state boards and racked our brains through impossible final examinations— only one week in the hospital remained.

Judith was back in the hospital again. There seemed no way to avoid the second amputation. "No choice," said Dr. Allen, "but first we've got to get the fluid off her lungs." Every word she spoke was with supreme effort, gurgling through the fluid that was drowning her. Still she kept up the narrative stream of the Holocaust.

The next day I came across a maintenance man changing the light fixtures in Judith's room on the second floor. I asked him what he was doing.

"The fire department says they're dangerous," he said. "Have to replace all five hundred fixtures . . . put up a safer kind."

"You're kidding!" I felt my face getting flushed. "Why now?"

"Oh, some dumb nurse put tubing on top of one a few weeks ago and it caused a fire. Just burned the corner of a bedspread, no one was hurt. Not many could reach this high . . . she musta been a tall one."

For the first time in my life, I wanted to be a midget.

"The fire" became Mrs. Erin's favorite topic—during conferences, classes, my performance evaluation, orientation for every new student thereafter, and during every chance meeting I had with her long after I had graduated.

"It could have happened to anyone," Faith Mason said.

"Just forget it." But neither she nor Mrs. Erin intended that I should forget it—it was a hot topic for years after it happened.

"They're changing all the light fixtures," I told Lani. "What a way to go out of here!" She and I were sitting in the fourth-floor conference room, thumbing through nursing journals. The class had unanimously voted her valedictorian for our graduation and we were looking for the Florence Nightingale pledge.

"What do you think? Should I use it?" she asked. "Maybe we could change the wording. Or would that be like changing the 'Star-Spangled Banner'?" She chuckled, not really wanting an answer. Classes before us had recited the pledge at their graduation, but our class had quibbled over the words the week before.

"I'm not reciting it," huffed Chelsee Jones. "Damned if I'm going to pledge to 'aid the physician in his work.' I'm no doctor's handmaiden! The Hippocratic oath doesn't tell him he has to aid me in *my* work." Chelsee had stayed in the program despite my prediction that she was "a token hippy" who would drop out. She was a good nurse, from what I had seen.

"If you use it," I told Lani, "Chelsee's apt to boo and hiss, right up there on stage."

"Code Blue, Two North! . . . Code Blue, Two North! . . ." The operator's metallic voice swept up the hairs on the back of my neck. "Judith?" Lani and I gasped together. We raced down the back stairs as if being chased by the devil.

"They can't . . . she has a Living Will," I shouted to Lani, hoping it wasn't Judith.

"Judith!" Lani cried out as we ran into the room. "No! Don't . . . she has a Living Will . . . it's on her chart." Nurses, doctors and technicians elbowed past her as if she had never said a word. The crash cart rolled in, two nurses were already doing cardiopulmonary resuscitation, and Dr. Gregory was clipping out orders in the same way a checker calls out prices in the grocery store. "He's good," Charlie had told me a year earlier.

"In a Code he's smooth as glass, never gets ruffled. If a patient can be saved, Gregory never misses. He's the best."

Dr. Gregory was also one of several physicians who attempted resuscitation no matter the circumstances. "He resuscitated Mac fifty-two times in one month," Charlie told me. I had been there for Mac's last Code. After wasting away for two years, his body finally rejected the efforts of the Code team— but not until the fifty-third time.

Judith had lived through the concentration camp, lived through watching her daughters and husband brutally murdered, lived through blindness, lived through one leg amputation, and all that lay ahead was the second leg amputation and eventual drowning in the fluid in her lungs. No amount of scientific or technological wizardry, no dazzling medical or nursing feat, could ever reverse her condition—she was doomed to suffering the rest of her days.

"She's had enough!" I hissed to Mrs. Erin. She had arrived with the throng—the Code Blue nurse from the emergency room, the supervisor, the EKG and respiratory therapy technicians, Faith Mason and two more staff nurses. I stood back in the corner, with Mrs. Erin, mentally disconnecting myself from the umbilical cord attached to Judith. This was not a human being with a personality being assaulted by an army of technicians. This was a Code, a "life-saving procedure," something I would be expected to do whether I agreed it should be done or not.

"This isn't right," I whispered to Mrs. Erin. "She's suffered enough." She looked at me sympathetically and bobbed her head toward Dr. Gregory. Only he could interrupt the Code. "You could be some help here. The student will inject the drugs." She nudged me toward the head of the bed, to Judith's IV line.

The Code Blue nurse handed me a syringe. "Upper port," she said. I reached for the top port on the line, then remembered we had been taught never to give a drug we hadn't drawn up ourselves. I started to hand it back to the nurse. "I can't give it . . . I didn't draw it."

"Inject it!" Mrs. Erin hissed. "Hurry up!"

As fast as I pushed a drug, someone handed me another. Everyone worked feverishly to save Judith's life. I never looked down to see if she was responding, but the technicians kept giving their reports, in flat monotone voices: "Nothing." "Flat line." "No pulse."

"Got it," Dr. Gregory said as he successfully slipped the tube into her lungs. It was a tricky procedure, not easily done—he was proud.

It seemed like hours before Dr. Allen walked into the room and asked what had happened.

"Full arrest," said Dr. Gregory. "We're not getting anything."

Dr. Allen watched the electrocardiogram machine while one of the nurses did chest compressions and another puffed oxygen into the tube to Judith's lungs. "She's lingered through two years of recovery and deterioration," he muttered. "I suppose there's no point in keeping this up . . she's gone . . . thank you all for trying so hard."

Within minutes the room was emptied of people, except for Lani and me—and Judith. The room looked like the remains of a chemists' laboratory after a crazed rage. Syringes, needles, electrodes, IV solutions and tubing, cellophane packages, broken ampules—the floor was a sticky, crunching icon to disaster. The red crash cart stood beside the bed, looking like a vandalized bureau, with oxygen tubing dripping from one of the drawers.

"She never missed a single turn of the screw . . . poor Judith." Lani leaned over and hugged her frail, lifeless body. "She's better off, Barb . . . she really is," she said, as much to convince herself as to convince me. "Some things are worse than death."

Mrs. Erin poked her head in the door. "There's some paper

work to be done on this, girls. Fill out the Code sheet, the disposition of personal belongings, the papers for the mortuary. You can come back and clean this mess later. I'll get a gown for the patient. Will relatives be coming in?"

"There's no one," I said. "No one will be coming." The people at Sunny Harbor were Judith's relatives, as were the students. We were her family.

"All things work together for good," Mr. Casper said, weeping pitifully. Lani and I had gone to tell him about Judith that afternoon. "She was much too ill to go on." He tried so hard not to cry, but the three of us sat there, holding hands, weeping all the tears that Judith could never shed herself.

The next two days at Oakmont County Hospital, our last two days as students, were marking time—nothing more. It was time to move on.

5　Graduation Day

"It is silliness to live when to live is torment; and then have we a prescription to die when death is our physician." Shakespeare's words were the solace for Judith's death. She had been released from more torment than most of us could bear, but still there was an emptiness. "Not a sad empty," I told Dean. "It's just that she had planned to be here . . . it feels like she belongs here, sitting in the front row."

"No tears now," he instructed, holding my chin in his hand. "This is the day you've wanted more than any other . . . you probably didn't want our *wedding* day as much as you've wanted this day, you creep!" It was the day before our twentieth anniversary. "I'm playing second fiddle to a funny-looking pointy nurse's cap." He feigned assault and rejection as only he could do it.

We were standing outside the auditorium, minutes before the ceremony was to start. "Now put on a smile, honey girl. We'll meet you out here when it's over." He kissed me on the forehead, squeezed my hand and whispered that he loved me. Then he kissed Lani and went with her husband, Lee, to find our kids in the auditorium.

"I'm scared, Barb." Lani's hands were ice cold. She shivered and then grinned. "Can you believe this? Did you ever think we'd make it? We're *done!*" Then she remembered she had the speech to give, before about a thousand people. "*Almost* done."

From the back of the auditorium, we filed up onto the stage, a dazzling group of crisp, white-clad, brand-new nurses, each with a pointy hat that had two navy-blue velvet bands across the cuff. The auditorium was old, elegant, massive, with deep crimson carpeting and enormous granite columns that sparkled in the dimmed lights. The pipe organ boomed out resounding chords that mirrored exactly the way I felt—incredibly triumphant!

I was always the tallest in every group, which meant I always stood in the last row for class pictures, graduation, chorus, whatever, from kindergarten on; but that night we were to stand in alphabetical order, on two sides of the stage, with an aisle down the center. I was in the front row. I laughed at myself when I thought of how significant that seemed—why should I care where I sat just so long as I graduated? At forty-one, I had finally made it to the front seat, I thought—it seemed a good omen.

Dean, our parents, the kids, were all sitting in about the third row, behind all our instructors, beaming as if I were the wonderful kid about to play a piano solo. I beamed back at them, feeling like that wonderful kid.

Mrs. Bills began a speech that probably consisted of carefully chosen words. It was the first time I ever looked at her without dread and animosity. She was not so bad. She would hand me my diploma, pin the class insignia on my collar, and I would say nice words of gratitude to her.

Lani's speech was beautiful, the kind where you tip back your head to keep tears from spilling. She had been valedictorian for her high-school class too, ten years earlier, and seemed the sort of person who spoke intuitively with deep wisdom and a clever, witty optimism.

I turned to wink at her as she came down from the podium. She cocked her head toward the audience and mouthed something I couldn't understand. Then she grinned and raised her eyes in a thank-God gesture.

I furrowed my brow to let her know I hadn't understood her, and then she looked urgent, as if the message couldn't wait. I thought she said, "Charlie," but wasn't sure. I barely stifled the urge to yell across the stage, "What?" Again I furrowed my brow—she looked exasperated but tried again.

Carefully I watched her mouth, puzzled by the blend of tears and a grin. As the chords of "Pomp and Circumstance" boomed out across the auditorium, she almost shouted, *"Charlie's here!"*

About the Author

Prize-winning essayist and author of *The Patient's Advocate,* Barbara Huttman, R.N., received her nursing degree in 1976. Since that time she has completed a Master of Science from the University of California at San Francisco in Nursing Administration, and has worked as Staff Nurse, Coordinating Nurse Supervisor and Clinical Coordinator in major metropolitan hospitals.

In 1980, Ms. Huttmann co-founded and has, since its inception, served as Director of Professional Health Care Consultants, a teaching, writing, lecturing and consulting service for hospitals, nursing organizations and health-care consumers.

In addition to her hospital work, Ms. Huttmann has distinguished herself as a writer. Her articles have appeared in the *American Journal of Nursing, Medical Self-Care, Nursing Life, RN Magazine* and other publications. She is first prize recipient of both the 1979 California–American Journal of Nursing Excellence in Writing Competition and the 1980 RN Magazine Writing Competition. *The Patient's Advocate,* a consumer's guide to effective negotiation with the health-care system, was published in 1981. *Code Blue* is her second book.

Ms. Huttmann lives with her husband in Lafayette, California.

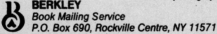

More Bestsellers from Berkley
The books you've been hearing about and want to read